Artificial Intelligence Applications in Education and Empowerment

nova
science publishers
www.novapublishers.com

Environmentalism - Transformation Acceleration

More information about this series can be found at
https://novapublishers.com/product-category/series/environmentalism-transformation-acceleration/

Medani P. Bhandari

Artificial Intelligence Applications in Education and Empowerment

nova
science publishers

www.novapublishers.com

DOI: https://doi.org/10.52305/JVRY0338

Library of Congress Cataloging-in-Publication Data

ISBN: 979-8-89530-914-8 (Hardcover)
ISBN: 979-8-89530-982-7 (eBook)

Published by Nova Science Publishers, Inc. † New York

To My Friend, Wife, Coauthor Mrs. Prajita Bhandari,
Without Your Help and Support This Book Was Impossible.

TOGETHER WE HAVE MILES TO GO

You have assumed a pivotal role akin to that of a true teacher, actively fostering an environmentally conscious atmosphere within your home, workplace, and community. Your impactful actions and exemplary behavior serve as an inspiration, motivating others to embrace sustainable practices and embrace a greener way of life. Your endeavors encompass a wide spectrum, from waste reduction to energy conservation and the advocacy for eco-friendly initiatives. Through these contributions, you actively participate in the creation of a better world for all. Your unwavering dedication to the stewardship of the environment shines as a guiding beacon, urging others to join the collective effort toward a healthier and more sustainable future. Amidst life's challenges, you provide me with a reassuring sense of comfort and a valuable lesson in resilience. For this, I extend my heartfelt gratitude to you.

Contents

Preface

In recent years, artificial intelligence (AI) has emerged as a transformative force across all sectors of society. Education is at the forefront of this change. This book, AI Applications in Education and Empowerment, offers a unique perspective on AI's multifaceted role in revolutionizing education systems, fostering empowerment, and bridging gaps that have historically hindered equitable access to knowledge. As we stand at the intersection of technological innovation and educational reform, this work provides insights into the potential of AI to address some of the most pressing challenges facing the global education landscape.

The power of AI to transform education lies not only in its ability to personalize learning and streamline administrative tasks but also in its capacity to foster lifelong learning, equip individuals with the skills needed for the future workforce, and empower underserved communities. This book is a call to action for educators, policymakers, and practitioners to embrace AI as a tool for empowerment, ensuring that its benefits are accessible to all, regardless of socioeconomic background or geographic location. It brings together diverse perspectives on how AI can be harnessed to drive educational innovation, from enhancing curriculum design and delivery to providing access to resources for marginalized groups.

The growing impact of AI on education necessitates a closer examination of its implications for equity, ethics, and societal transformation. As AI technologies become more integrated into educational systems, it is crucial to address issues of bias, accessibility, and cultural sensitivity in AI systems to ensure that they promote inclusive and just learning environments. This book delves into these concerns, offering a comprehensive look at how AI can challenge and support existing educational structures, fostering a future where learning is more efficient and equitable.

This work emphasizes the need for a thoughtful, human-centered approach to AI in education. AI's potential to enhance learning outcomes and empower individuals will be realized only if it is used responsibly and ethically. This book underscores the importance of designing AI-driven educational solutions that align with the values of inclusivity, diversity, and social justice. It highlights the importance of global collaboration in developing policies and frameworks that govern AI in education, ensuring its use supports the well-being and development of individuals and societies worldwide.

This book aims to bridge the knowledge gap by comprehensively exploring the intersection between artificial intelligence and education, providing academic and practical insights. With AI rapidly transforming educational landscapes, there is a growing need for a resource that explains the technology and explores how it can be applied effectively to address real-world educational challenges. Many educators, policymakers, and technologists are eager to understand AI's potential, but the gap between technological innovation and practical application remains wide. This book aims to bridge that divide by providing concrete examples, theoretical foundations, and actionable strategies that will enable readers to navigate this complex field.

One of the key takeaways from this book is the understanding that AI is not a one-size-fits-all solution. Instead, its application in education must be contextually grounded and tailored to specific needs, whether in curriculum design, personalized learning, or addressing systemic inequities in education. The book emphasizes the importance of considering AI's social and ethical implications, urging readers to think critically about issues such as equity, access, and bias. It highlights the critical need for policymakers and educational institutions to craft strategies that harness AI's potential for positive change while ensuring that vulnerable and underserved populations are not left behind.

This book's major message is that AI can empower learners, educators, and communities when used thoughtfully. By automating certain administrative tasks, AI can allow educators to focus more on individualized instruction. In addition, AI-driven tools can provide personalized learning experiences for students, enhancing educational outcomes for diverse learning needs. However, this power also comes with responsibility. We must be vigilant in designing AI systems that are ethical, transparent, and aligned with the values of social justice. Furthermore, AI has the potential to revolutionize lifelong learning, equipping individuals with the skills they need to adapt to an ever-changing workforce.

Who can benefit from this book? This work is designed for a wide range of readers, including educators, policymakers, technologists, researchers, and anyone interested in the intersection of technology and education. Educators will find valuable insights on integrating AI into their classrooms, curriculum design, and strategies for using AI to support diverse learners. Policymakers will better understand the regulatory frameworks and governance needed to ensure that AI in education is implemented responsibly and inclusively. Researchers will benefit from discussing current trends, challenges, and future directions in AI research, while technologists can explore how their innovations can be adapted for educational contexts.

This book also serves as a resource for social justice and educational equity. By exploring AI's role in empowering marginalized communities, we aim to inspire readers to consider how technology can be a tool for social transformation. Through examining case studies from various regions, we provide practical examples of how AI is already being utilized to make education more accessible and equitable, offering lessons that can be adapted globally.

Ultimately, this book is for anyone looking to understand the transformative potential of AI in education and how it can be harnessed to create a more inclusive, equitable, and empowered society. Whether you are an educator striving to integrate technology into your teaching practice, a policymaker shaping the future of education, or a technologist designing AI-driven tools, this book will guide you in using AI to shape the future of education better. As AI continues to evolve, this book provides the foundational knowledge and practical insights needed to navigate its complexities and unlock its full potential in the educational sphere.

We hope that this book serves as a guide for educators, policymakers, and technologists seeking to navigate the complex terrain of AI in education. By providing a broad range of perspectives and practical insights, we aim to bridge the knowledge gap in this rapidly evolving field, offering a foundation for new knowledge in the era of AI. As we look to the future, we believe AI can reshape the educational landscape, offering new opportunities for learning and empowerment and fostering a more inclusive and just global society.

Thank you!

Professor Medani P. Bhandari, PhD

Acknowledgments

This book, *AI Applications in Education and Empowerment*, explores the transformative role of artificial intelligence (AI) in revolutionizing education systems, fostering empowerment, and addressing longstanding inequities in access to knowledge. It highlights AI's potential to personalize learning and promote lifelong learning, equip individuals with the skills required for the future workforce, and empower underserved communities. As AI continues to reshape the educational landscape, this work calls on educators, policymakers, and practitioners to embrace AI as a tool for equitable empowerment, offering hope and optimism for the future of education.

The book emphasizes addressing critical issues such as bias, accessibility, and cultural sensitivity in AI systems to ensure inclusive learning environments. It advocates for a human-centered approach, ensuring that AI's deployment in education remains ethical, transparent, and aligned with social justice values. The insights shared in this book aim to bridge the knowledge gap between technological innovation and its practical application, equipping educators, technologists, and policymakers with the tools and strategies needed to navigate this complex field.

This book illustrates how AI can enhance curriculum design, provide personalized learning experiences, and empower marginalized communities. It serves as a comprehensive guide for those looking to understand AI's transformative potential in education. It is intended as a beacon for educators, policymakers, researchers, and technologists, underscoring your vital role in creating a more inclusive, equitable, and empowered educational landscape.

I extend my deepest gratitude to those who have shaped and influenced my work. This book, a culmination of our collective efforts, reflects their contributions as much as it does my own aspirations for a sustainable and equitable world. May it inspire action, innovation, and cooperation toward a brighter, more sustainable future.

I am deeply grateful to all the stakeholders who have contributed to my understanding and insights—academic peers, policymakers, technologists, environmentalists, and community leaders. Your interactions have not only enriched my perspective but also made a significant impact on the content of this book. I also owe much to my family, friends, and colleagues for their unwavering support and encouragement, a constant source of inspiration. Finally, I acknowledge the contributions of those advancing AI, Education, and Innovation whose work provides the foundation for this book.

My heartfelt gratitude extends to the many scholars, educators, and researchers whose work has shaped and informed my understanding of AI in education. The vast knowledge in educational technology, artificial intelligence, and empowerment has provided the foundation for the ideas and strategies presented here. I am deeply thankful for your intellectual generosity and dedication to advancing the field.

To my dear friends—Kshitiz Raj Prasai, Rajan Adhikari, Dr. Medini Adhikari, Govinda Luitel, Binod Luitel, and Prof. Bishwa Kalyan Parajuli—your constant encouragement, insistence on the continuation of my research, and shared vision have been instrumental in driving this work forward. Your belief in this project has been invaluable.

I also wish to thank Prof. Ganesh Man Gurung, Pratibha Koirala, Gopal Khatri, Goma Chapagain, Januka Prof. Jacek Piotr Binda, Prof. Keshav Bhattarai, Dr. Shvindina Hanna, Dr. Aleksander Łukasz Sapiński, Prof. Durga Paudel, Mr. Jay Bhandari, and all those who have supported my academic and professional growth throughout this journey.

I want to thank the Board Chairperson of Kathmandu Forestry College (KAFCOL), Mr. Kishor Chandra Gautam, Board Members Ms. Netra Kumari Aryal, and Mr. Baikuntha Pd. Khanal, Mr. Rajendra Poudyal, Mr. Nabin Prakash Upadhyaya, Mr. Kumar Jung Thakuri, Mr Ishwor Man Shrestha, Ms. Sovita Pariyar, Dr. Ambika Prasad Gautam, Dr. Bishnu Hari Pandit, Ms. Sarita Jnawali, KAFCOL Faculties Mr. Arun Sharma Poudyal, Mr. Shiva Shankar Neupane, Mr. Murari Joshi, Mr. Nabin Upadhyaya, Ms. Leena Sah, Mr. Prashid Kandel, and KAFCOL Staff- Mr. Gopal Khatri, Mr. Bidur Koirala, Ms. Januka Adhikari, Mr. Krishna Hari Maharjan, Ms. Januka Lamsal, Ms. Menuka Shrestha, Mr. Santamani Aryal, Ms. Goma Chapagain, Mr. Ram Bahadur Majhi, Ms. Saraswati Lamichhane for their help and support.

"Janani Janmabhoomischa Swargadapi Gariyasi," the timeless adage honoring the significance of mother and motherland, resonates deeply within me. I extend my deepest gratitude to my mother, Heema Devi, whose boundless love and care reflect the nurturing spirit of Mother Earth. I would also like to remember and dedicate this work to my late father, Lok Nath

Bhandari. If he were with us today, he would be incredibly proud and encourage me to continue pursuing projects like this.

I also wish to thank my family—my wife Prajita, son Prameya, daughter Manaslu, daughter-in-law Kelsey, son-in-law Abhimanyu, and their families—for their unwavering support and insightful contributions. To my grandchildren Neena and Neelok, your presence brings immeasurable joy, and to Prasmin and Aahana Bhandari, I look forward to the day you read this book with pride.

My brothers, sisters, extended family, and siblings in Nepal and abroad have consistently given me strength, encouragement, and love. To Prajita's family and close friends, your unwavering support has made my conservation journey possible.

A special acknowledgment goes to my wife, Prajita Bhandari, whose meticulous editing and insightful contributions have been crucial in shaping this book into its final form. Your steadfast support has been my anchor throughout this journey, and this work is as much yours as it is mine.

I also thank Nova Publishers for their professional support in publishing this book. Your expertise and dedication have been instrumental in shaping it and bringing it to a wider audience.

Finally, to future generations whose well-being we must safeguard, thank you for inspiring me to dedicate my life to creating a sustainable and thriving world. To all the readers engaging with this work, your interest and commitment to environmental sustainability continue to fuel my passion for conservation and social empowerment.

With deep appreciation,

Professor Medani P. Bhandari, PhD

Chapter 1

AI Applications in Education and Empowerment

1.1. Introduction

AI Applications in Education and Empowerment explores the transformative potential of artificial intelligence (AI) in reshaping educational practices and fostering empowerment across diverse contexts. AI technologies, such as machine learning, natural language processing, and intelligent systems, have introduced new possibilities for personalized learning, skill development, and equitable access to education. This book examines how AI can address educational challenges, enhance teaching methodologies, and empower individuals and communities by fostering digital literacy and inclusion.

By leveraging theoretical frameworks, case studies, and interdisciplinary approaches, the book delves into key areas such as adaptive learning systems, vocational training, inclusive technologies for marginalized groups, and AI-driven policy recommendations. It also critically analyzes ethical considerations, such as fairness, transparency, and data privacy, while proposing strategies for scaling AI adoption in under-resourced regions. Through a forward-looking lens, the book envisions how AI can contribute to sustainable development, lifelong learning, and a more equitable global educational landscape.

This comprehensive resource guides educators, policymakers, technologists, and researchers, offering insights into integrating AI to create transformative, inclusive, and scalable solutions in education and beyond.

1.1.1. AI Applications in Education and Empowerment

The rapid advancements in artificial intelligence (AI) are redefining the boundaries of human potential across numerous fields. Among these, education and empowerment stand out as critical areas where AI has the potential to foster profound, transformative change. The vision of this book, is to explore how AI technologies can be harnessed to address persistent inequalities, enhance learning outcomes, and promote individual and societal empowerment. By examining innovative applications of AI, the book aims to highlight opportunities, address challenges, and provide a roadmap for integrating AI into educational systems and empowerment initiatives.

One of the core purposes of this book is to bridge the gap between technology and its real-world implications for education. Traditional educational systems often struggle to cater to diverse learner needs, particularly in underserved and remote areas. AI can customize learning experiences through adaptive technologies, enabling personalized education tailored to each student's strengths, weaknesses, and learning pace (Holmes et al., 2019). These systems can democratize access to quality education, breaking geographical and economic barriers and fostering inclusivity. By showcasing global examples and case studies, this book emphasizes AI's potential to enhance educational equity and accessibility.

Another critical objective is to investigate the role of AI in empowerment—particularly in fostering skills, agency, and self-reliance among individuals and communities. Empowerment involves providing individuals with the tools, knowledge, and confidence to effect change in their lives and society. AI-powered platforms can offer vocational training, language learning, and technical upskilling to prepare individuals for a technology-dominated future (Luckin et al., 2016). These tools are essential for bridging the digital divide and enabling marginalized groups to access education, employment, and civic participation opportunities.

The book also addresses the ethical dimensions of AI in education and empowerment. As AI becomes increasingly integrated into these domains, concerns about equity, privacy, algorithmic bias, and the potential misuse of data have emerged (West et al., 2019). The purpose is to provide a balanced narrative, exploring AI's transformative potential and the governance frameworks and ethical principles required to ensure that AI-driven education and empowerment initiatives are fair, inclusive, and sustainable.

Furthermore, this book is envisioned as a resource for educators, policymakers, technologists, and activists working at the intersection of AI and human development. It aspires to comprehensively understand how AI technologies can be effectively deployed in diverse contexts, from formal education systems to informal learning environments and community-driven empowerment projects. The book seeks to inspire stakeholders to leverage AI's potential while addressing its limitations by focusing on practical insights and actionable strategies.

AI Applications in Education and Empowerment aims to highlight the interplay between technology, education, and social change. It underscores the need for collaborative efforts between governments, private organizations, and civil society to ensure that AI is a tool for universal empowerment and sustainable progress. The book envisions a future where AI is not just a technological advancement but a cornerstone of equitable education systems and empowered communities worldwide.

1.1.2. Importance of AI in Transforming Education and Empowerment

Artificial intelligence (AI) has emerged as a transformative force in addressing complex global challenges, including education and empowerment. Traditional approaches to learning and personal development must be revised in the face of rapidly changing societal needs, technological advancements, and the growing demand for equitable access to knowledge and opportunities. AI offers innovative solutions to these challenges by enabling personalized, inclusive, and scalable educational and empowerment models.

1.1.2.1. Transforming Education: Personalization and Inclusivity

AI-driven tools in education enable personalized learning experiences that adapt to individual needs, preferences, and abilities. For instance, intelligent tutoring systems (ITS) use AI algorithms to analyze a learner's progress and provide customized feedback, allowing students to learn at their own pace (Chen et al., 2020). These systems are particularly effective in addressing the diverse learning needs of students, including those with disabilities or those in underserved communities. For example, platforms like Microsoft's Seeing AI assist visually impaired learners by converting text to speech, demonstrating how AI fosters inclusivity in education.

Moreover, AI can bridge geographical and economic disparities by offering access to quality education through online learning platforms. AI-powered systems like Coursera and Khan Academy leverage natural language processing (NLP) and machine learning to provide tailored content and assessments. By doing so, they empower learners worldwide to access high-quality educational resources, regardless of socioeconomic or geographic constraints (Luckin et al., 2016).

1.1.2.2. Empowerment Through Skills and Lifelong Learning

Empowerment fundamentally equips individuals and communities with the tools, knowledge, and confidence to shape their futures. AI is pivotal in fostering this empowerment by facilitating skills development and lifelong learning. AI-driven vocational training platforms like IBM's SkillsBuild use simulations and adaptive learning to prepare individuals for the future workforce, addressing skill gaps and enhancing employability (Holmes et al., 2019).

In addition, AI fosters empowerment by providing language translation tools like Google Translate, which breaks down linguistic barriers and promotes cross-cultural communication. This capability is particularly significant in empowering marginalized communities to participate in global education and professional networks. Furthermore, AI's ability to analyze large datasets enables policymakers and educators to identify disparities and tailor interventions, ensuring more equitable outcomes for all learners.

1.1.2.3. Tackling Systemic Inequalities and Promoting Equity

AI's role in transforming education and empowerment also extends to addressing systemic inequalities. Data-driven insights generated by AI can identify educational gaps and suggest strategies to close them, ensuring that resources are allocated where they are most needed (West et al., 2019). For instance, AI-powered predictive analytics can help educators identify at-risk students and provide timely interventions to prevent dropouts.

In the context of empowerment, AI can democratize access to financial resources, healthcare, and job opportunities. For example, platforms like the Grameen Foundation's AI-powered microfinance tools provide financial literacy training and credit access to underserved populations, empowering them economically and socially.

Looking forward, integrating AI into education and empowerment initiatives promises to redefine how individuals and societies learn, grow, and thrive. However, realizing this potential requires careful consideration of ethical, cultural, and policy dimensions. AI systems must be designed to promote inclusivity, avoid reinforcing biases, and ensure data privacy and security (UNESCO, 2021). Collaborative efforts among governments, private organizations, and civil society are essential to ensure that AI is a force for equity and empowerment.

AI has the potential to revolutionize education and empowerment by enabling personalized learning, fostering inclusivity, addressing systemic inequalities, and promoting lifelong skills development. By leveraging AI responsibly, societies can build a future where education and empowerment are accessible to all, driving global progress and social equity.

1.1.3. Methodology and Scope

The success of this book relies on a robust methodology and a clearly defined scope that ensures a comprehensive and insightful exploration of the subject matter. By adopting an interdisciplinary approach and integrating theoretical and practical perspectives, the book aims to serve as a foundational resource for academics, practitioners, policymakers, and technology developers.

1.1.3.1. Methodological Approach to AI in Education and Empowerment

The book employs interdisciplinary methodology, integrating insights from artificial intelligence, education, sociology, psychology, and development studies. This approach fosters a comprehensive understanding of AI's impact on education and empowerment by examining its technological, social, cultural, and ethical dimensions.

1.1.3.2. Literature Review

The book reviews academic research, industry reports, and policy documents to establish a solid theoretical foundation. This desktop research synthesizes diverse perspectives on AI's role in education and empowerment, drawing on sources like peer-reviewed journals, white papers, government publications, and case studies from organizations such as UNESCO, OECD, and the World Bank.

Integrating artificial intelligence (AI) into education and empowerment has transformed traditional learning paradigms and presented new opportunities for personalized and inclusive education. This literature review examines the theoretical foundations, practical implementations, and challenges associated with AI in education and its role in fostering empowerment and equity in learning environments.

1.1.3.2.1. AI as a Transformative Force in Education

AI is widely regarded as a transformative tool for modern education, redefining how knowledge is imparted, acquired, and assessed. Luckin (2018) articulates the potential of AI to complement human intelligence, fostering environments where machines support educators in creating engaging and responsive learning systems. AI-powered tools like chatbots, intelligent tutoring systems, and adaptive learning platforms have shifted the focus from a one-size-fits-all approach to one that is learner-centric and adaptable (Holmes et al., 2019).

Adaptive learning systems have gained significant traction due to their ability to tailor educational experiences to individual students. According to Chen and Chen (2020), these systems analyze learners' progress, adapting content and pacing to meet unique needs. Such personalized approaches are particularly impactful for students with learning disabilities, as AI tools provide real-time support and interventions, ensuring equitable access to education. The ability of AI to break down traditional barriers and foster inclusivity marks a critical advancement in educational practice.

1.1.3.2.2. Empowering Educators and Students Through AI

AI enhances learning and empowers educators by alleviating administrative burdens and enriching teaching methodologies. Automated grading systems, for instance, streamline the evaluation process, allowing educators to allocate more time to student engagement and curriculum development (Baker, 2016). Moreover, intelligent tutoring systems provide real-time data analytics, enabling teachers to identify learning gaps and intervene effectively.

In addition to supporting educators, AI fosters a sense of agency among learners by offering tools for autonomous and self-directed learning. Integrating AI-powered learning assistants has democratized access to quality educational resources, enabling students from diverse backgrounds to engage in meaningful and impactful learning experiences (Lin & Chiou, 2020). AI tools designed to support underserved communities are pivotal in bridging digital divides and addressing systemic inequities in education (UNESCO, 2019).

1.1.3.2.3. Ethical Dimensions and Emerging Challenges

While AI offers numerous benefits, its adoption raises critical ethical concerns. Holmes and Porayska-Pomsta (2021) identify issues such as data privacy, algorithmic bias, and transparency as significant challenges. These concerns necessitate the development of robust ethical frameworks to guide AI implementation in education. For example, AI systems must ensure the equitable treatment of all students, avoiding the perpetuation of existing biases in data or algorithms.

The role of educators in AI-driven learning environments also warrants attention. Selwyn (2019) explores the tension between technology and traditional teaching, urging caution against overreliance on AI systems. The human element in education—characterized by empathy, adaptability, and mentorship—remains irreplaceable, emphasizing the importance of maintaining human-centric learning environments even as AI systems become more prevalent.

1.1.3.2.4. Innovations and Future Directions

Recent advancements in AI-driven technologies have introduced immersive tools such as augmented reality (AR) and virtual reality (VR), which enhance experiential learning (Holmes et al., 2019). These technologies create dynamic and interactive environments, enabling students to explore complex concepts through simulations and visualizations. For instance, virtual labs and field trips offer opportunities for hands-on learning in contexts where physical resources may be limited.

Emotional intelligence and social-emotional learning (SEL) are emerging areas of focus in AI research. Rashid and Aslam (2021) highlight the potential of AI to analyze and respond to students' emotional states, fostering supportive learning environments. This capability enables educators to address the holistic needs of learners, promoting both academic success and emotional well-being.

Policy frameworks and global collaborations are essential for maximizing AI's educational potential. The OECD (2021) emphasizes the need for international cooperation to establish standards for ethical AI deployment, promote workforce reskilling, and ensure lifelong learning opportunities. Similarly, the World Economic Forum (2020) underscores the importance of preparing students for AI-driven economies by integrating AI literacy and computational thinking into curricula.

The importance and application of AI are growing, with numerous scholars delving into its transformative potential across various domains, particularly education and empowerment. Their contributions provide valuable insights into the opportunities and challenges of integrating AI into these fields.

Artificial Intelligence (AI) is increasingly recognized for its transformative potential in education and empowerment. Scholars have contributed extensively to understanding its applications, exploring various facets, from enhancing learning environments to addressing broader societal implications. Among these contributions, Luckin (2018) stands out for exploring the synergy between machine learning and human intelligence. Her work emphasizes how AI can complement and enhance educational practices, paving the way for more effective and learner-centric approaches that combine the strengths of both human and artificial intelligence.

Holmes, Bialik, and Fadel (2019) comprehensively analyze the promises and implications of AI in education. Their research highlights the role of AI in fostering adaptive learning, personalized instruction, and data-driven decision-making, offering critical insights into how technology can address diverse learner needs and optimize educational outcomes. Similarly, Chen and Chen (2020) delve into the application of AI in creating personalized learning environments, particularly for students with disabilities. Their work underscores the potential of AI to ensure equitable access to quality education by tailoring learning experiences to individual needs.

Baker (2016) focuses on the intersection of learning analytics and educational data mining, exploring how big data can be harnessed through AI technologies to identify and address individual learning needs. This research highlights the transformative role of data in shaping responsive and personalized education systems. Rashid and Aslam (2021) extend this discourse to social-emotional learning (SEL), investigating how AI tools can identify and respond to emotional cues, thereby supporting students' holistic development. Their findings illustrate the potential of AI to foster emotional well-being alongside cognitive growth.

Selwyn (2019) critically examines AI's implications for the teaching profession. His research cautions against an overreliance on technology and advocates for preserving human-centric elements in education, emphasizing the need to balance technological innovation with the irreplaceable value of human teachers. Holmes and Porayska-Pomsta (2021) further contribute to the ethical discourse by focusing on AI systems' fairness, accountability, and transparency. Their work addresses the risks of biases and inequities, calling for ethical frameworks to guide AI integration in education.

Beyond the classroom, UNESCO (2019) explores how AI can support sustainable development goals (SDGs), highlighting its role in democratizing access to education and fostering global collaboration. This perspective is complemented by the OECD (2021), which discusses the policy and practical implications of AI in education—their work advocates for establishing international standards and frameworks to ensure AI technologies' ethical and equitable deployment. The World Economic Forum (2020) addresses the broader implications of AI on employment and workforce readiness. Their research emphasizes the necessity of reskilling and AI literacy to prepare learners for an evolving job market shaped by technological advancements.

This underscores the importance of aligning educational objectives with future workforce demands.

Collectively, these resources provide a robust foundation for understanding AI's growing role in education and empowerment. They offer theoretical, practical, and ethical insights essential for shaping the development and application of AI technologies, ensuring they contribute to equitable and transformative educational practices.

As noted above, a growing body of literature addresses the general issues surrounding AI and its implications for education. Researchers have explored themes such as personalized learning, adaptive systems, ethical considerations, and AI's role in fostering social-emotional learning. Despite these valuable contributions, there remains a significant knowledge gap in specific domains, particularly in understanding how AI can be systematically applied to create equitable, inclusive, and innovative educational practices. For instance, the intersection of AI with education in underrepresented communities, its role in addressing cultural and linguistic diversity, and its potential for fostering creativity and critical thinking in learners still need to be explored.

Moreover, the practical implementation of AI in education—particularly in resource-constrained settings—lacks detailed analysis. While general discussions highlight AI's potential, there is insufficient focus on how educators, policymakers, and institutions can effectively deploy AI tools in diverse and dynamic learning environments. Additionally, the implications of AI for teacher training, curriculum design, and the broader educational ecosystem often remain vague, leaving educators and administrators without clear strategies for integration.

This book seeks to bridge these knowledge gaps by delving into AI's nuanced applications and usefulness in education and innovation. It aims to provide a foundational knowledge base that is both theoretical and practical, addressing how AI can be utilized not only to personalize and enhance learning experiences but also to democratize access to education globally. By exploring case studies, emerging trends, and real-world implementations, this book offers insights into how AI can be a transformative force in education, driving creativity, fostering innovation, and supporting lifelong learning.

Furthermore, this work emphasizes the importance of ethical considerations, cultural sensitivity, and inclusive design in AI-driven educational tools. It examines how AI can empower educators, learners, and communities while addressing its integration challenges and limitations. By filling these critical gaps, the book aspires to serve as a comprehensive resource for scholars, practitioners, policymakers, and anyone invested in harnessing AI's potential to redefine education for a more equitable and innovative future.

The body of literature demonstrates that AI is a powerful tool for transforming education and empowerment, offering innovative solutions to long-standing challenges. Its capacity to personalize learning, foster inclusivity, and empower educators and learners underscores its potential to reshape educational landscapes. However, ethical considerations and systemic challenges remain significant barriers that must be addressed through deliberate policy design, technological innovation, and ongoing research.

This literature review provides a foundation for exploring the diverse applications of AI in education and empowerment, as elaborated in subsequent chapters. By balancing innovation with ethical responsibility, AI can be harnessed to create equitable, inclusive, and transformative learning environments for all.

1.1.3.3. Theoretical Frameworks

The analysis is anchored in established theoretical frameworks from education, empowerment, and AI ethics. For instance, Amartya Sen and Martha Nussbaum's Capability Approach offers a perspective on how AI can enhance opportunities for individuals to realize their potential. Theories of personalized learning and digital inclusion also guide the exploration of AI's applications in education.

The analysis presented in this book is firmly rooted in established theoretical frameworks that span the fields of education, empowerment, and AI ethics. The book aims to offer a comprehensive and multidimensional understanding of AI's potential to transform education and empower individuals by grounding the discussion in these perspectives.

One significant theoretical lens is the Capability Approach, developed by Amartya Sen (1999) and expanded by Martha Nussbaum (2000). This approach emphasizes enhancing individuals' freedoms and opportunities to achieve what they value in life. Applying this framework to AI in education, the book explores how AI technologies can expand students' capabilities by personalizing learning experiences, facilitating access to diverse resources, and providing tools that cater to individual needs and aspirations. For instance, AI-driven platforms that adapt to learners' unique paces and styles can ensure equitable opportunities for realizing their potential, addressing not only academic but also social and emotional development.

Theories of personalized learning also play a pivotal role in this analysis. Personalized learning, rooted in constructivist principles, posits that learning is most effective when it aligns with an individual's prior knowledge, interests, and pace of understanding (Holmes, Bialik, & Fadel, 2019). AI applications, such as adaptive learning platforms and intelligent tutoring systems, embody this principle by tailoring educational content to each learner. These technologies promise to democratize education by making high-quality, personalized instruction accessible to all, regardless of geographic or socioeconomic barriers.

The concept of digital inclusion further guides the exploration of AI in education. Digital inclusion emphasizes equitable technology access and benefits, especially for marginalized or underserved populations (UNESCO, 2019). The book highlights strategies to bridge the digital divide by examining case studies and emerging AI tools, such as AI's role in supporting learners with disabilities (Chen & Chen, 2020) and its potential to deliver multilingual and culturally sensitive educational content to diverse populations.

Ethical considerations in AI, such as fairness, accountability, and transparency, are another cornerstone of the book's framework (Holmes & Porayska-Pomsta, 2021). The integration of these principles ensures that AI systems in education not only enhance learning but also uphold equity and trust. For example, addressing algorithmic bias and ensuring that AI tools are designed to respect cultural and individual differences are critical to creating inclusive educational environments.

The intersection of these frameworks provides a robust analytical foundation for this book, ensuring that discussions about AI's applications in education and empowerment are theoretically grounded and practically relevant. Drawing on these theories, the book seeks to illuminate pathways for leveraging AI to foster human flourishing, address systemic inequities, and create a more inclusive and empowering educational landscape.

1.1.3.4. Case Study Analysis

The book incorporates case studies to contextualize theoretical discussions with real-world applications. These studies examine AI-driven innovations like adaptive learning platforms, intelligent tutoring systems, vocational training programs, and digital inclusion initiatives. Examples include Google's AI for Social Good and IBM's SkillsBuild platform, highlighting best practices and lessons learned (Holmes et al., 2019).

The book integrates various case studies to ground theoretical discussions in practical, real-world applications. These case studies serve as illustrative examples, demonstrating how AI-driven innovations can reshape education and empowerment initiatives. By examining specific programs and tools, the book highlights how theoretical concepts translate into tangible outcomes, offering readers a nuanced understanding of the opportunities and challenges in this domain.

One area of focus is adaptive learning platforms, which leverage AI algorithms to customize educational content to meet individual learners' needs. These platforms, such as those developed by DreamBox and Knewton, dynamically adjust instructional material based on learners' progress, thereby ensuring personalized and efficient learning pathways. Through these tools, the book explores how AI-driven adaptability can cater to diverse learning styles and help address disparities in educational achievement (Holmes, Bialik, & Fadel, 2019).

Intelligent tutoring systems (ITS) are also prominently featured in the discussion. These systems, such as Carnegie Learning's Cognitive Tutor, utilize AI to provide real-time feedback and guidance, simulating a one-on-one tutoring experience. The book examines the impact of ITS on improving learning outcomes, particularly in STEM education, where students often require tailored support to master complex concepts.

Vocational training and skill development are further contextualized through initiatives like IBM's SkillsBuild platform, which offers free, AI-powered training programs tailored to upskill individuals for the workforce. The platform provides resources for digital literacy, data analysis, and AI fundamentals, empowering learners to remain competitive in a rapidly evolving job market. By analyzing such programs, the book highlights the role of AI in bridging the skills gap and promoting lifelong learning.

The book also delves into digital inclusion initiatives, focusing on efforts to extend AI-powered educational tools to marginalized and underserved communities. For example, Google's AI for Social Good program has supported projects that leverage AI to develop low-cost, scalable education solutions. Case studies of these initiatives demonstrate how AI can enhance access to quality education for remote or economically disadvantaged populations, aligning with global efforts to achieve equity in education (UNESCO, 2019).

These case studies provide rich insights into the practical applications of AI in education and empowerment, illustrating both best practices and challenges. By examining these real-world examples, the book emphasizes the importance of innovation, collaboration, and ethical considerations in harnessing AI for societal benefit.

1.1.3.5. Qualitative Analysis of Case Studies

A secondary analysis of documented case studies showcases successful AI implementations in education and empowerment. Examples include AI-powered tutoring systems, inclusive educational technologies, and skill development platforms. This approach highlights practical applications and insights for policymakers and educators.

The book employs a secondary analysis of documented case studies to illuminate successful implementations of AI in education and empowerment. This methodological approach involves analyzing existing case studies to draw insights and lessons to guide future efforts. The book bridges theoretical frameworks and practical applications by focusing on well-documented examples, providing valuable insights for policymakers, educators, and researchers.

One prominent area of focus is AI-powered tutoring systems. These systems, such as Carnegie Learning's Cognitive Tutor and ALEKS, are designed to offer personalized guidance and real-time feedback, replicating the advantages of one-on-one tutoring. The analysis showcases how these systems have significantly improved learning outcomes, particularly in STEM subjects. For example, studies have demonstrated that intelligent tutoring systems can enhance problem-solving skills and conceptual understanding by adapting to students' unique learning trajectories (Holmes, Bialik, & Fadel, 2019).

The book also explores inclusive educational technologies, which aim to ensure equitable access to quality education for all learners, including those with disabilities. Tools like Microsoft's Seeing AI and AI-driven speech-to-text applications have created accessible learning environments. These technologies break down barriers for students with visual, auditory, or physical impairments, fostering inclusivity and equal opportunities for success (Chen & Chen, 2020).

Another significant case study area is AI in skill development platforms. Initiatives such as IBM's SkillsBuild and Coursera's AI-powered learning recommendations highlight how AI can support workforce readiness and lifelong learning. These platforms use algorithms to tailor learning paths based on user goals and progress, ensuring learners acquire the skills most relevant to their personal and professional development. This approach addresses the growing demand for reskilling in an AI-driven economy and supports economic empowerment (World Economic Forum, 2020).

By employing a secondary analysis of these case studies, the book illustrates AI's transformative potential in education and empowerment and identifies critical success factors and challenges. This evidence-based approach offers practical insights for designing, implementing, and scaling AI solutions in diverse educational contexts. The analysis further emphasizes the importance of ethical considerations, data privacy, and collaboration among stakeholders to maximize the benefits of AI for all.

1.1.3.6. Mixed-Methods Research

The book's analysis is based on a combination of qualitative and quantitative research. Quantitative data is sourced from global reports, surveys, and studies on AI adoption in education and empowerment (UNESCO, 2021). Qualitative insights are drawn from interviews, focus groups, and expert opinions, capturing the lived experiences of those directly affected by AI technologies.

The book's analysis is underpinned by a combination of qualitative and quantitative research methodologies, which provide a comprehensive understanding of AI's impact and potential in education and empowerment. This mixed-methods approach allows for both broad statistical insights and an in-depth, contextual understanding of how AI technologies are being applied in real-world educational settings.

Quantitative data forms the foundation for assessing AI adoption's global scope and scale in education and empowerment. This data is primarily sourced from various global reports, surveys, and studies on integrating AI in education. Key sources include UNESCO's 2021 report on AI and education, which provides data on how countries adopt AI technologies in educational systems, highlighting the challenges and opportunities faced by different regions. According to UNESCO (2021), AI has the potential to revolutionize education by enhancing access, improving learning outcomes, and fostering personalized learning pathways for students worldwide. Additionally, large-scale surveys on AI adoption among educators and learners provide statistical insights into trends such as the use of AI for personalized learning, the development of adaptive learning platforms, and the implementation of AI-powered tutoring systems. These quantitative findings offer a broad understanding of the patterns and effectiveness of AI technologies in various educational contexts.

In contrast, qualitative research captures the lived experiences of individuals directly affected by AI technologies. Data for this qualitative analysis is gathered through interviews, focus groups, and expert opinions, ensuring a rich and nuanced understanding of AI's real-world applications and challenges in education. Interviews with educators, students, and policymakers reveal the diverse ways in which AI is transforming teaching and learning. Focus groups with learners and teachers highlight the personal and emotional impact of AI-driven educational tools, such as the adaptability and inclusivity of AI systems and the perceived value of personalized learning experiences. Expert opinions from thought leaders in AI ethics, education, and technology provide critical insights into the broader implications of AI deployment in educational settings, particularly around issues of equity, privacy, and ethical use.

These qualitative and quantitative insights provide a holistic view of AI's role in education and empowerment. The combination of statistical data and personal narratives ensures that the book reflects both the macro-level trends and the micro-level experiences of AI's impact on individuals and societies. The integration of these methods allows for a comprehensive analysis that informs policymakers, educators, and researchers on the practical, ethical, and technological considerations of AI in education.

1.1.3.7. Comparative Analysis

The book employs comparative analysis to investigate variations in AI adoption across regions, socioeconomic groups, and educational systems. This method illuminates disparities in access, resources, and outcomes, forming a basis for policy recommendations and targeted interventions.

The book employs comparative analysis as a key methodological approach to investigate the variations in AI adoption across different regions, socioeconomic groups, and educational systems. By analyzing the global landscape of AI implementation in education, this method highlights critical disparities in access, resources, and outcomes associated with AI-driven educational initiatives. These disparities often reflect broader social, economic, and infrastructural inequalities, and understanding them is crucial for formulating effective policy responses and interventions.

The comparative analysis begins by exploring how AI technologies are integrated into educational systems across various regions, considering economic development, technological infrastructure, and governmental support. For instance, high-income countries with well-established digital infrastructure, such as the United States, Germany, and South Korea, have seen relatively advanced AI applications in education, including personalized learning platforms, AI tutors, and large-scale data-driven assessments (Holmes et al., 2019). In contrast, low- and middle-income countries need help accessing the necessary resources for AI adoption, including limited internet connectivity, a lack of AI-trained educators, and insufficient investment in digital infrastructure. This regional disparity in AI implementation results in varying levels of educational equity, with marginalized groups often bearing the brunt of these inequalities.

Furthermore, the book investigates how socioeconomic factors influence AI adoption and its educational impact. In wealthier areas, AI tools may enhance already strong educational practices, leading to improved learning outcomes, increased engagement, and higher levels of personalized instruction. However, in socioeconomically disadvantaged communities, students may need more access to AI-driven technologies, which could exacerbate existing achievement gaps (OECD, 2021). The comparative analysis examines these differences to understand how AI can perpetuate or help mitigate educational inequalities.

The analysis also includes examining educational systems with differing philosophies and practices. For example, some countries prioritize personalized learning and the use of AI for individualized education, while others emphasize collective, collaborative learning with limited AI integration. The variations in how AI is applied across these systems can affect both the efficacy and equity of educational outcomes. This leads to nuanced insights into how AI can be best utilized in diverse educational contexts.

By shedding light on these disparities, the book forms a foundation for policy recommendations that advocate for equitable access to AI technologies in education. Recommendations may include increasing investment in digital infrastructure, providing targeted support for marginalized communities, ensuring the training of educators in AI technologies, and fostering international collaboration to share best practices and resources. The comparative analysis also calls for targeted interventions that address the specific needs of disadvantaged regions and socioeconomic groups, ensuring that the benefits of AI in education are distributed more equitably across the globe.

This comparative method thus provides a critical lens for understanding the complexities of AI integration in education, helping to ensure that future implementations are inclusive, accessible, and capable of improving educational outcomes for all learners, regardless of their background or location.

1.1.3.8. Comparative Synthesis

Desktop research further enables a comparative synthesis of AI adoption and its implications across sectors and regions. The analysis provides a balanced and inclusive perspective by examining disparities in AI access, effectiveness, and ethical concerns.

Desktop research plays a crucial role in the book's approach by providing a comprehensive framework for the comparative synthesis of AI adoption across different sectors and regions. This form of research involves a thorough review of secondary data sources, including academic journals, policy reports, industry white papers, and global surveys. This allows the analysis to capture a broad spectrum of perspectives on AI's impact on education and empowerment.

One of the key outcomes of desktop research is its ability to highlight disparities in AI access. Across various regions, there are significant differences in the availability and quality of AI technologies. For example, in high-income countries, AI tools such as intelligent tutoring systems, adaptive learning platforms, and automated assessment tools are more commonly available and integrated into mainstream educational practices. In contrast, low-income countries may need help with the infrastructure and resources necessary to deploy these technologies effectively (UNESCO, 2021). The digital divide is a persistent challenge where marginalized communities, particularly in rural or underserved areas, may lack the internet connectivity or technical resources needed to benefit from AI applications.

Furthermore, desktop research also enables examining AI effectiveness across various contexts. For instance, in regions with advanced technological infrastructure, AI applications often lead to significant improvements in personalized learning, providing real-time feedback to students and adapting to their learning styles (Holmes et al., 2019). In contrast, in areas with limited resources, AI may not be fully optimized, and its impact can be more uneven, sometimes exacerbating existing educational inequalities rather than alleviating them.

Another critical aspect that desktop research facilitates is the exploration of ethical concerns associated with AI adoption in education. Ethical issues such as bias in AI algorithms, privacy concerns, and the potential for surveillance are pervasive and must be carefully considered in the global context. In countries with strong regulations around data privacy, such as those in the European Union, there are robust frameworks for ensuring that AI technologies adhere to ethical standards. However, in regions where such regulations are less stringent, AI systems may inadvertently perpetuate inequalities by reinforcing existing biases or violating user privacy (Holmes & Porayska-Pomsta, 2021).

By synthesizing these various factors—disparities in access, effectiveness, and ethical concerns—desktop research provides a balanced and inclusive perspective on AI's role in education and empowerment. It ensures that the analysis is not overly optimistic about AI's potential, nor overly cautious, but instead offers a nuanced understanding of how AI can be a force for good if deployed thoughtfully and equitably. This approach supports the development of evidence-based recommendations that take into account the global diversity of educational contexts, ensuring that the adoption of AI is ethical, inclusive, and effective across all sectors.

In conclusion, desktop research enables a broad and in-depth comparison of AI adoption, helping to bridge knowledge gaps regarding its practical implications, ethical considerations, and regional differences. This methodological approach ensures that the book provides a well-rounded perspective on the future of AI in education and empowerment, grounded in real-world data and contextual understanding.

1.1.3.9. Foresight Analysis

Recognizing the dynamic nature of artificial intelligence (AI), this book adopts foresight methodologies to anticipate and prepare for its evolving role in education and empowerment. As AI continues to advance at an unprecedented pace, understanding the long-term implications and emerging trends is crucial for ensuring its potential is maximized for the benefit of learners and educators worldwide.

Scenario planning is one of the primary foresight methodologies employed in this analysis. This approach involves creating a series of plausible future scenarios based on current trends, technological advancements, and potential disruptions. By considering a range of possible futures—from highly optimistic to more cautious or even dystopian scenarios—scenario planning helps identify both the opportunities and risks associated with AI's integration into education systems. For instance, a positive scenario could involve AI-powered personalized learning systems that drastically improve student outcomes by adapting to individual learning needs, fostering greater equity and inclusivity. On the other hand, a more cautious scenario might focus on the ethical challenges of widespread AI adoption, such as increased surveillance, algorithmic biases, and the exacerbation of existing inequalities in education (Selwyn, 2019).

Incorporating expert consultations further enriches the foresight process. Experts from diverse fields—such as AI research, educational technology, ethics, and policy—provide valuable insights into the potential evolution of AI in education. Their input offers a broader perspective on both the technical capabilities of AI and the societal implications of its deployment. For example, consultations with AI technologists may shed light on the future capabilities of AI systems, while discussions with educational theorists and policymakers help identify the ethical, cultural, and regulatory considerations that must be addressed to ensure AI is used responsibly in education (Holmes & Porayska-Pomsta, 2021).

Additionally, expert consultations help forecast key challenges that may arise, including issues related to data privacy, algorithmic accountability, and the impact of AI on the workforce. As AI continues to play a significant role in shaping learning experiences and outcomes, understanding these challenges is crucial for developing policies that ensure AI systems are fair, transparent, and equitable in their application (OECD, 2021). For instance, discussions surrounding the digital divide—where access to AI technologies remains limited in certain geographic regions or among marginalized groups—are crucial for ensuring that AI's benefits are shared more equally across global educational systems.

By utilizing foresight methodologies like scenario planning and expert consultations, this book does not only address current trends in AI's role in education and empowerment, but also provides strategic insights into how AI may evolve in the future. This forward-looking perspective allows educators, policymakers, and technology developers to anticipate and prepare for potential challenges and opportunities, ensuring that AI's integration into education remains adaptive, inclusive, and ethically responsible.

1.1.3.10. Foresight and Scenario Planning

The long-term implications of AI in education and empowerment are thoroughly explored in this book using foresight and scenario planning methodologies. As AI technologies continue to evolve, it is essential to anticipate and prepare for the potential impacts that AI may have on global education systems and empowerment efforts. Foresight helps identify emerging risks, opportunities, and ethical challenges, ensuring that the book provides valuable perspectives that remain relevant as the technological landscape shifts.

Through scenario planning, the book considers various future possibilities based on current trends, technological advancements, and societal changes. These scenarios serve as a tool for examining how AI could reshape education in the coming years. For instance, one emerging opportunity is the potential for AI to further personalize education, providing tailored learning experiences that respond to individual students' needs, abilities, and interests. This could lead to greater educational equity and accessibility, particularly for marginalized and underserved communities (Holmes, Bialik, & Fadel, 2019).

However, this opportunity also raises important questions about the digital divide, as disparities in access to technology could limit the benefits of AI in education for some students.

At the same time, the foresight analysis identifies risks associated with the widespread adoption of AI. One pressing concern is the ethical implications of AI in education, including issues of bias in algorithmic decision-making, data privacy and security, and the potential for surveillance and control in educational environments. For example, AI systems used for personalized learning may inadvertently reinforce existing biases if they are trained on biased data, leading to unfair outcomes for certain groups of students (Selwyn, 2019). Moreover, the use of AI to monitor and track student progress raises questions about the boundaries of privacy and autonomy, particularly when it comes to sensitive data.

The book also addresses ethical challenges that AI poses in the context of empowerment. For instance, how can AI be used to empower learners without reinforcing societal inequalities or marginalizing certain groups? How can AI be designed to promote critical thinking, creativity, and social-emotional skills, which are essential for human flourishing but are often neglected by technology-driven education systems? These challenges require careful consideration of design principles that prioritize human agency, dignity, and autonomy (UNESCO, 2019).

This structured methodology of foresight and scenario planning ensures a rigorous and multidimensional examination of AI's transformative potential in education and empowerment. By analyzing future trends and examining the potential risks and rewards associated with AI technologies, the book provides actionable insights that are relevant to scholars, educators, and policymakers alike. These insights are not only aimed at understanding the present applications of AI in education but also at preparing for a future in which AI plays an even more central role in shaping educational practices and fostering social empowerment.

1.1.4. Scope - AI in Education and Empowerment

1.1.4.1. Education

The book examines the application of AI in formal, informal, and non-formal educational contexts. Key areas include personalized learning, intelligent tutoring systems, curriculum development, and accessibility tools for learners with disabilities. Additionally, the role of AI in lifelong learning and professional development is explored, addressing the evolving needs of individuals in a rapidly advancing technological landscape (Luckin et al., 2016).

1.1.4.1.1. Adaptive Learning Technologies

Adaptive learning technologies harness the power of AI to create personalized learning experiences that adapt in real time to a learner's progress, strengths, and weaknesses. These technologies analyze data from assessments, interactions, and behaviors to adjust instructional content, pacing, and feedback dynamically. For example, platforms like DreamBox Learning and ALEKS provide tailored math and science instruction based on students' unique learning needs. This customization increases engagement and supports mastery of complex concepts by ensuring learners are neither overwhelmed nor under-challenged (Pane et al., 2014). Adaptive learning also has significant potential in addressing learning disparities and providing equitable access to quality education for diverse learners.

1.1.4.1.2. Intelligent Tutoring Systems

Intelligent tutoring systems (ITS) simulate the guidance and feedback of human tutors using AI technologies like natural language processing and machine learning. These systems, such as Carnegie Learning's MATHia and AutoTutor, deliver personalized instruction, offer instant feedback, and facilitate interactive problem-solving. ITS platforms engage learners through conversational interfaces and adaptive problem-solving exercises, making education accessible and tailored to individual learning needs. Studies show that ITS can significantly improve learning outcomes, particularly in STEM subjects, by replicating one-on-one tutoring experiences (VanLehn, 2011).

1.1.4.1.3. Curriculum Design Enhanced by AI

AI offers innovative solutions for curriculum design by analyzing large datasets to uncover learning patterns, skills in demand, and effective pedagogical strategies. AI-driven tools like Knewton suggest curriculum modifications to align with industry needs and learner progress. These systems enable dynamic, data-informed curriculum updates that ensure relevance and responsiveness to evolving societal and technological trends. For instance, integrating AI insights into curriculum design can help educators address skills gaps in data science and renewable energy, preparing students for future opportunities (Luckin et al., 2016).

1.1.4.1.4. Accessibility Tools for Learners with Diverse Needs

AI-powered accessibility tools significantly enhance inclusivity in education by addressing the diverse needs of learners with disabilities or other challenges. Technologies such as text-to-speech, speech-to-text, real-time language translation, and visual recognition systems provide critical support for students who might otherwise face barriers to learning. For example, Microsoft's Seeing AI app assists visually impaired learners by describing text, objects, and surroundings. AI can also personalize education for neurodiverse learners, enabling a more equitable and supportive learning environment. These tools align with global efforts to create inclusive education systems that leave no learner behind (World Economic Forum, 2020).

1.1.4.1.5. AI's Contribution to Lifelong Learning and Workforce Development

AI transforms lifelong learning and workforce development by offering flexible, scalable, and personalized learning pathways. Platforms like LinkedIn Learning and Coursera utilize AI algorithms to recommend tailored courses and skill-building programs aligned with individual goals and labor market trends. AI also plays a pivotal role in reskilling and upskilling, especially in industries affected by automation and technological disruption. For example, IBM's SkillsBuild platform uses AI to provide personalized career resources for marginalized communities. By aligning education with employment opportunities, AI contributes to economic mobility and workforce readiness (OECD, 2021).

These AI-driven applications highlight the transformative potential of technology in creating more personalized, inclusive, and impactful educational and empowerment experiences globally.

1.1.4.2. Empowerment

The book delves into AI-driven initiatives that empower individuals and communities. This includes applications in skill-building, vocational training, and digital literacy. It highlights how AI fosters agency and participation, particularly among marginalized communities, by enabling tools for language translation, financial inclusion, and career development.

1.1.4.2.1. Skill-Building and Vocational Training Platforms

AI-powered platforms play a pivotal role in skill-building and vocational training by providing targeted, personalized, and scalable learning experiences. Tools like IBM's SkillsBuild and Microsoft's Global Skills Initiative leverage AI to identify skill gaps and recommend tailored training modules. These platforms integrate virtual labs, simulations, and interactive assessments to prepare learners for industry-specific roles in technology, healthcare, manufacturing, and other sectors. By providing accessible and flexible training opportunities, AI platforms contribute to workforce development, especially in regions facing employment challenges due to automation and economic transitions (Schwab & Malleret, 2020).

1.1.4.2.2. AI Tools for Digital Literacy and Economic Inclusion

AI tools are essential for fostering digital literacy, equipping individuals with the skills needed to navigate and thrive in a technology-driven world. Platforms like Google's Applied Digital Skills and UNESCO's ICT Competency Framework use AI to create personalized digital literacy curricula, enabling learners to acquire basic and advanced technological skills. Additionally, AI supports economic inclusion by offering tools for financial literacy, entrepreneurial training, and e-commerce. For example, AI-driven chatbots and learning apps help users in developing regions understand digital banking systems, enabling broader access to economic opportunities (West et al., 2019).

1.1.4.2.3. Applications Like Language Translation and Microfinance for Underserved Populations

AI applications such as language translation and microfinance platforms have transformative impacts on underserved populations. Tools like Google Translate and Microsoft's Translator use natural language processing (NLP) to break language barriers, fostering inclusivity in education, commerce, and communication. Meanwhile, AI-powered microfinance platforms, such as Tala and Kiva, use machine learning algorithms to analyze creditworthiness and provide small loans to individuals without formal credit histories. These applications empower marginalized communities by enabling access to global markets, educational resources, and financial services, reducing disparities and promoting sustainable development (UNESCO, 2021).

These AI applications highlight their transformative potential in skill-building, digital literacy, and economic empowerment, particularly for vulnerable and underserved communities worldwide.

1.1.4.3. Ethical and Social Considerations

Ethical and social dimensions are integral to the book's analysis. Issues such as data privacy, algorithmic bias, and equity in AI implementation are critically examined. Emphasis is placed on developing ethical frameworks and governance models that prioritize inclusivity, fairness, and accountability (West et al., 2019).

1.1.4.3.1. Data Privacy and Security Concerns

One of the primary challenges in the integration of AI into education and empowerment is safeguarding data privacy and ensuring robust security measures. AI systems rely on vast amounts of personal data to deliver personalized learning experiences and empowerment tools. However, this data collection raises significant concerns regarding individual privacy and the risk of misuse. Educators, learners, and vulnerable communities are especially vulnerable to breaches or unauthorized access to their sensitive information. For example, in AI-driven education, data such as student performance, personal preferences, and behavioral patterns are collected, potentially exposing learners to privacy violations if not properly protected. Solutions like differential privacy, end-to-end encryption, and transparent data policies are crucial to addressing these concerns (Zeng et al., 2020). Moreover, clear regulatory frameworks and ethical data practices, such as those outlined in the General Data Protection Regulation (GDPR), play a critical role in mitigating security risks.

1.1.4.3.2. Algorithmic Bias and Fairness

AI systems, particularly in education and empowerment, are often subject to algorithmic bias, which can inadvertently reinforce existing inequalities. Algorithms are designed to process large datasets to make decisions, but if these datasets reflect historical biases—whether related to race, gender, socioeconomic status, or other factors—AI models may perpetuate or even exacerbate these biases. In educational settings, biased AI algorithms could lead to unequal treatment of students, such as lower grades for certain demographics or exclusion from advanced learning opportunities. Similarly, in empowerment programs, biased algorithms can hinder access to resources like job opportunities or financial support. Ensuring fairness in AI requires strategies such as bias detection, transparent model development, and continuous monitoring to reduce discriminatory outcomes. The implementation of fairness metrics, as proposed by scholars like Angwin et al. (2016), is critical in evaluating and rectifying algorithmic bias.

1.1.4.3.3. The Digital Divide and Equitable AI Access

The digital divide remains a persistent global issue, with disparities in access to digital technologies and the internet creating significant inequalities in educational and economic opportunities. AI applications in education and empowerment have the potential to either bridge or widen these gaps. For individuals in underserved communities, limited access to AI-powered tools, digital devices, and internet connectivity can exclude them from the benefits of AI-driven education, such as personalized learning platforms or online vocational training. The digital divide also reflects disparities in the availability of AI-related skills and knowledge, which are critical for navigating an increasingly tech-driven world. To ensure equitable access, it is essential for policymakers to prioritize infrastructure investments, affordable internet access, and digital literacy programs. Initiatives like the UNESCO Broadband Commission and the AI for Good Foundation aim to promote digital equity and ensure that AI tools are accessible to all, regardless of geographic location or socioeconomic status.

1.1.4.3.4. Ethical Theories and Policy Frameworks for AI Governance

AI governance must be guided by ethical principles to ensure that the technology is used for the collective good. Various ethical frameworks can inform the development and deployment of AI in education and empowerment. Utilitarianism, deontology, and virtue ethics offer different approaches to evaluating AI's societal impact. For instance, a utilitarian approach might prioritize the greatest good for the largest number, while a deontological framework might focus on upholding individual rights and autonomy. In the context of AI, these theories can be used to navigate complex decisions about privacy, consent, and fairness. Furthermore, policy frameworks such as the OECD AI Principles and EU Artificial Intelligence Act advocate for ethical governance by establishing guidelines on transparency, accountability, and fairness. A multidisciplinary approach that integrates law, ethics, and technology is essential to ensure that AI is developed and implemented in a way that promotes human dignity, social justice, and sustainability.

These key issues highlight the critical importance of addressing ethical, legal, and social concerns in AI development, particularly in the fields of education and empowerment, to ensure that AI serves as a tool for equity, inclusion, and social progress.

1.1.4.4. Global and Contextual Relevance

The book adopts a global perspective, analyzing the challenges and opportunities AI presents in diverse cultural and socioeconomic contexts. Insights are drawn from both developed and developing nations to ensure a comprehensive understanding of AI's varying impacts.

1.1.4.4.1. Disparities in AI Adoption and Resource Allocation

The global adoption of AI is marked by significant disparities in access to resources, infrastructure, and technological know-how. High-income countries typically have the financial capacity to invest in cutting-edge AI technologies, including advanced machine learning algorithms, personalized learning platforms, and intelligent tutoring systems. In contrast, low- and middle-income countries face challenges such as limited access to the internet, insufficient educational infrastructure, and a lack of skilled personnel to develop and implement AI solutions. These disparities exacerbate existing inequalities in education and empowerment, limiting the potential benefits AI can offer to be marginalized populations. A critical analysis of global AI adoption reveals that nations in the Global South often face barriers such as inadequate digital infrastructure, high costs of technology, and lack of localized content, which restrict the transformative power of AI in education and empowerment. Addressing these disparities requires international collaboration, increased investment in AI infrastructure, and policies that foster equitable access to technology.

1.1.4.4.2. Cultural and Economic Influences on AI Effectiveness

Cultural and economic factors significantly influence the effectiveness and adoption of AI in both education and empowerment. In developed nations, where economic resources and technological infrastructures are advanced, AI tools can be deployed more effectively across educational settings, providing personalized learning and skills development opportunities. In contrast, developing countries often face cultural and economic barriers that hinder AI adoption. For example, AI solutions in education may need to be adapted to local languages, learning styles, and cultural contexts to be effective in different regions. Additionally, economic factors such as affordability, access to technology, and the availability of skilled labor are key determinants in the success of AI initiatives. In many African, Asian, and Latin American countries, AI adoption is slowed by high costs, limited access to technology, and a lack of local capacity for implementing these tools. Therefore, understanding and addressing the cultural and economic contexts is essential for maximizing the effectiveness of AI in diverse settings.

1.1.4.4.3. Case Studies Showcasing Regional and Global Best Practices

To better understand how AI can be effectively leveraged in education and empowerment, the book highlights case studies from both developed and developing regions. These case studies showcase successful AI-driven initiatives and offer lessons for other regions facing similar challenges. In developed countries, initiatives such as AI-powered personalized learning systems in the United States and Europe demonstrate the potential of AI to address educational inequities and improve learning outcomes. In contrast, case studies from developing regions highlight AI-driven solutions that tackle unique challenges, such as language barriers, limited internet access, and cultural relevancy. For instance, the AI for Social Good initiative by Google and IBM's SkillsBuild platform have successfully provided scalable solutions to foster digital literacy and skills training in underserved communities globally. Moreover, countries like India and Kenya are experimenting with AI-powered mobile platforms for educational delivery and financial inclusion, which are proving effective in expanding access to education and economic opportunities.

These sections underscore the global dimension of AI in education and empowerment, emphasizing the importance of contextual understanding, resource allocation, and international cooperation in harnessing the full potential of AI. By learning from case studies that span the globe, policymakers, educators, and technology developers can foster more inclusive and equitable AI applications

1.1.4.5. Practical Applications and Policy Recommendations

To bridge theory and practice, the book provides actionable insights and strategic recommendations for practitioners, educators, and policymakers. It offers guidance on effectively integrating AI into education and empowerment initiatives, emphasizing strategies for driving meaningful and equitable change.

1.1.4.5.1. Best Practices for AI Integration in Educational Settings

Integrating AI into educational settings requires a strategic approach to ensure that the technology enhances the learning experience while addressing challenges such as inclusivity, accessibility, and equity. Best practices for AI integration include:

1.1.4.5.1.1. Personalized Learning

AI can be used to tailor educational content to individual learning needs, creating customized learning pathways. For example, adaptive learning platforms such as Knewton and DreamBox adjust the difficulty of lessons based on a learner's progress, allowing students to work at their own pace and improving retention and engagement (Linn, 2019).

AI has the potential to revolutionize education by personalizing learning and tailoring content to the individual needs of each student, fostering a more adaptive and engaging learning experience. One key application of AI in this domain is through adaptive learning platforms, which can adjust the difficulty and pacing of lessons according to a learner's progress and performance. Such platforms allow students to learn at their own pace, ensuring they fully grasp concepts before moving forward, which improves retention and engagement.

For instance, Knewton and DreamBox are two prominent adaptive learning technologies that leverage AI to optimize learning pathways. Knewton's AI engine personalizes lessons by continuously assessing students' strengths and weaknesses and modifying content to meet their evolving needs. This personalization not only helps students learn at a pace that suits them, but it also promotes deeper understanding, as the system dynamically provides additional support when it detects a learner struggling with specific concepts (Linn, 2019). Similarly, DreamBox adjusts lessons based on real-time feedback from students, enabling them to work through math problems at a level that corresponds to their individual mastery, creating a more individualized and effective learning experience.

The ability to customize learning pathways through AI is particularly beneficial for learners with diverse educational needs, such as those needing additional support or advanced learners requiring more challenging materials. By facilitating personalized instruction, AI platforms like Knewton and DreamBox can reduce educational disparities, ensuring that every student receives the appropriate level of challenge and support to succeed. As a result, students become more engaged and develop a greater sense of ownership over their learning journey.

Moreover, these technologies provide educators with real-time analytics, giving them actionable insights into student performance. This allows for more data-driven decision-making and enables teachers to provide timely interventions when necessary, ensuring no student falls behind.

As such, integrating AI into education through platforms like Knewton and DreamBox represents a decisive step toward creating learner-centric environments that cater to individual needs, fostering academic achievement and personalized growth.

1.1.4.5.1.2. Teacher Support

AI can assist teachers in automating administrative tasks, such as grading and curriculum mapping, thus freeing up more time for personalized student support. Tools like Turnitin for plagiarism detection and AI-based grading systems can enhance efficiency in educational environments (Chase et al., 2019).

AI offers significant potential to assist educators by automating administrative tasks, enabling teachers to allocate more time and resources to providing personalized student support. One area where AI has made notable strides is in the automation of grading and curriculum mapping, both of which are typically time-consuming for teachers.

For example, AI-based grading systems can assess assignments and tests more efficiently, often providing faster feedback to students than traditional methods. These systems are designed to analyze and grade both objective assessments (e.g., multiple-choice questions) and more complex, subjective responses (e.g., essays). AI systems can evaluate student work based on various factors, including grammar, coherence, and argument structure, and then provide personalized feedback that can help students improve their work. This automation reduces the burden on educators and speeds up the feedback loop, essential for maintaining student engagement and improving learning outcomes (Chase et al., 2019).

Turnitin, a widely used tool in many educational settings, is another example of how AI can help automate administrative tasks. Designed initially as a plagiarism detection tool, Turnitin uses advanced algorithms to identify similarities between student submissions and a vast database of sources. This helps ensure academic integrity and saves teachers time that would otherwise be spent manually reviewing and comparing student work for potential plagiarism.

Additionally, AI can assist with curriculum mapping, aligning teaching objectives, content, and assessments with desired learning outcomes. AI tools can analyze vast amounts of educational data to identify trends, gaps, and areas for improvement in the curriculum, helping educators to design their courses better and tailor them to meet students' needs. By automating this process, AI ensures the curriculum is dynamic, data-driven, and aligned with educational goals.

These technologies enable educators to focus more on student interaction and individualized instruction while increasing the overall efficiency and effectiveness of teaching. With AI tools handling repetitive and administrative tasks, educators are empowered to engage more meaningfully with their students, fostering a more prosperous, more personalized learning environment.

1.1.4.5.1.3. Data-Driven Insights

AI-powered analytics can provide valuable insights into student performance, helping educators identify at-risk students and intervene early. Learning management systems (LMS) like Blackboard and Moodle incorporate AI capabilities that allow instructors to track learner behavior and personalize interactions accordingly.

AI-powered analytics are revolutionizing how educators track and support student progress by providing valuable insights into student performance. These insights help instructors identify at-risk students and implement early intervention strategies, ultimately improving student outcomes.

One of the most significant contributions of AI in this area is its ability to analyze vast amounts of data generated by students as they interact with educational content. For instance, learning management systems (LMS) like Blackboard and Moodle, which incorporate AI capabilities, can track a range of student behaviors, including the frequency of logins, time spent on assignments, participation in discussions, and quiz performance. By applying predictive analytics, these systems can identify patterns that indicate when a student is struggling or falling behind in their learning, enabling instructors to intervene in a timely manner (Liu et al., 2021).

AI systems in LMS platforms go beyond simply identifying students at risk; they can also help personalize learning experiences. For example, if a student shows signs of difficulty in a particular subject area, the AI can suggest additional resources or assignments tailored to that student's needs. By offering personalized support, AI helps maintain engagement and motivation, which are critical factors in student retention and success (Shute & Zapata-Rivera, 2020).

Furthermore, AI-powered analytics allow for a holistic view of student performance, integrating data from various sources such as course grades, participation in online activities, and social interactions in collaborative learning environments. This comprehensive view enables instructors to understand each student's learning journey better and adapt their teaching methods accordingly.

The use of AI for student performance tracking and early intervention is particularly beneficial in large-scale online education environments, where instructors may interact differently with each student than in traditional classroom settings. With AI systems handling data analysis and feedback generation, instructors are better equipped to manage large numbers of students effectively, ensuring that each learner receives the attention they need.

Overall, integrating AI into learning management systems improves efficiency and enhances the personalized learning experience for students, fostering a more inclusive, responsive, and supportive educational environment.

1.1.4.5.1.4. Scalable Solutions

For AI to be successfully integrated, educational institutions need to prioritize scalability. Solutions like Google Classroom or Microsoft Teams for Education have demonstrated how AI can scale to large populations, offering virtual learning environments that integrate with other technologies and foster collaboration (Holmes et al., 2019).

Institutions must prioritize scalability for AI to be successfully integrated into educational systems. As the demand for personalized learning and data-driven decision-making grows, AI solutions must adapt and function effectively across large populations of students. Scalable AI solutions help ensure that personalized learning, real-time feedback, and targeted interventions are accessible to all learners, regardless of their geographic location or the size of their educational institution.

One of the most notable examples of scalable AI in education is Google Classroom, which allows educators to create and manage digital classrooms for large numbers of students. Google Classroom integrates seamlessly with other Google services, such as Google Drive and Google Docs, making it a comprehensive platform that supports communication, content sharing, and collaborative learning. By leveraging AI tools, Google Classroom can offer personalized recommendations, assess student progress, and streamline administrative tasks, making it a powerful resource for both teachers and students (Holmes et al., 2019).

Similarly, Microsoft Teams for Education provides an AI-enabled virtual learning environment that supports real-time collaboration, content sharing, and communication. Its AI features can help automate routine tasks like scheduling, grading, and organizing assignments, allowing teachers to focus on delivering quality instruction and engaging with students meaningfully.

Integrating AI into these platforms also makes tracking student progress and customizing learning experiences easier, which is particularly important for supporting students with diverse learning needs (Chase et al., 2019).

These platforms demonstrate the scalability of AI-powered solutions in education by catering to large, diverse populations while maintaining effective personalization. Through AI-driven analytics and adaptive learning tools, these platforms can adjust content, provide immediate feedback, and create individualized learning pathways for each student. This scalability ensures that AI's benefits are not limited to small, specialized programs but can extend to global education systems.

Moreover, integrating AI in tools like Google Classroom and Microsoft Teams promotes collaboration among students and educators, fostering a dynamic learning environment where information is shared seamlessly. As such, these platforms serve as valuable models for educational institutions looking to implement AI solutions that can grow and evolve with changing educational needs.

The scalability of AI in education is a key factor in its successful integration. Platforms like Google Classroom and Microsoft Teams provide powerful examples of how AI can support large-scale, personalized learning experiences while fostering collaboration and enhancing efficiency across diverse educational settings.

1.1.4.6. Strategies for Scaling AI-Driven Empowerment Tools

Scaling AI-driven tools for empowerment requires a comprehensive strategy that considers both technological and socio-economic factors. Key strategies for scaling AI tools for empowerment include:

1.1.4.6.1. Building Localized Solutions

AI tools must be adapted to local contexts to have a lasting impact. This involves designing linguistically and culturally appropriate systems and ensuring they are accessible on low-cost devices, such as mobile phones. For example, AI-based language translation tools like Google Translate can help break down language barriers and increase access to global knowledge and services, especially for marginalized populations.

1.1.4.6.2. Partnerships and Collaboration

Scaling AI tools requires collaboration between governments, NGOs, private sector players, and local communities. Initiatives like IBM's SkillsBuild platform show how partnerships can leverage AI to offer vocational training programs that can be scaled across different regions, improving access to skill development and enhancing employability in underserved areas.

1.1.4.6.3. Capacity Building

Empowering local communities to use AI tools requires investment in digital literacy programs and ongoing training for users and facilitators. This includes offering workshops and certifications on AI usage, digital skills, and data privacy. Programs such as AI4Good and Microsoft's Digital Literacy Initiative help build the capacity of local educators and community leaders to facilitate these technologies in their regions.

Empowering local communities to use AI tools effectively goes beyond simply providing access to technology; it involves fostering digital literacy and equipping users and facilitators with the necessary skills to navigate, use, and benefit from these tools. In regions with limited experience with technology, particularly in low-income or rural areas, targeted digital literacy programs are essential to ensure that individuals can use AI-powered solutions confidently and competently. These programs must focus on building fundamental digital skills, understanding AI's potential and limitations, and addressing crucial issues such as data privacy and ethical AI use.

One of the key components of these empowerment initiatives is offering workshops and certifications that cover a range of skills—from basic digital competencies to more advanced topics like AI development, programming, and the ethical implications of using AI. For example, AI4Good, an initiative that connects AI technologies with social impact, focuses on fostering the use of AI to address global challenges such as poverty, health, and education (UNICEF, 2020). Through such programs, local communities can learn how to apply AI tools in ways that are contextually relevant and beneficial to their needs, whether in education, healthcare, agriculture, or other sectors.

Similarly, Microsoft's Digital Literacy Initiative provides training resources and certification programs aimed at equipping individuals with essential digital skills, including understanding how to safely and ethically use AI technologies (Microsoft, 2020). These initiatives often target community leaders, educators, and local facilitators who can serve as multipliers, spreading knowledge and empowering others in their communities to adopt and use AI tools. By training a core group of individuals within a community, these programs create a sustainable framework for ongoing technology adoption and use, as local facilitators can support and mentor others in their peer networks.

In addition to digital literacy, ongoing training is necessary to keep users up-to-date with rapidly evolving AI technologies. Since AI tools and platforms are constantly being updated, it is crucial that training programs include continuous learning modules to ensure that community members are always prepared to take advantage of new features, platforms, and best practices. Facilitators must also be equipped to teach others about the evolving landscape of AI, ensuring that the knowledge shared is accurate, ethical, and in line with the latest advancements.

One of the significant benefits of these initiatives is the empowerment of local educators and community leaders who can bridge the gap between the global technological landscape and the unique needs of their communities. Through targeted training, these individuals can become champions of AI integration, helping contextualize and apply AI solutions in culturally and regionally appropriate ways. Educators can incorporate AI tools into their teaching practices, while community leaders can guide the implementation of AI-based programs that foster local development.

Furthermore, including data privacy and ethical considerations in these training programs is critical. As AI systems often rely on vast amounts of personal data, ensuring that community members understand the importance of safeguarding privacy and upholding ethical standards is fundamental. This aspect of digital literacy prepares individuals to use AI tools and advocate for their responsible and ethical deployment in their communities. Educators and facilitators must be well-versed in the ethical dilemmas surrounding AI, including bias, discrimination, and accountability, to ensure that AI technologies benefit all members of society, particularly those historically marginalized.

Investing in digital literacy and providing ongoing training for local communities is crucial for successfully adopting and integrating AI tools in education and beyond. Programs such as AI4Good and Microsoft's Digital Literacy Initiative play a pivotal role in building local capacity and ensuring that communities are equipped to harness the full potential of AI technologies. By empowering local educators, community leaders, and users, these initiatives create sustainable, inclusive ecosystems that enable AI to serve as a tool for empowerment, social good, and community development.

1.1.4.6.4. Ensuring Affordability and Accessibility

Scaling AI tools must also reduce access barriers, particularly in low-income regions. Subsidized devices, free internet access, and open-source software can ensure that more people benefit from AI-powered tools. Governments and international organizations are critical in ensuring that digital infrastructures support large-scale adoption.

Scaling AI tools in education is about expanding their reach to larger populations and ensuring that all learners, regardless of their socio-economic background, have equal access to the benefits of AI-powered education. This requires a concerted effort to reduce barriers to access, particularly in low-income regions where infrastructure, technology, and digital literacy may be limited. By addressing these challenges, AI can become an inclusive tool that promotes equity in education and helps bridge the digital divide.

One of the primary barriers to AI adoption in low-income regions is the lack of access to devices and reliable internet connectivity. For AI to function effectively in education, it often requires students to have access to smartphones, laptops, or desktop computers, as well as stable internet connections. In many underdeveloped or rural areas, these resources are limited or unavailable, which creates a digital divide that can prevent students from benefiting from AI-based learning tools.

To address this issue, subsidized devices and free internet access can play a crucial role. Governments and organizations can collaborate with tech companies to provide affordable devices such as tablets, laptops, or even smartphones specifically designed for educational purposes. For example, the One Laptop Per Child initiative has been working to provide low-cost, durable laptops to children in underserved regions. Similarly, projects like Google's Project Loon and Facebook's Internet.org have focused on providing free internet access to remote areas. By reducing the cost of devices and expanding internet connectivity, educational institutions can ensure that more students can access AI-powered learning tools.

Open-source software is a powerful tool for scaling AI in education, particularly in regions with limited resources. Open-source platforms, like Moodle for learning management or TensorFlow for AI development, provide free and accessible alternatives to costly proprietary software. These platforms can be customized to meet the specific needs of local education systems, allowing schools in low-income areas to deploy AI solutions without the financial burden of licensing fees. Open-source software also encourages community-driven innovation, where local educators and developers can contribute to developing tools tailored to their region's unique needs.

In addition to providing access to devices and software, building the digital infrastructure necessary to support AI adoption is essential. This includes ensuring that educational institutions in low-income regions have access to the cloud computing resources needed to run AI applications. Many

AI tools rely on cloud-based systems to process large amounts of data and deliver personalized learning experiences. Governments and international organizations can support this infrastructure by investing in broadband expansion and cloud services in underserved areas.

Digital literacy is another critical aspect of scaling AI tools. In many low-income regions, students and teachers may need the necessary skills to use AI-powered platforms effectively. Governments and NGOs can help by offering training programs focusing on digital literacy and AI literacy, ensuring that educators and students are equipped with the knowledge needed to use AI tools effectively. This could include professional development programs for teachers on integrating AI into the classroom and community-based workshops for students on using AI-powered educational platforms.

Governments, international organizations, and private-sector stakeholders have a critical role in reducing these barriers and ensuring the large-scale adoption of AI in education. By investing in digital infrastructure, providing affordable devices, offering free internet access, supporting open-source solutions, and fostering digital literacy, these entities can help bridge the gap between different regions and create a more equitable educational landscape. These efforts will enable AI to fulfill its potential as a transformative force in education, ensuring that all learners, regardless of their socio-economic status, can access its opportunities and benefits.

Scaling AI tools in education is about expanding access to technology and reducing the barriers preventing low-income students from benefiting from AI-powered learning solutions. Governments, international organizations, and other stakeholders can ensure that AI contributes to a more inclusive and equitable education system by focusing on affordability, infrastructure, and digital literacy.

1.1.4.7. Policy Frameworks to Ensure Ethical AI Deployment

Ensuring that AI is deployed ethically in education and empowerment contexts requires the establishment of robust policy frameworks. These frameworks should guide AI design, development, and deployment to prioritize fairness, transparency, and accountability. Key policy considerations include:

- *Inclusive Design Standards:* Policymakers must ensure that AI systems are designed with inclusivity. This includes creating guidelines for building AI tools that are accessible to all learners, particularly those with disabilities. Ensuring accessibility for visually impaired learners, for instance, involves integrating text-to-speech or speech-to-text functionality into AI applications.

- *Ethical Guidelines for Data Use:* AI systems rely on data to function, raising significant concerns about data privacy and security. Policies should establish clear guidelines on data collection, usage, and storage, emphasizing the need for informed consent and protecting users' personal information. Organizations like UNESCO have emphasized the importance of safeguarding human rights and promoting ethical AI use (UNESCO, 2021).
- *Transparency and Accountability*: Policymakers should demand transparency from AI developers regarding how their systems make decisions. Clear documentation of algorithms, underlying assumptions, and decision-making processes can help mitigate biases and ensure that AI deployment is accountable. This includes fostering public trust by ensuring that AI systems are explainable to non-experts, particularly in critical sectors like education and financial inclusion.
- *Global Ethical Standards:* As AI systems are increasingly deployed worldwide, it is vital to establish global ethical standards that can guide their implementation across different cultural and socio-economic contexts. Organizations like the OECD and the EU have developed frameworks for AI ethics that aim to ensure fairness, accountability, and transparency in AI use across borders (OECD, 2020).

By following these practical guidelines, educational institutions, policymakers, and technology developers can effectively integrate AI into education and empowerment programs while ensuring that AI tools are accessible, scalable, and ethically sound. This approach ensures that AI serves as a tool for transformation, addressing critical gaps in education and empowerment globally.

1.1.4.8. Theoretical and Practical Insights

The book balances theoretical exploration with practical application, ensuring a nuanced understanding of AI's potential and challenges.

1.1.4.8.1. AI in Education

- *Revolutionizing Education through Adaptive Technologies and Data-Driven Insights*
AI transforms education by utilizing adaptive learning technologies and personalizing student learning experiences. These systems use data-driven insights to adjust content, pace, and difficulty based on individual progress. Tools such as AI-powered learning platforms like Knewton and DreamBox Learning enable students to learn at their own pace, enhancing engagement and retention. AI also provides real-time analytics to educators, helping them track student performance and make data-driven decisions to improve learning outcomes (Holmes et al., 2019).
- *Addressing Educational Inequities, Particularly in Underserved Communities*
AI can play a crucial role in reducing educational inequities by providing access to high-quality learning materials in underserved communities. For instance, AI-based tutoring systems can offer personalized learning experiences even in areas without qualified teachers. Additionally, AI-powered platforms can make educational resources available to learners in remote or economically disadvantaged regions, overcoming barriers related to infrastructure and teacher availability (Luckin et al., 2016). By providing adaptive tools, AI helps ensure that all students, regardless of background, have access to effective educational resources.
- *Rethinking Curricula to Align with a Technology-Driven World*
The rapid evolution of technology calls for an overhaul of traditional curricula. AI allows curricula to reflect the skills needed in a technology-driven world, such as problem-solving, critical thinking, and digital literacy. By integrating AI into the curriculum, educational systems can prepare students for future challenges and equip them with the skills needed in the evolving job market. AI tools can also help reimagine the teaching process, moving from traditional lecture-based models to more interactive and personalized learning experiences (Chase et al., 2019).

1.1.4.8.2. AI in Empowerment

- *Enhancing Skill-Building, Economic Participation, and Global Connectivity*
  AI-driven technologies can enhance skills development and economic participation, particularly in marginalized communities. AI platforms can help individuals acquire job-ready skills tailored to specific industries by providing personalized learning pathways. For example, platforms like Coursera and edX offer online courses, often powered by AI, that allow individuals to gain skills relevant to the global job market. These tools democratize access to education and enable people to participate more fully in the worldwide economy, irrespective of their geographic location or socioeconomic status (Saini & Agarwal, 2021).
- *Examining Tools Like Microfinance Technologies and Vocational Platforms for Empowerment*
  AI-based tools in microfinance, such as mobile banking platforms and credit scoring algorithms, empower individuals in developing countries by providing access to financial resources. Microfinance platforms like M-Pesa leverage AI to enable financial inclusion by offering mobile phone services such as money transfers, savings, and loans. Additionally, AI-powered vocational training platforms, such as IBM's SkillsBuild, equip individuals with the skills necessary to enter the workforce and improve their economic status. These platforms often include mentorship, job matching, and career development tools to facilitate long-term economic empowerment (Liu et al., 2020).

1.1.4.8.3. Ethical Considerations

- *Addressing Issues Like the Digital Divide, Algorithmic Fairness, and Responsible AI Governance*
  The digital divide remains a significant challenge in ensuring equitable access to AI-driven education and empowerment tools. Policymakers and organizations must work to bridge this gap by promoting affordable access to technology and the Internet. Additionally, AI systems must be designed to be fair and unbiased. Algorithmic fairness ensures that AI does not perpetuate or amplify existing social inequalities. This requires the development of AI

models that are transparent and accountable. Ethical AI governance frameworks, such as those proposed by UNESCO and other global organizations, provide guidelines for ensuring that AI technologies are developed and deployed in ways that prioritize inclusivity and equity (West et al., 2019).

- *Leveraging Ethical Theories and International Policy Guidelines*
  Ethical theories, including deontological and utilitarian perspectives, can guide AI development and deployment by ensuring that AI systems respect fundamental human rights while maximizing societal benefits. International policy guidelines, such as UNESCO's *Ethical Guidelines for Artificial Intelligence* and the EU's *Artificial Intelligence Act*, provide frameworks for regulating AI. These frameworks address data privacy, transparency, and accountability in AI systems. These policies promote responsible AI deployment that upholds ethical standards and protects vulnerable populations (UNESCO, 2021; OECD, 2020).

1.1.4.8.3.1. Global Context

- *Highlighting Regional Disparities in AI Adoption and Its Cultural Impacts*
  AI adoption varies significantly across regions and is influenced by economic development, infrastructure, and governmental policies. In developed countries, AI is being integrated into education systems faster, while developing nations face challenges related to access to technology and skilled personnel. The cultural context also plays a role in the implementation and perception of AI. For example, AI systems in some regions may need to be tailored to local languages, customs, and educational practices. Understanding these regional disparities is crucial for ensuring AI benefits are equitably distributed globally (Liu et al., 2020).
- *Analyzing AI's Role in Achieving Global Education and Empowerment Goals*
  AI has the potential to significantly contribute to achieving global education and empowerment goals, particularly the United Nations' Sustainable Development Goals (SDGs). AI can support SDG 4 (Quality Education) by providing personalized learning opportunities to people in under-resourced areas. It can also aid in SDG 8 (Decent

Work and Economic Growth) by offering skill-building platforms that empower individuals economically. By leveraging AI in these ways, countries can accelerate progress toward meeting global development goals and promoting more equitable, sustainable growth (Holmes et al., 2019).

These elements explore AI's transformative role in education and empowerment and the ethical considerations and global implications of its adoption, offering insights into how AI can create more equitable and inclusive societies worldwide.

This comprehensive scope ensures that the book is both a theoretical guide and a practical resource for understanding and leveraging AI in education and empowerment.

1.1.4.8.3.2. Relevance of AI Today

The book is anchored in the understanding that AI is a transformative force in addressing contemporary challenges. Its theoretical exploration underscores how AI can democratize access to education, enhance learning outcomes, and empower marginalized communities. By synthesizing insights from desktop research and global case studies, the book positions itself as a resource for understanding the profound implications of AI for education and empowerment in the modern era.

The methodology and scope of this study are designed to provide a rigorous and comprehensive analysis of AI's transformative potential. The book aims to contribute to global efforts to foster equitable education and empower communities worldwide through interdisciplinary research, real-world case studies, and forward-looking insights.

References

Angwin, J., Larson, J., Mattu, S., & Kirchner, L. (2016). Machine bias: There's software used nationwide to predict future criminals. And it's biased. *ProPublica*. https://www.propublica.org/article/machine-bias-risk-assessments-in-criminal-sentencing.

Aoun, J. E. (2017). *Robot-proof: Higher education in the age of artificial intelligence.* MIT Press.

Baker, R. S. (2016). Big data and education: Learning analytics and educational data mining. *Review of Research in Education*, 40(1), 33-68.

Baker, R. S. (2016). Stupid tutoring systems, intelligent humans. *International Journal of Artificial Intelligence in Education, 26*(2), 600–614. https://doi.org/10.1007/s40593-016-0105-0.

Binns, R. (2018). On the ethical implications of AI in developing countries. *AI & Society, 33*(3), 427-433. https://doi.org/10.1007/s00146-018-0802-7.

Center for Curriculum Redesign. (n.d.). AI and the future of learning. Retrieved from https://curriculumredesign.org.

Chase, A., Maher, C., & Alavi, M. (2019). The role of AI in improving educational outcomes: Best practices for integration. *International Journal of Educational Technology, 16*(3), 45-57.

Chase, B., Thomas, R., & Hartman, M. (2019). *AI in education: Exploring the potential of scalable solutions*. Journal of Educational Technology & Society, 22(4), 49-60.

Chase, P., Parson, L., & Ross, S. (2019). *AI in education: Tools for improving teaching and learning*. In J. S. D. Chan & A. E. T. Klein (Eds.), *Technologies shaping the future of education* (pp. 125-140). Springer.

Chen, J., & Chen, J. (2020). Personalized learning with AI: Methods and applications. *Journal of Artificial Intelligence in Education*, 29(2), 1-18.

Chen, J., & Chen, L. (2020). AI for inclusive education: Addressing challenges for learners with disabilities. *Journal of Educational Technology*, 35(2), 123-136.

Chen, X., & Chen, S. (2020). AI-enabled personalized learning for students with disabilities: Challenges and opportunities. *Educational Technology Research and Development*, 68(4), 1471–1493.

EdSurge. (n.d.). The intersection of AI and education. Retrieved from https://www.edsurge.com.

Facebook. (2021). *Internet.org: Connecting the world.* Retrieved from https://www.internet.org.

Google AI. (2019). AI for Social Good. Retrieved from Google AI for Social Good.

Google. (2020). *Project Loon: Bringing internet access to remote areas*. Retrieved from https://www.projectloon.com

Haider, S., & Tandon, R. (2022). Integrating AI into digital learning ecosystems. In *Proceedings of the IEEE Conference on Learning Technologies* (pp. 125–132).

Holmes, W., & Porayska-Pomsta, K. (2021). *Ethical implications of artificial intelligence in education*. Springer.

Holmes, W., & Porayska-Pomsta, K. (2021). Ethics in AI and education: Balancing risks and opportunities. *AI & Society, 36*(3), 639–656. https://doi.org/10.1007/s00146-020-01055-0.

Holmes, W., & Porayska-Pomsta, K. (2021). Ethics in AI education: Transparency, fairness, and accountability. *AI & Society*, 36, 1-17.

Holmes, W., & Porayska-Pomsta, K. (2021). Ethics in AI education: Towards a framework for fairness and accountability. *AI and Ethics*.

Holmes, W., Bialik, M., & Fadel, C. (2019). *Artificial intelligence in education: Promises and implications for teaching and learning*. Boston: Center for Curriculum Redesign.

IBM. (2021). SkillsBuild: Empowering individuals with skills for the future. Retrieved from IBM SkillsBuild.

Lin, C. H., & Chiou, H. J. (2020). The role of AI in equitable education: A systematic review. *Computers & Education*, 150, 103857.

Lin, J., & Chiou, W. (2020). AI and digital equity: Overcoming barriers to learning in underserved communities. *Journal of Educational Innovation, 15*(3), 245–258.

Linn, M. C. (2019). The role of artificial intelligence in personalized education. *Educational Psychologist, 54*(2), 127-138. https://doi.org/10.1080/00461520.2019.1594016.

Linn, R. L. (2019). *The role of artificial intelligence in personalized learning*. In B. L. Bialik & C. Fadel (Eds.), *Artificial intelligence in education: Promises and implications for teaching and learning* (pp. 45-62). Center for Curriculum Redesign.

Liu, M., Tapan, M., & Syed, J. (2021). *AI-driven learning management systems: Enhancing student engagement and performance monitoring*. Journal of Educational Technology, 42(1), 58-72.

Shute, V. J., & Zapata-Rivera, D. (2020). *Personalized learning and AI: Tools and techniques for effective educational interventions*. Educational Technology Research and Development, 68(3), 973-993.

Liu, W., Chen, Y., & Zhang, Q. (2020). Scaling AI for development: Strategies for empowering communities. *Journal of Technology in Society, 41*, 77-89. https://doi.org/10.1016/j.techsoc.2020.100348.

Luckin, R. (2018). *Machine learning and human intelligence: The future of education for the 21st century*. Routledge.

Luckin, R., Holmes, W., Griffiths, M., & Forcier, L. B. (2016). *Intelligence Unleashed: An argument for AI in education*. Pearson Education.

Microsoft. (2020). *Microsoft digital literacy initiative*. Retrieved from https://www.microsoft.com/digital-literacy.

Munyua, H., & Njiru, N. (2020). Digital transformation and AI: Lessons from Kenya's educational and vocational training sectors. *Journal of African Development, 22*(2), 121-130.

Nussbaum, M. C. (2000). *Women and human development: The capabilities approach*. Cambridge: Cambridge University Press.

OECD. (2020). *AI in education: Policies for a fairer and more inclusive future*. OECD Publishing.

OECD. (2021). *AI and the future of skills: Education 2030*. Organization for Economic Co-operation and Development.

OECD. (2021). *AI in education: Challenges and opportunities for sustainable development*. Organization for Economic Co-operation and Development.

OECD. (2021). *AI in education: Challenges and opportunities*. Paris: OECD Publishing.

OECD. (2021). *Artificial intelligence in education: Insights and policy recommendations*. Organization for Economic Co-operation and Development.

OECD. (2021). *The future of education and skills: Education 2030*. Organization for Economic Cooperation and Development.

One Laptop Per Child. (2021). *About OLPC*. Retrieved from http://www.laptop.org.

Rashid, T., & Aslam, M. (2021). AI and social-emotional learning: Opportunities and challenges. *International Journal of Educational Technology in Higher Education*, 18(3), 22-39.

Rashid, T., & Aslam, N. (2021). Exploring AI-driven emotional learning systems. *AI in Education Research Quarterly, 14*(1), 98–105.

Saini, P., & Agarwal, R. (2021). Digital literacy and AI-driven tools for empowerment: Strategies for scaling across developing nations. *Journal of Information Technology, 24*(1), 54-67.

Schwab, K., & Malleret, T. (2020). *The Great Reset*. Forum Publishing.

Selwyn, N. (2019). Should robots replace teachers? AI and the future of education. *British Journal of Educational Technology*, 50(6), 1-17.

Selwyn, N. (2019). *Should robots replace teachers? AI and the future of education.* Wiley.

Sen, A. (1999). *Development as freedom*. New York: Alfred A. Knopf.

UNESCO. (2019). *Artificial intelligence in education: Challenges and opportunities for sustainable development*. United Nations Educational, Scientific and Cultural Organization.

UNESCO. (2021). *AI and education: A guide for policymakers*. Paris: United Nations Educational, Scientific and Cultural Organization.

UNESCO. (2021). *AI for good: Bridging the digital divide*. United Nations Educational, Scientific and Cultural Organization.

UNESCO. (2021). *Artificial intelligence and education: Guidance for policymakers*. UNESCO Publishing.

UNESCO. (2021). *Artificial intelligence and inclusion: Bridging the divide*. United Nations Educational, Scientific and Cultural Organization.

UNESCO. (2021). *Artificial intelligence in education: Challenges and opportunities for sustainable development*. United Nations Educational, Scientific and Cultural Organization.

UNESCO. (2021). *Artificial intelligence in education: Challenges and opportunities*. United Nations Educational, Scientific and Cultural Organization.

UNESCO. (2021). *Ethical guidelines for artificial intelligence: Fostering inclusive and equitable development*. UNESCO Publishing.

UNICEF. (2020). *AI for good: Leveraging AI to meet the SDGs*. Retrieved from https://www.unicef.org.

VanLehn, K. (2011). The relative effectiveness of human tutoring, intelligent tutoring systems, and other tutoring systems. *Educational Psychologist, 46*(4), 197-221. https://doi.org/10.1080/00461520.2011.607258.

Vinuesa, R., Azizpour, H., Lehtimäki, J., et al. (2020). The role of artificial intelligence in achieving sustainable development goals. *Nature Communications, 11*(1), 233. https://doi.org/10.1038/s41467-019-14108-y.

West, D. M., & Allen, J. R. (2019). *How artificial intelligence is transforming the future of work*. Brookings Institution Press.

West, S. M., Whittaker, M., & Crawford, K. (2019). *Discriminating systems: Gender, race, and power in AI*. Data & Society. https://datasociety.net/pubs/ia_ds_2019_discriminating_systems_2019.pdf.

Woolf, B. P., Lane, H. C., Chaudhri, V. K., & Kolodner, J. L. (2013). AI grand challenges for education. In *Proceedings of the 27th AAAI Conference on Artificial Intelligence* (pp. 1936–1941).

World Economic Forum. (2020). *Schools of the future: Defining new models of education for the fourth industrial revolution*. World Economic Forum.

World Economic Forum. (2020). *The future of AI in education: Preparing students for the AI-driven economy*. WEF Report Series.

World Economic Forum. (2020). *The future of jobs report*. Geneva: World Economic Forum.

Zawacki-Richter, O., Marín, V. I., Bond, M., & Gouverneur, F. (2019). Systematic review of research on artificial intelligence applications in higher education. *International Journal of Educational Technology in Higher Education, 16*(1), 39. https://doi.org/10.1186/s41239-019-0177-8.

Zeng, J., & Han, Y. (2020). *Artificial intelligence and privacy concerns: Exploring the future of digital privacy in AI governance*. Springer. https://doi.org/10.1007/978-3-030-27944-5.

Chapter 2

The Age of Artificial Intelligence

2.1. Introduction

Artificial Intelligence's (AI's) rapid evolution has been a technological advancement but a transformative force that has reshaped various aspects of society. This era, commonly referred to as 'The Age of Artificial Intelligence,' has seen AI, the simulation of human intelligence processes by machines, particularly computer systems, move from the realm of science fiction to reality. AI systems are now capable of learning, problem-solving, and even decision-making, offering unprecedented opportunities and challenges. The integration of AI technologies has moved beyond simple automation. It is now deeply intertwined with data science, machine learning, and natural language processing, resulting in systems that can process vast amounts of information with accuracy and speed unparalleled by human capabilities (Brynjolfsson & McAfee, 2014).

AI's rapid advancement is driven by several factors: the exponential growth of computational power, vast amounts of available data, and improvements in algorithmic techniques. As a result, AI is no longer confined to narrow applications but increasingly influences complex areas such as autonomous vehicles, personalized medicine, and AI-enhanced learning environments (Chui et al., 2016). For instance, AI-driven technologies in education, such as intelligent tutoring systems and adaptive learning platforms, are redefining traditional pedagogical approaches and offering tailored educational experiences to meet individual learner needs (Holmes et al., 2019). In healthcare, AI tools like predictive analytics and machine learning models improve diagnostic accuracy and treatment planning, thus transforming patient care delivery (Topol, 2019).

However, this technological revolution also brings forward significant ethical and societal concerns. The increased reliance on AI systems raises critical questions about privacy, security, bias, and the potential for job displacement due to automation. Algorithmic bias, for example, can perpetuate systemic inequalities, particularly when AI systems are trained on biased data sets or fail to account for diverse societal needs (West et al., 2019). Additionally, the digital divide—unequal access to AI technologies between different regions and socioeconomic groups—exacerbates existing inequalities, limiting the ability of marginalized populations to benefit from AI advancements (OECD, 2020) fully. These challenges highlight the need for robust ethical frameworks and policies to guide the development and implementation of AI technologies, underscoring the responsibility of all stakeholders in the AI ecosystem.

As we move into the age of AI, it is crucial to address these concerns while embracing AI's immense potential for solving some of the world's most pressing issues, such as climate change, global health disparities, and educational inequities. AI has the potential to revolutionize these areas, offering innovative solutions and inspiring hope for a better future. Policymakers, educators, and technologists must collaborate to ensure that AI is developed and deployed in ways that promote inclusivity, fairness, and transparency. The future of AI will likely be shaped not only by its technological capabilities but also by how society chooses to regulate and integrate these systems into existing structures, ensuring that AI serves as a force for good while mitigating potential risks.

2.1.1. Historical Overview and Development of AI

The history of Artificial Intelligence (AI) spans over seven decades and reflects the evolution of human thought on intelligence, computation, and automation. The concept of AI can be traced back to ancient myths and stories of artificial beings endowed with intelligence, such as the Greek myth of Talos, the giant automaton, or the golem in Jewish folklore. However, the formalization of AI as a field of study began in the mid-20th century with the rise of modern computer science and the development of theoretical foundations for machine learning and logic (Russell & Norvig, 2016). Early AI research was heavily influenced by the work of Alan Turing, who in 1950 published the seminal paper "Computing Machinery and Intelligence," proposing the question "Can machines think?" and introducing what is now known as the Turing Test, a benchmark for evaluating a machine's ability to exhibit intelligent behavior indistinguishable from that of a human (Turing, 1950).

The formal birth of AI as a research discipline occurred in 1956 at the Dartmouth Conference, organized by John McCarthy, Marvin Minsky, Nathaniel Rochester, and Claude Shannon. This conference set the tone for AI research to create "thinking machines." Early efforts in AI were focused on symbolic approaches, where problems were solved through predefined sets of rules and logic. These early AI systems, such as the Logic Theorist and the General Problem Solver developed by Allen Newell and Herbert A. Simon, relied on symbolic reasoning to emulate human problem-solving capabilities (Newell & Simon, 1972). During this period, AI research garnered significant optimism, with scholars believing that machines would soon be capable of performing a wide range of cognitive tasks.

However, the initial optimism was followed by what is commonly referred to as the "AI winter," a period of stagnation in the field during the 1970s and 1980s. Several factors contributed to this slowdown, including the limitations of early computational power, the inability of symbolic AI to handle real-world complexity, and the failure to meet the high expectations set in earlier decades. During this time, AI research faced criticism for its inability to produce practical, scalable applications, leading to reduced funding and interest from academia and industry (Crevier, 1993). Nevertheless, AI continued progressing in niche areas such as expert systems, which used rule-based approaches to make decisions in specialized domains like medical diagnosis and financial forecasting.

The resurgence of AI in the late 20th and early 21st centuries can be attributed to several technological advancements. First, the exponential growth in computational power and the availability of large datasets laid the foundation for developing machine learning (ML) and deep learning (DL) algorithms. These approaches, which rely on statistical models and pattern recognition rather than explicit rule-based systems, have enabled machines to learn from data and improve their performance over time (Goodfellow et al., 2016). One of the pivotal moments in this resurgence was the success of deep learning models, particularly the convolutional neural networks (CNNs) developed for image recognition tasks, which achieved breakthroughs in performance on tasks such as speech recognition, computer vision, and natural language processing (LeCun et al., 2015). This era marked a shift from symbolic AI to statistical and data-driven AI, focusing less on replicating human reasoning and more on creating systems that could identify patterns and make predictions from vast amounts of data.

The 21st century has seen the proliferation of AI in various sectors, from healthcare to finance to education. One of the key drivers of AI adoption in recent years has been the integration of AI with cloud computing and big data analytics, enabling scalable and efficient AI solutions. AI applications such as autonomous vehicles, facial recognition technology, and personalized recommendation systems have become part of daily life, showcasing AI's potential to transform industries and society (Brynjolfsson & McAfee, 2014). However, as AI systems have become more powerful and ubiquitous, they have also raised important ethical and societal concerns, such as algorithmic bias, privacy violations, and the impact of automation on the workforce. The growing influence of AI has prompted the development of ethical frameworks and regulatory guidelines to ensure that AI technologies are deployed responsibly and equitably (Jobin et al., 2019).

In conclusion, the development of AI has been a long and dynamic journey, marked by periods of optimism, setbacks, and eventual breakthroughs. From its conceptual beginnings in the mid-20th century to its current position as a transformative force across industries, AI has evolved from theoretical musings to practical, data-driven technologies with the potential to reshape the future. As AI advances, it will be crucial to balance its technological capabilities with ethical considerations to ensure its benefits are distributed equitably and its risks are mitigated.

2.1.2. Intersection of AI with Education and Empowerment

The intersection of Artificial Intelligence (AI) with education and empowerment is a rapidly evolving area that holds the potential to reshape learning environments and foster greater opportunities for individuals worldwide. As AI technologies continue to mature, their integration into educational contexts has opened new possibilities for personalized learning, student empowerment, and equitable access to academic resources. AI's role in education extends beyond the enhancement of learning processes; it also provides the tools for expanding human potential and addressing existing disparities in access to quality education.

One of the key ways AI influences education is through personalized learning. AI-powered tools like intelligent tutoring systems (ITS) and adaptive learning platforms enable a more tailored educational experience. These systems leverage machine learning algorithms to assess students' strengths, weaknesses, and learning styles, adapting the content and pace of lessons to suit individual needs (VanLehn, 2011). For instance, AI applications like personalized reading programs or math tutoring systems can provide instant feedback and guidance, helping students master topics at their own pace, regardless of their physical location or access to qualified educators. This shift from a one-size-fits-all model to personalized instruction has significant implications for both student learning outcomes and the overall effectiveness of educational systems (Luckin et al., 2016).

In addition to personalized learning, AI can facilitate empowerment by making education more inclusive and accessible. In many regions, particularly in low-income or rural areas, access to quality education is limited by a shortage of teachers, infrastructure, and resources. AI can help bridge these gaps by providing scalable and cost-effective solutions. For example, AI-driven platforms can offer virtual tutoring, language translation, and specialized resources for students with disabilities, enabling greater inclusion for marginalized groups (Holmes et al., 2019). Furthermore, AI can assist in overcoming language barriers, enabling non-native speakers to engage with educational content in their preferred language or through real-time translation services. These advancements can reduce educational inequality and ensure that more learners, regardless of their geographic location or socio-economic background, can access quality education (UNESCO, 2021).

Empowerment through AI in education also involves enhancing the skills and capabilities of educators. AI systems can assist teachers in various administrative tasks, such as grading and scheduling, allowing them to focus more on pedagogy and student engagement (West et al., 2019). In addition, AI can support teachers in identifying at-risk students or those who may need additional help, providing insights that enable early intervention. By automating routine tasks, AI can reduce teacher burnout and increase job satisfaction, ultimately contributing to a more sustainable and effective educational workforce. Additionally, AI tools can offer professional development opportunities, helping educators stay up to date with the latest pedagogical approaches and integrate innovative technologies into their teaching practices (Luckin et al., 2016).

Despite its potential, integrating AI into education raises several critical challenges, particularly concerning equity and ethics. As AI becomes more prevalent in educational settings, concerns about algorithmic bias and privacy issues must be addressed. Research has shown that AI systems can unintentionally perpetuate biases, particularly when trained on data sets that reflect societal inequalities related to race, gender, or socioeconomic status (West et al., 2019). In education, biased algorithms could impact how students are assessed, which resources are recommended, or even the opportunities offered. Therefore, it is essential to develop and implement AI systems that are transparent, fair, and accountable, ensuring that they contribute to, rather than hinder, social equity (Holmes et al., 2019).

Moreover, the rise of AI in education presents a significant opportunity to promote lifelong learning and skills development. As automation continues to disrupt traditional job markets, there is an increasing demand for individuals to acquire new skills throughout their lives. AI can facilitate this transition by providing personalized, flexible learning experiences that enable people to upskill or reskill at any stage of their careers. For example, AI-powered platforms can help individuals learn new languages, technical skills, or vocational competencies, equipping them with the tools to adapt to changing labor markets (Brynjolfsson & McAfee, 2014). This approach aligns with the principles of empowerment, as it enables individuals to take control of their learning journeys and better navigate the complexities of modern society.

In conclusion, AI's intersection with education and empowerment offers transformative possibilities for learners, educators, and society. By enhancing personalized learning, increasing accessibility, and supporting lifelong learning, AI has the potential to revolutionize education and provide equitable opportunities for all. However, this transformation must be approached cautiously, ensuring that ethical considerations, such as bias and privacy, are integrated into the design and deployment of AI systems. With the right frameworks in place, AI can play a pivotal role in creating more inclusive, personalized, and empowering educational experiences that contribute to the development of individuals and communities worldwide.

References

Brynjolfsson, E., & McAfee, A. (2014). The second Machine Age: Work, progress, and Prosperity in a time of brilliant technologies. W. W. Norton & Company.

Chui, M., Manyika, J., & Miremadi, M. (2016). Where machines could replace humans—and where they cannot (yet). McKinsey & Company. https://www.mckinsey.com/featured-insights/future-of-work/where-machines-could-replace-humans-and-where-they-cant-yet.

Crevier, D. (1993). AI: The tumultuous history of the search for artificial intelligence. Basic Books.

Goodfellow, I., Bengio, Y., & Courville, A. (2016). *Deep learning*. MIT Press.

Holmes, W., Bialik, M., & Fadel, C. (2019). Artificial Intelligence in Education: Promises and Implications for Teaching and Learning. Center for Curriculum Redesign.

Jobin, A., Ienca, M., & Vayena, E. (2019). The global landscape of AI ethics guidelines. Nature Machine Intelligence, 1(9), 389-399. https://doi.org/10.1038/s42256-019-0088-2.

LeCun, Y., Bengio, Y., & Hinton, G. (2015). *Deep learning. Nature*, 521(7553), 436-444. https://doi.org/10.1038/nature14539.

Luckin, R., Holmes, W., Griffiths, M., & Forcier, L. B. (2016). *Intelligence Unleashed: An Argument for AI in Education*. Pearson Education.

Newell, A., & Simon, H. A. (1972). *Human problem solving*. Prentice-Hall.

OECD. (2020). *AI in education: Policies for a fairer and more inclusive future*. OECD Publishing.

Russell, S., & Norvig, P. (2016). *Artificial intelligence: A modern approac*h (3rd ed.). Pearson.

Topol, E. (2019). Deep medicine: How artificial intelligence can make healthcare human again—basic Books.

Turing, A. (1950). Computing machinery and intelligence. *Mind,* 59(236), 433-460.

UNESCO. (2021). *Artificial Intelligence and Education: Guidance for Policy-Makers.* UNESCO Publishing.

VanLehn, K. (2011). The relative effectiveness of human tutoring, intelligent tutoring systems, and other tutoring systems. *Educational Psychologist*, 46(4), 197-221.

West, S. M., Whittaker, M., & Crawford, K. (2019). *Discriminating systems: Gender, race, and power in AI*. AI Now Institute.

West, S. M., Whittaker, M., & Crawford, K. (2019). *Discriminating systems: Gender, race, and power in AI.* AI Now Institute.

Chapter 3

The Need for Transformation in Education and Empowerment

3.1. Introduction

Transformation in education and empowerment is not just a distant possibility but an urgent necessity in the face of global challenges such as inequality, climate change, technological disruption, and shifting societal needs. Traditional educational systems have often been critiqued for their inability to address the evolving demands of a rapidly changing world. As society transitions into the digital age, education must undergo significant reforms to equip individuals with the skills, knowledge, and agency necessary for navigating an interconnected, complex world. In this context, transformation in education is not merely about improving existing practices but about fundamentally reimagining how learning occurs, what is learned, and for whom.

One of the primary drivers of this transformation is the increasing recognition of the limitations of traditional educational models, which often prioritize rote memorization, standardized testing, and passive learning. While these approaches have been historically effective in specific contexts, they need to foster critical thinking, creativity, or the ability to adapt to new and unforeseen challenges (Saavedra & Opfer, 2012). In a world where the nature of work and society is rapidly evolving due to advances in technology, automation, and globalization, there is an urgent need for educational systems to foster skills that enable individuals to thrive in a constantly changing landscape. This includes technical skills and socio-emotional competencies such as problem-solving, collaboration, adaptability, and emotional intelligence, all of which are essential for human flourishing and societal progress.

The global rise in educational inequality has underscored the need to transform how education is delivered and accessed. According to the United Nations Educational, Scientific and Cultural Organization (UNESCO, 2021), over 260 million children and adolescents worldwide are still out of school, while millions more face poor-quality education due to factors like poverty, gender discrimination, and geographic location. Such disparities exacerbate existing social inequalities and limit opportunities for upward mobility. In this context, educational reform is not just about improving the quality of education but also about ensuring that education is inclusive, equitable, and accessible to all learners, regardless of their background or circumstances. The transformative potential of education lies in its capacity to level the playing field and empower individuals to escape cycles of poverty, marginalization, and disenfranchisement.

Empowerment is another crucial aspect of the educational transformation needed today. The concept of empowerment encompasses enabling individuals and communities to gain control over their lives, make informed decisions, and shape their future. In the educational context, this means creating learning environments where students are not passive recipients of knowledge but active participants in their learning processes. Empowering students requires a shift from teacher-centered to student-centered pedagogies, where learners are encouraged to take responsibility for their learning, pursue their interests, and develop the skills necessary for lifelong learning. As Freire (2000) highlighted, education must be a tool for liberation, helping individuals critically examine their social, political, and economic environments and take action to transform them.

Technology plays a pivotal role in this transformation, particularly in expanding access to education and enhancing the quality of learning experiences. Integrating digital tools, online platforms, and Artificial Intelligence (AI) into education provides unprecedented opportunities for personalized learning, as it allows for the creation of tailored educational experiences that cater to individual learning styles, paces, and needs (Holmes et al., 2019). AI, for instance, can help bridge gaps in educational access by providing scalable tutoring services, real-time feedback, and adaptive learning environments, particularly in areas where qualified teachers are in short supply. In addition, AI can help democratize education by providing learners worldwide with access to high-quality educational content that may otherwise be inaccessible due to geographic or financial barriers. This aligns with the broader goal of empowerment, as education becomes not just a means of acquiring knowledge but a tool for personal and social transformation.

The globalized and interconnected world also necessitates a transformation in education content. Traditional curricula often prioritize disciplinary knowledge, which, while important, may not adequately prepare students for the interdisciplinary, complex problems they will face in the future. There is a growing emphasis on teaching students to think critically about global issues such as climate change, social justice, and sustainability, as well as how they can contribute to positive change in their communities and beyond (UNESCO, 2017). This shift towards a more holistic, interdisciplinary approach to education reflects the need for individuals to possess specific knowledge and the ability to apply that knowledge in real-world contexts to solve complex, global challenges. The ability to critically engage with equity, justice, and sustainability issues is paramount for creating a more just, peaceful, and sustainable world.

Education's transformative potential is closely linked to its ability to foster agency and self-efficacy among individuals. Empowering learners means helping them develop a sense of ownership over their learning and lives. This requires an education system that emphasizes academic success, personal growth, resilience, and developing a growth mindset (Dweck, 2006). When individuals believe in their ability to grow, learn, and make meaningful contributions to society, they are more likely to take the initiative to improve their circumstances and those of others. Education, therefore, becomes a vehicle for both personal empowerment and collective social change, where individuals are equipped to actively participate in shaping a better future.

The need for transformation in education and empowerment is urgent and multifaceted. As the world faces complex challenges, education must evolve to provide learners with the skills, knowledge, and agency to thrive in a rapidly changing, interconnected world. This transformation should focus on inclusivity, critical thinking, and personal agency, ensuring that all individuals, regardless of their background, have access to education that empowers them to contribute to the collective well-being. By reimagining education in this way, we can harness its full potential as a tool for personal and social empowerment, helping to create a more equitable, sustainable, and just society.

3.1.1. Current Challenges in Global Education

Global education faces many challenges impacting the quality, accessibility, and relevance of learning worldwide. These challenges are multifaceted and interconnected, spanning issues of inequality, technology integration, pedagogical approaches, and the changing demands of the labor market. Addressing these challenges is crucial for ensuring that education systems can effectively prepare learners for the complex, interconnected world of the future. The following paragraphs explore some of the key challenges facing global education today.

One of the most pressing challenges in global education is the persistent issue of educational inequality. According to UNESCO (2020), more than 260 million children and adolescents are out of school, and many others face poor-quality education, often due to factors such as poverty, gender, geographical location, and disability. The COVID-19 pandemic exacerbated these disparities, with millions of learners in low-income countries losing access to education due to school closures and the digital divide. Even within high-income countries, marginalized communities often struggle to access quality education due to systemic inequalities in the education system, such as insufficient resources, unqualified teachers, and inadequate support for students with special needs (UNICEF, 2020). Tackling educational inequality requires improving access to education and addressing the quality of education students receive, ensuring that all learners can succeed, regardless of their socio-economic background.

Another significant challenge is the rapid pace of technological change and its impact on education. While technology has the potential to enhance learning, increase access to education, and enable personalized learning experiences, it also presents challenges, particularly in terms of the digital divide. Technology integration in education has not been uniform, with many low-income regions lacking the necessary infrastructure, such as reliable internet access, devices, and trained teachers, to fully benefit from digital learning tools (Selwyn, 2016). Furthermore, the rise of digital learning platforms and Artificial Intelligence (AI) in education raises questions about the quality and equity of learning experiences. There is a growing concern that the increasing reliance on technology may further marginalize those already disadvantaged, creating a new form of inequality. As Holmes, Bialik, and Fadel (2019) argue, technology can be a great equalizer or divider, depending on how it is implemented and who has access to it. To ensure that technology contributes positively to education, addressing the digital divide and ensuring that all learners have equitable access to the resources they need to succeed is essential.

The need for education systems to adapt to the changing demands of the labor market is another critical challenge. The skills required to succeed in the workforce rapidly evolve in an increasingly globalized and technology-driven world. According to the World Economic Forum (2020), critical thinking, creativity, emotional intelligence, and digital literacy skills are becoming more important than ever. However, many education systems continue to focus heavily on traditional academic subjects and rote learning, which may not adequately prepare students for the complex, interdisciplinary challenges they will face in the future (Saavedra & Opfer, 2012). There is a growing need to reform curricula to focus on academic knowledge and developing 21st-century skills that enable learners to adapt to new technologies, work collaboratively, and solve complex problems. Moreover, education systems must be more flexible and responsive to the changing needs of the workforce, ensuring that learners are equipped with skills relevant to the rapidly evolving job market.

The focus on standardized testing and rigid curricula in many countries has been criticized for stifling creativity, critical thinking, and innovation. Standardized testing often prioritizes the ability to memorize and regurgitate information rather than encouraging students to engage with material in a deeper, more meaningful way (Popham, 2018). This approach may limit students' ability to think critically and creatively and fail to consider the diverse ways in which students learn. The one-size-fits-all model of education is increasingly seen as inadequate for addressing students' diverse needs and learning styles. Education systems must shift towards more flexible, personalized approaches emphasizing inquiry-based learning, project-based learning, and collaborative problem-solving (Saavedra & Opfer, 2012). Such approaches can foster the development of higher-order thinking skills and better prepare students to navigate the complexities of the modern world.

A further challenge is the lack of focus on socio-emotional learning (SEL) in many educational systems. While academic skills are essential, socio-emotional skills such as resilience, empathy, collaboration, and self-regulation are equally important for personal development and social integration (Durlak et al., 2011). The increasing stress and mental health challenges faced by students, especially in the wake of the pandemic, highlight the importance of SEL in education. Without adequate support for socio-emotional well-being, students may struggle to develop the emotional intelligence necessary for success in both personal and professional life. Educational systems must incorporate SEL into curricula and provide students with the tools to navigate the social and emotional challenges of growing up in a rapidly changing world.

Climate change and environmental degradation are emerging as critical issues that education systems must address. As the effects of climate change become more apparent, education systems must equip students with the knowledge, skills, and values needed to tackle these global challenges. UNESCO (2017) has emphasized the importance of Education for Sustainable Development (ESD), which focuses on understanding sustainability issues and empowering learners to contribute to solutions. However, many education systems have yet to fully integrate sustainability into their curricula, leaving students ill-prepared to address the urgent environmental challenges of the future. Education must become a key tool in driving global sustainability efforts, teaching students about environmental issues and how to take meaningful action in their communities and beyond.

Global education faces a number of significant challenges, including educational inequality, the digital divide, the need for curriculum reform, and the lack of emphasis on socio-emotional learning. These challenges require urgent attention and a comprehensive approach to reform that prioritizes access, equity, and relevance in education. Addressing these issues is crucial for ensuring that all learners, regardless of their background, are equipped with the skills and knowledge they need to succeed in the complex, interconnected world of the 21st century. Educational systems must evolve to meet the demands of a rapidly changing global landscape, fostering creativity, critical thinking, and socio-emotional resilience while empowering learners to tackle the pressing challenges of our time.

3.1.2. Addressing Inequalities and Barriers to Empowerment

Education inequality, particularly regarding access and quality, remains a significant barrier to empowerment for many individuals worldwide. Empowerment refers to the process by which individuals gain the capacity to make choices and act upon them in a way that enhances their ability to shape their own lives and the lives of others. However, for many, societal structures such as poverty, gender discrimination, race, disability, and geographic location continue to limit access to education and opportunities for empowerment. Addressing these inequalities is fundamental to creating inclusive and equitable societies that foster empowerment at all levels.

One of the most pervasive barriers to empowerment is gender inequality in education. Despite significant progress in many parts of the world, girls and women still face considerable barriers to education, particularly in low-income countries and conflict zones. According to the United Nations Girls' Education Initiative (UNGEI, 2020), approximately 130 million girls worldwide are out of school, with many girls forced to drop out due to early marriage, poverty, gender-based violence, and cultural norms that prioritize boys' education over girls. This gender disparity in education limits women's access to economic opportunities and their ability to participate fully in society, perpetuating cycles of poverty and social inequality. Addressing gender inequality requires improving access to education and creating a supportive environment that challenges traditional gender norms, provides safe learning spaces, and empowers girls and women to pursue their educational and professional aspirations.

In addition to gender, socio-economic status is a key determinant of educational opportunities. Poverty is one of the most significant barriers to access to quality education. As UNESCO (2019) notes, children from low-income households are more likely to be out of school or attend substandard schools with limited resources. Furthermore, the financial burden of education, including the costs of tuition, uniforms, books, and transportation, often makes schooling unaffordable for disadvantaged families. In many rural and remote areas, schools may be poorly equipped or too far for children to attend regularly. This lack of access to education restricts individual potential and stymies social and economic development in these communities. To address these inequalities, it is necessary to implement policies that make education more affordable, such as scholarships, free schooling, and community-based initiatives that bring educational opportunities closer to marginalized populations.

Disability is another significant barrier to education and empowerment. According to the World Health Organization (WHO, 2011), over a billion people worldwide experience some form of disability, and many of them face substantial barriers to accessing education. In many countries, educational systems are not adequately equipped to meet the needs of students with disabilities. Schools may lack the necessary infrastructure, resources, or trained personnel to provide inclusive education that accommodates the diverse learning needs of students with disabilities. Moreover, societal attitudes toward disability often result in discrimination and marginalization, further limiting the empowerment of these individuals. Inclusive education policies that promote accessibility, adaptability, and support services are critical for ensuring that all students, regardless of their physical or cognitive abilities, have equal access to educational opportunities and can reach their full potential.

Racial and ethnic inequalities also play a crucial role in hindering empowerment through education. Discriminatory practices based on race or ethnicity can create hostile learning environments where students may face bias, prejudice, and exclusion. In many countries, students from minority ethnic groups or indigenous populations are disproportionately affected by low-quality education, inadequate resources, and lower expectations from teachers (UNESCO, 2017). This educational inequality limits the opportunities available to these students and perpetuates broader societal inequalities. Educational systems must work to deconstruct racial biases, provide culturally relevant curricula, and ensure that all students, regardless of their ethnic background, are empowered to succeed in school and beyond. Anti-racist education, teacher training, and promoting diversity and inclusion are essential to addressing racial educational disparities.

Geographic location is another determinant of access to education and empowerment. Students in many rural and remote areas face significant barriers to attending school, including long travel distances, lack of transportation, and insufficient infrastructure. According to the World Bank (2020), children in rural areas are less likely to complete their education compared to their urban counterparts. Rural schools often face underfunding, overcrowded classrooms, and a shortage of qualified teachers. The lack of access to technology and digital learning resources further exacerbates these inequalities, particularly in the context of the COVID-19 pandemic, which forced many schools to shift to online learning (OECD, 2020). To address these geographical disparities, governments must prioritize the development of rural education infrastructure, improve access to technology, and provide incentives for teachers to work in underserved areas. Mobile and digital learning solutions can also be leveraged to bring education to remote communities.

The intersectionality of multiple forms of disadvantage also compounds the barriers to empowerment through education. For example, a girl from a low-income, rural community with a disability may face compounded challenges that hinder her access to education. The concept of intersectionality highlights how various forms of inequality, such as gender, race, socio-economic status, and disability, intersect and create unique experiences of marginalization (Crenshaw, 1991). To effectively address these interconnected barriers, education policies and interventions must adopt an intersectional approach that considers the multiple layers of disadvantage and tailors solutions to the specific needs of marginalized groups.

Finally, the digital divide represents a growing barrier to empowerment in the context of the global knowledge economy. As technology becomes increasingly central to education and economic participation, those without access to digital tools and the internet are disadvantaged. The UNESCO Institute for Statistics (2020) reports that while internet access has increased globally, significant disparities remain, particularly in low-income countries and rural areas. The lack of digital infrastructure, affordable internet, and access to devices means that many students are excluded from online learning opportunities, exacerbating educational inequalities. Addressing the digital divide requires infrastructure investments, affordable digital tools, and digital literacy programs to ensure all learners have the skills they need to thrive in the digital age.

In conclusion, addressing inequalities and barriers to empowerment requires comprehensive efforts to tackle the root causes of educational disparities, whether they are based on gender, socio-economic status, disability, race, geographic location, or other forms of marginalization. Governments, educators, and organizations must work collaboratively to create inclusive, equitable educational systems that provide all learners with the opportunities, resources, and support they need to succeed. This includes improving access to education and ensuring that educational environments are supportive, inclusive, and responsive to the diverse needs of learners. Through such transformative efforts, education can only be a tool for empowerment and social change.

References

Crenshaw, K. (1991). Mapping the margins: Intersectionality, identity politics, and violence against women of color. *Stanford Law Review*, 43(6), 1241-1299.

Durlak, J. A., Weissberg, R. P., Dymnicki, A. B., Taylor, R. D., & Schellinger, K. B. (2011). The impact of enhancing students' social and emotional learning: A meta-analysis of school-based universal interventions. *Child Development*, 82(1), 405-432.

Dweck, C. S. (2006). *Mindset: The new psychology of success*. Random House.

Freire, P. (2000). *Pedagogy of the oppressed*. Continuum.

Holmes, W., Bialik, M., & Fadel, C. (2019). *Artificial Intelligence in Education: Promises and Implications for Teaching and Learning*. Center for Curriculum Redesign.

OECD. (2020). The impact of COVID-19 on education: Insights from education at a glance 2020. OECD Publishing.

Popham, W. J. (2018). *Everything school leaders need to know about assessment*. ASCD.

Saavedra, A. R., & Opfer, V. D. (2012). *Learning 21st-century skills requires 21st-century teaching*. Phi Delta Kappan, 93(3), 8-13.

Sclwyn, N. (2016). *Education and technology: Key issues and debates*. Bloomsbury Academic.

UNESCO. (2017). *Education for Sustainable Development Goals: Learning Objectives*. UNESCO Publishing.

UNESCO. (2017). *Racial and ethnic equality in education: A global perspective*. UNESCO Publishing.

UNESCO. (2019). Global Education Monitoring Report 2019: Migration, displacement, and education – Building bridges, not walls. UNESCO Publishing.

UNESCO. (2020). *Global Education Monitoring Report 2020: Inclusion and* education: All means all. UNESCO Publishing.
UNESCO. (2021). *Artificial Intelligence and Education: Guidance for Policy-Makers.* UNESCO Publishing.
UNICEF. (2020). The State of the World's Children 2020: Children, food, and Nutrition: Growing well in a changing world. UNICEF.
United Nations Girls' Education Initiative (UNGEI). (2020). Gender and education: Breaking barriers to equality. UNGEI. Retrieved from https://www.ungei.org.
WHO. (2011). *World Report on Disability.* World Health Organization.
World Bank. (2020). *Education in rural areas: A global perspective.* World Bank Group.
World Economic Forum. (2020). *The Future of Jobs Report 2020.* World Economic Forum.

Part I: Foundations of AI in Education

Introduction

Integrating Artificial Intelligence (AI) into education represents a profound transformation in how learning and teaching are conceptualized, delivered, and experienced. AI in education is underpinned by several foundational principles that combine advancements in machine learning, cognitive science, data analytics, and educational psychology. The primary objective is to enhance educational processes by tailoring learning experiences to individual needs, improving administrative efficiencies, and fostering innovative educational practices. By automating administrative tasks, offering personalized learning paths, and providing real-time feedback, AI can bridge education gaps, promote accessibility, and contribute to equitable learning opportunities.

One of the foundational pillars of AI in education is personalized learning. Traditional education systems often rely on a one-size-fits-all approach, where students are expected to learn at the same pace and in the same manner. However, AI technologies can tailor learning experiences based on individual student needs, preferences, and learning styles. Machine learning algorithms can analyze vast amounts of data from students' interactions with educational platforms, identifying patterns and providing insights to guide personalized learning interventions. Adaptive learning systems, for example, adjust the difficulty level of tasks or lessons based on real-time data about the learner's performance (Luckin et al., 2016). This dynamic adjustment allows for differentiated instruction, ensuring that students are neither bored by content that is too easy nor frustrated by material that is too difficult. As a result, AI facilitates more efficient learning, catering to each student's specific strengths and weaknesses, thereby supporting their educational development.

AI's potential to support personalized learning is also deeply connected to the foundation of educational psychology. The concept of scaffolding, introduced by Vygotsky (1978), emphasizes the importance of providing learners with the necessary support to reach their potential. AI-powered educational tools can serve as digital scaffolds, offering students immediate assistance, feedback, and hints when they struggle with tasks. This real-time support boosts student confidence and ensures that learners receive the guidance they need to succeed in their educational endeavors. For example, intelligent tutoring systems (ITS) can mimic one-on-one tutoring experiences by providing explanations, hints, and corrective feedback based on the learner's specific needs, much like a human tutor would (VanLehn, 2011).

Another foundational aspect of AI in education is its capacity to improve administrative and operational processes. Education systems globally face significant challenges in managing large student populations, tracking academic progress, and providing feedback. AI can automate administrative tasks such as grading, scheduling, and attendance tracking, allowing educators to focus more on teaching and student interaction. Educators play a crucial role in the design and implementation of AI systems, ensuring that they align with pedagogical strategies and individualized student support. For example, AI systems can grade assignments that require open-ended responses, such as essays, by assessing content quality, coherence, and relevance to the prompt (Shermis & Hamner, 2013). This reduces the time educators spend on administrative tasks and allows them to focus more on pedagogical strategies and individualized student support. Moreover, AI's data analytics capabilities enable institutions to track student performance and predict outcomes, offering valuable insights that can guide curriculum adjustments, intervention strategies, and resource allocation (Holmes et al., 2019).

The integration of AI into education also benefits from its ability to foster collaboration and communication. Educational tools powered by AI can facilitate collaborative learning environments where students work together on tasks, share knowledge, and solve problems. AI can provide real-time translation services, allowing students from diverse linguistic backgrounds to interact without language barriers. Additionally, AI-based platforms can offer personalized feedback on collaborative projects, helping students learn not only from their own work but also from their peers. These technologies, when applied effectively, support the development of critical skills such as teamwork, communication, and problem-solving—skills that are essential for success in the 21st-century workforce.

The concept of the "learning analytics" framework is another foundational element of AI in education. Learning analytics involves collecting and analyzing student behavior, engagement, and performance data to inform instructional practices and institutional decision-making. AI algorithms can process vast amounts of data to detect patterns that might be invisible to human educators, providing insights into student needs, learning trends, and potential risks (Siemens, 2013). For instance, predictive analytics can identify students who may be at risk of dropping out or underperforming, allowing educators to intervene early with targeted support. Moreover, AI-driven learning analytics can help refine the design of educational materials, ensuring that content is relevant, engaging, and aligned with students' learning goals.

However, it is important to recognize that AI in education is not without its challenges. The foundational principles of AI must be approached with caution to ensure that they align with ethical standards, promote equity, and avoid exacerbating existing disparities in education. The responsible and ethical use of AI is crucial to its successful implementation in educational systems. There are concerns related to privacy, bias, and accessibility, which need to be addressed in the implementation of AI in educational systems. As AI technologies analyze vast amounts of personal data, including students' learning behaviors, academic records, and demographic information, there is a risk of data breaches or misuse. Moreover, if AI systems are not properly designed, they may perpetuate biases in educational outcomes, such as racial, gender, or socio-economic bias (West et al., 2019). Ethical considerations regarding transparency, accountability, and fairness must therefore be integrated into the design and deployment of AI tools in education, reassuring the audience about the responsible use of technology.

In conclusion, the foundations of AI in education hold the potential to revolutionize learning. By personalizing learning, automating administrative tasks, improving educational outcomes, and fostering collaboration, AI can create more inclusive, accessible, and effective learning environments. However, to ensure that AI's role in education is beneficial and equitable, careful attention must be paid to its ethical implementation, privacy protection, and the elimination of biases. As AI continues to evolve, its application in education promises to reshape traditional teaching and learning paradigms, offering unprecedented opportunities for students and educators and inspiring hope for the future of learning.

Chapter 4

AI and Learning Paradigms

4.1. Introduction

The emergence of Artificial Intelligence (AI) in education has fundamentally reshaped traditional learning paradigms, offering new avenues for personalized, flexible, and efficient teaching and learning experiences. AI has introduced innovative tools and methods that enhance learning, catering to diverse student needs, learning styles, and educational contexts. Integrating AI into education has created opportunities to rethink conventional approaches to learning, extending beyond the limitations of traditional pedagogies. As a result, AI is transforming the content and structure of learning experiences, facilitating a shift toward more individualized, student-centered models that prioritize active engagement, feedback, and continuous improvement.

One of the key transformations in learning paradigms with the introduction of AI is the move from teacher-centered instruction to learner-centered models. Traditional educational systems have typically relied on a one-size-fits-all approach, where the teacher is the primary source of knowledge, and students passively receive content. However, AI technologies enable a more personalized learning experience, where students can progress at their own pace, choose learning paths that align with their interests, and receive individualized support. Adaptive learning systems, powered by AI, adjust the difficulty and pace of instructional content based on a student's performance, allowing learners to move through the material at a speed that suits their abilities and needs (Siemens, 2013). This model encourages active participation, self-regulation, and independent learning, empowering students to take control of their educational journeys.

AI also facilitates the transition from knowledge acquisition to developing critical thinking, problem-solving, and higher-order cognitive skills. Traditional education models often focus on rote memorization and passive content consumption, whereas AI-enabled systems encourage deeper engagement with content. For instance, AI-powered platforms can challenge students with complex scenarios that require them to apply their knowledge, collaborate with others, and engage in real-world problem-solving. These systems can provide immediate feedback, guiding students through the problem-solving process and helping them to refine their thinking. By promoting inquiry-based learning, AI helps cultivate a mindset of curiosity and critical reflection, moving students beyond memorization to more meaningful, transformative learning experiences (Luckin et al., 2016).

Another significant shift in learning paradigms due to AI is the reimagining of the role of educators. Rather than being the sole disseminators of knowledge, teachers in AI-enhanced environments act as facilitators and mentors. AI tools can handle administrative tasks like grading and scheduling, enabling educators to focus on higher-level instructional duties and student interaction. This shift allows teachers to dedicate more time to providing personalized feedback, supporting students' emotional and social development, and fostering a collaborative learning environment. AI also serves as a valuable tool for professional development, as it can analyze teacher performance, identify areas for growth, and provide recommendations for improving instructional practices (Holmes et al., 2019). In this way, AI impacts students and transforms educators' roles and professional development, creating a more dynamic and adaptive learning ecosystem.

The application of AI also aligns with the principles of constructivist learning theories, particularly those influenced by the work of Vygotsky (1978). Constructivist learning emphasizes active learning, where learners construct their understanding through experiences and interactions. AI-powered educational tools support this model by offering interactive, exploratory learning environments where students can engage with content hands-on. For example, virtual simulations and gamified learning platforms allow students to experiment, solve problems, and test hypotheses in safe, controlled environments. AI's real-time ability to track and analyze student progress enables these tools to offer personalized learning experiences that align with students' developmental stages and cognitive abilities (Siemens, 2013). This individualized approach supports the social constructivist idea that learning is a collaborative process, as AI can also facilitate peer interaction and collaborative problem-solving within digital spaces.

In addition to personalized learning and teacher facilitation, AI contributes to the democratization of education by providing access to high-quality learning resources and experiences. AI-powered platforms can offer content in various formats, including video, text, simulations, and interactive exercises, making education more accessible to learners with diverse needs. AI tools can also provide real-time language translation, helping bridge linguistic barriers in multicultural and multilingual classrooms. Moreover, AI enables learners in remote or underserved areas to access world-class educational content, overcoming geographical limitations and expanding learning opportunities. As a result, AI is playing a crucial role in addressing educational inequities and ensuring that more students have access to personalized, high-quality learning experiences regardless of their background or location (West et al., 2019).

Despite the promising potential of AI to reshape learning paradigms, some challenges and considerations must be addressed. Equity, data privacy, algorithmic bias, and the digital divide must be considered when implementing AI in educational contexts. AI systems can inadvertently reinforce existing biases if they are not carefully designed and tested, potentially exacerbating disparities in educational outcomes. Furthermore, the reliance on AI technologies raises concerns about data privacy and the security of student information, particularly as these systems collect vast amounts of personal and behavioral data. As AI evolves, policymakers, educators, and technologists must work together to ensure that AI is used ethically, responsibly, and inclusively to benefit all learners.

In conclusion, AI is driving a significant shift in learning paradigms, moving away from traditional, teacher-centered models toward more personalized, learner-centered, and collaborative approaches. By empowering students to take control of their learning, providing real-time feedback, and enhancing the role of educators, AI can transform education in previously unimaginable ways. However, it is crucial to approach the integration of AI into education with careful consideration of ethical implications, equity, and inclusivity, ensuring that all learners benefit from the opportunities AI offers.

4.1.1. Personalized Learning Systems

Personalized learning systems powered by Artificial Intelligence (AI) can revolutionize the educational landscape by adapting learning experiences to meet each student's unique needs, abilities, and interests. This shift represents a move away from the traditional, one-size-fits-all approach to teaching, enabling learners to engage with content in ways that align with their learning styles, pace, and preferences. Personalized learning empowers students to take control of their educational journeys, promoting autonomy, motivation, and deep engagement. AI-driven personalized learning systems leverage advanced algorithms and data analytics to assess students' strengths and weaknesses, tailoring the learning experience to maximize individual success.

One of the key features of personalized learning systems is their ability to provide real-time feedback and adjust learning content based on a student's performance. These systems track students' interactions with educational material, such as quizzes, assignments, and assessments, and use this data to create a dynamic learning path. If a student excels in a particular area, the system may introduce more challenging content, while if a student struggles, it can provide additional support or alternative resources. This individualized feedback loop fosters continuous improvement, ensuring that students are always engaged at an appropriate level of challenge (Siemens, 2013). For example, platforms like DreamBox Learning and Knewton offer adaptive learning environments that respond to students' needs, adjusting in real time to optimize their learning experience.

Personalized learning systems also empower students to set learning goals and choose their learning paths. Traditional classrooms often follow a rigid curriculum and fixed pace, leaving little room for students to explore areas of personal interest or work at their speed. AI-based systems, however, enable students to pursue their interests and passions, encouraging self-directed learning. For instance, tools like the Khan Academy and Coursera allow learners to select topics, choose courses, and determine their learning pace. This flexibility enhances student engagement, as they are more likely to invest time in topics that they find personally meaningful. Additionally, students can revisit material whenever needed, reinforcing mastery through repetition, a feature that is difficult to achieve in traditional classroom settings.

In addition to providing personalized learning paths, AI-powered systems can also support diverse learning needs by offering multiple modalities for learning. Students can engage with content through various formats, such as text, video, audio, and interactive simulations, catering to different learning preferences and styles. This multimedia approach enhances comprehension, as students can access information in the format that best suits their learning style. For example, visual learners may benefit from video tutorials or infographics, while auditory learners may prefer podcasts or recorded lectures. The availability of these diverse learning modes helps ensure that all students, regardless of their individual learning needs, can access and engage with educational content effectively (Holmes et al., 2019).

Moreover, AI-driven personalized learning systems are critical in promoting inclusivity and addressing equity in education. By providing tailored support, these systems can help students from various backgrounds overcome barriers to learning, such as language differences, disabilities, or gaps in prior knowledge. AI tools can offer instant translation services, enabling non-native speakers to engage with content in their preferred language. Additionally, students with learning disabilities can benefit from assistive technologies such as text-to-speech or speech-to-text tools, which facilitate their learning experience by providing alternative ways to access and interact with content (West et al., 2019). This level of customization ensures that all students, regardless of their challenges, can succeed in an educational environment that recognizes their unique needs.

Another significant benefit of personalized learning systems is their ability to promote lifelong learning. In the modern world, where knowledge and skills constantly evolve, individuals need to continue learning. AI-based systems allow learners to develop and refine skills over time, whether for academic achievement, career development, or personal enrichment. These systems can offer ongoing support, recommending new topics or areas of study based on learners' previous interactions and progress. As such, personalized learning systems support the development of critical 21st-century skills such as self-regulation, critical thinking, and problem-solving, which are crucial for success in a rapidly changing world (Luckin et al., 2016).

While personalized learning systems present numerous benefits, their implementation and use have certain challenges. One of the primary concerns is the potential for data privacy issues. Personalized learning systems rely on extensive data collection to track student's learning behaviors and preferences, raising concerns about protecting sensitive personal information. Ensuring that these systems comply with privacy regulations and are transparent about how data is collected and used is essential for maintaining trust between students, educators, and technology providers. Additionally, while AI can significantly enhance learning experiences, over-reliance on technology could reduce face-to-face interactions between students and teachers, potentially impacting social learning experiences.

Furthermore, AI-driven personalized learning systems are only as effective as the algorithms and data they are based on. If these systems are not carefully designed or if the data used to train the algorithms is biased, the learning paths they generate could inadvertently reinforce existing inequalities. For example, a system may provide certain students with more challenging content based on their previous performance. However, if the data is skewed or incomplete, it could limit opportunities for those students to progress. Therefore, these systems must be continuously monitored and refined to ensure they promote fairness, equity, and inclusivity (Siemens, 2013).

Personalized learning systems powered by AI offer transformative possibilities for the future of education. These systems promote engagement, mastery, and lifelong learning by tailoring learning experiences to individual students' needs, abilities, and interests. However, addressing the challenges associated with data privacy, equity, and algorithmic bias is important to ensure that AI in education serves all learners effectively and ethically. As AI continues to evolve, the potential for these systems to enhance personalized learning will only expand, offering new opportunities for students to thrive in an increasingly complex and dynamic educational landscape.

4.1.2. Intelligent Tutoring Systems (ITS)

Intelligent Tutoring Systems (ITS) are a key application of Artificial Intelligence (AI) in education, designed to provide personalized, interactive learning experiences that mimic the one-on-one tutoring process. By leveraging AI and machine learning algorithms, ITS can assess a student's current knowledge, adapt learning materials to suit their needs, and offer real-time feedback, thus fostering an environment conducive to self-directed learning. These systems aim to provide individualized instruction without the need for a human tutor, utilizing the power of technology to improve learning outcomes across various subjects and educational levels.

At the core of ITS is the ability to assess students' performance and make adaptive adjustments based on their responses. The system collects data on a student's interactions with the learning material—such as answering questions, completing exercises, and making decisions—and uses this data to create a dynamic learning experience that responds to the student's progress and struggles. For example, suppose a student answers a question incorrectly. In that case, the ITS may adjust the next question's difficulty, offer hints, or provide additional explanations to help the learner understand the material better. This adaptability ensures that each student receives the appropriate level of challenge, avoiding frustration from overly difficult tasks or boredom from too easy tasks (VanLehn, 2011).

The process of feedback is a central feature of ITS, as it helps students identify gaps in their knowledge and offers guidance for improvement. Real-time feedback, delivered as the student works through exercises, is crucial in enhancing learning outcomes. Studies have shown that immediate feedback helps learners correct mistakes, reinforce correct answers, and maintain motivation, all of which contribute to a deeper understanding of the material

(VanLehn, 2011). By simulating the role of a tutor, ITS provides a more interactive learning environment compared to traditional, passive learning models, where feedback may only come after the fact, often delaying correction and learning reinforcement.

Moreover, ITS can incorporate a variety of learning strategies to accommodate different learning styles and preferences. These systems may use a range of teaching techniques, including problem-solving exercises, simulations, and interactive scenarios, to engage students in active learning. In a mathematics ITS, for example, the system might present students with problems that require them to demonstrate step-by-step reasoning. In contrast, in a language-learning ITS, the system may use dialogue systems to simulate conversations, allowing students to practice vocabulary and grammar in context. This flexibility ensures learners can engage with content in ways that suit their individual learning preferences, fostering a deeper understanding of the subject matter (Baker et al., 2009).

One notable benefit of ITS is their ability to offer scalable, cost-effective educational support. While one-on-one tutoring is traditionally expensive and resource-intensive, ITS can provide personalized support to a large number of students simultaneously. This scalability can potentially democratize access to high-quality education, particularly when qualified human tutors are scarce or unavailable. For instance, systems like Carnegie Learning and AutoTutor have been used in various educational settings to provide tutoring for subjects ranging from mathematics to science, helping students who might otherwise lack access to individualized instruction (Koedinger et al., 2013).

ITS is also designed to monitor and track student progress, providing valuable insights into individual learning trajectories and overall class performance. Teachers can access detailed reports on how students interact with the material, including data on which concepts they are struggling with and which they have mastered. This data can inform instructional decisions, enabling teachers to provide targeted support for students who need it most. By analyzing the patterns in student performance, ITS can also identify broader trends in class performance, helping to optimize teaching methods and curricula (Baker et al., 2009).

Despite the many benefits, there are also challenges and limitations associated with ITS. One of the primary concerns is the reliance on high-quality data to ensure the system's effectiveness. For an ITS to adapt successfully to a student's needs, it must have accurate data on their performance, learning style, and potential misconceptions. This data collection raises issues regarding privacy and security, particularly when personal student information is involved. Ensuring these systems comply with data protection regulations is essential to protect students' privacy and maintain trust in these technologies (West et al., 2019).

Another challenge lies in the scope of subjects that ITS can effectively cover. While it has made significant progress in subjects like mathematics, language learning, and basic sciences, there are still limitations in its ability to teach more complex subjects, such as the humanities or creative fields. These areas often require nuanced, critical thinking and complex problem-solving that AI systems may not easily simulate. Furthermore, ITS cannot yet replicate the rich, social aspects of learning that occur in human-to-human interactions, such as collaborative problem-solving and peer discussions, which are critical for developing higher-order thinking skills (VanLehn, 2011).

In addition, the design of the tutoring system itself is crucial to its success. If the system is not well-designed, it can fail to engage students, provide inaccurate feedback, or address learning needs appropriately. The quality of the underlying AI algorithms, the content delivered, and the user interface influence how effective ITS can be. As such, ongoing research and development are required to ensure that ITS meets the diverse needs of learners and is aligned with best pedagogical practices (Koedinger et al., 2013).

Intelligent Tutoring Systems represent a promising educational development, offering personalized, scalable, and interactive learning experiences to help students learn more effectively and efficiently. By adapting to the individual needs of learners, providing real-time feedback, and offering diverse learning strategies, ITS can transform education and democratize access to high-quality tutoring. However, the success of ITS depends on its ability to handle data effectively, address privacy concerns, and cover a broad range of subjects. With ongoing advancements in AI and machine learning, ITS is likely to play an increasingly significant role in the future of education.

References

Baker, R. S., Corbett, A. T., & Koedinger, K. R. (2009). The dynamics of feedback in intelligent tutoring systems. In D. P. Thomas & J. E. Beck (Eds.), *Proceedings of the 12th International Conference on Artificial Intelligence in Education* (AIED 2009) (pp. 29-36).

Holmes, W., Bialik, M., & Fadel, C. (2019). *Artificial Intelligence in Education: Promises and Implications for Teaching and Learning.* Center for Curriculum Redesign.

Koedinger, K. R., McLaughlin, E. A., & Stamper, J. C. (2013). Designing the future of education with intelligent tutoring systems. In J. A. Cerri, G. Gouardères, & F. Paraguacu (Eds.), *Intelligent Tutoring Systems: 12th International Conference*, ITS 2013, Montreux, Switzerland (pp. 27-34). Springer.

Luckin, R., Holmes, W., Griffiths, M., & Forcier, L. B. (2016). *Intelligence Unleashed: An Argument for AI in Education.* Pearson Education.

Shermis, M. D., & Hamner, B. (2013). *The validity of automated essay scoring.* Educational Testing Service.

Siemens, G. (2013). Learning Analytics: The Emergence of Discipline. *American Behavioral Scientist*, 57(10), 1-16.

VanLehn, K. (2011). The relative effectiveness of human tutoring, intelligent tutoring systems, and other tutoring systems. *Educational Psychologist*, 46(4), 197-221.

Vygotsky, L. S. (1978). *Mind in Society: The Development of Higher Psychological Processes.* Harvard University Press.

West, S. M., Whittaker, M., & Crawford, K. (2019). *Discriminating Systems: Gender, Race, and Power in AI.* AI Now Institute.

Chapter 5

AI in Curriculum Design and Development

5.1. Introduction

The integration of Artificial Intelligence (AI) in curriculum design and development is a transformative approach that aligns with the evolving needs of educators and students. AI technologies, particularly machine learning, natural language processing, and data analytics, have the potential to significantly enhance curriculum development. By creating adaptive, personalized learning experiences, optimizing content delivery, and providing valuable insights into student progress, AI becomes a powerful tool for reimagining how curricula are structured, delivered, and assessed. This ultimately leads to improved educational outcomes.

At the heart of AI's impact on curriculum design is its ability to personalize learning. Traditional curricula often follow a one-size-fits-all approach, which may not be effective for all students, especially those with diverse learning needs and preferences. AI, however, can analyze individual learning patterns, preferences, and progress, enabling the development of personalized learning pathways that cater to each student's strengths, weaknesses, and pace. For instance, AI can identify when a student struggles with a particular concept and adjust the curriculum in real time, offering additional resources, exercises, or explanations tailored to the learner's specific needs (Holmes et al., 2019). This dynamic approach ensures that students are continuously engaged and challenged at an appropriate level, fostering deeper learning and better retention.

Incorporating AI into curriculum design also allows for the development of adaptive learning systems. These systems use algorithms to assess and respond to students' progress, dynamically adjusting the content and sequence of lessons to optimize learning. Adaptive learning tools powered by AI can provide instant feedback to learners, which is essential for reinforcing concepts and correcting misconceptions. These systems can also track a student's learning journey over time, enabling teachers to monitor progress and intervene when necessary (Luckin et al., 2016). This flexibility in curriculum design can help bridge gaps in student achievement, ensuring that all learners are given the support they need to succeed, regardless of their starting point or learning pace.

Moreover, AI-powered analytics are revolutionizing how educators design and refine curricula. By collecting and analyzing vast amounts of data on student performance, behavior, and engagement, AI systems can offer valuable insights into how well the curriculum works and where improvements are needed. For example, data analysis can reveal patterns in which students are most likely to struggle with specific topics or which teaching strategies yield the best results. Teachers and curriculum designers can use this information to continuously refine and adapt the curriculum to meet student's needs better. Additionally, AI can be used to analyze the efficacy of different instructional materials, helping educators identify the most effective resources for promoting learning outcomes (West et al., 2019).

AI's role in curriculum development extends to supporting project-based and inquiry-based learning models. These models encourage students to explore real-world problems and engage in critical thinking, problem-solving, and collaboration. AI tools can facilitate these types of learning by providing resources and guidance for students as they work through complex projects. By integrating AI into project-based learning environments, educators can foster the development of critical skills such as collaboration, creativity, and problem-solving, which are essential for success in the modern workforce.

The potential of AI in curriculum design extends beyond the classroom into more personalized and flexible learning environments. AI can facilitate the creation of hybrid or fully online curricula customized to suit different learning contexts and student needs. In a globalized world, where students may have varying educational backgrounds, access to resources, and learning environments, AI can help bridge these gaps. This potential of AI to ensure inclusivity and equity in education should make policymakers feel hopeful and optimistic about the future of education.

Despite its promising potential, integrating AI into curriculum design also presents challenges. One significant challenge is ensuring that AI systems are used ethically and transparently, particularly regarding data privacy and security. The data used to train AI algorithms often include sensitive student information, and safeguarding this data is critical to maintaining trust and ensuring compliance with privacy laws (West et al., 2019). Additionally, curriculum designers must ensure that AI systems are not reinforcing biases in terms of content or how students are assessed. There is a risk that AI algorithms may inadvertently perpetuate existing inequalities in the educational system, which could undermine the goal of providing equitable education for all (Holmes et al., 2019).

Another challenge is that educators and curriculum designers need to develop the necessary digital literacy and technical expertise to implement AI effectively in curriculum development. While AI offers immense potential, it requires a deep understanding of educational theory and AI technology. Teachers and instructional designers need professional development opportunities to learn how to integrate AI into their teaching practices and curriculum designs in pedagogically sound and ethically responsible ways. This requires a collaborative approach, where educators, AI experts, and policymakers work together to ensure that AI is used effectively to enhance educational experiences (Luckin et al., 2016).

In conclusion, AI has the potential to revolutionize curriculum design and development. By providing personalized, adaptive learning experiences, optimizing teaching strategies, and offering valuable insights into student progress, AI can help create more flexible, inclusive, and effective learning environments. However, to fully realize the benefits of AI in education, it is crucial to address challenges related to data privacy, equity, and the professional development of educators. With careful planning and ethical considerations, AI can play a transformative role in shaping the future of education.

5.1.1. Dynamic Curriculum Adaptation

Dynamic curriculum adaptation refers to continually adjusting the curriculum to meet the evolving needs of students, educational contexts, and broader societal demands. This approach is particularly relevant in the educational context of Artificial Intelligence (AI). AI's ability to analyze real-time data and respond to student progress enables a more flexible, individualized, and responsive curriculum. By leveraging AI technologies such as machine learning, natural language processing, and data analytics, educational systems can create adaptive curricula that are continuously refined based on students' learning patterns, preferences, and needs. This ensures that each student receives a challenging and supportive education, ultimately improving learning outcomes.

AI-driven dynamic curriculum adaptation provides a more personalized approach to learning, shifting away from the traditional "one-size-fits-all" model. Traditional curricula often follow a fixed sequence of lessons and assessments that may not align with individual students' varying abilities and learning paces. AI systems, however, can continuously assess a student's progress and adjust the curriculum to accommodate their learning needs in real-time (Holmes et al., 2019). For instance, if a student struggles with a particular topic, the AI system can automatically modify the content, offering additional explanations, practice exercises, or alternative learning materials to support the student's understanding. Conversely, the system can introduce more advanced concepts for students who demonstrate mastery of a subject, ensuring that they remain engaged and appropriately challenged.

Incorporating dynamic curriculum adaptation also allows for greater flexibility in assessment and feedback. Traditional assessment methods, such as standardized tests, are often inflexible and do not provide immediate insights into student progress. AI-powered systems, however, can track student performance in real time, offering immediate feedback and adjusting the learning materials as needed. For example, suppose a student answers a question incorrectly. In that case, the system can provide hints, explanations, or resources to help the student understand the correct answer, all while adjusting the subsequent lessons based on this information (Luckin et al., 2016). This form of assessment, known as formative assessment, is continuous and integrated into the learning process, which fosters a more supportive and effective learning environment.

Furthermore, dynamic curriculum adaptation offers a significant advantage in addressing students' diverse learning styles and needs. Students learn in different ways, whether through visual, auditory, or kinesthetic methods, and their engagement with content may vary based on these preferences. AI systems can analyze data on how students interact with various types of content and tailor the curriculum to align with their preferred learning modalities. For instance, some students may benefit from video-based explanations, while others may prefer interactive simulations or written explanations (Holmes et al., 2019). By utilizing AI to adjust the curriculum dynamically, educators can ensure that each student has access to the learning experiences that best suit their needs, promoting deeper engagement and better knowledge retention.

In addition to individual student adaptation, AI-enabled dynamic curriculum systems can respond to changes in the broader educational landscape. As societal needs evolve, curricula must be updated to reflect new skills, knowledge, and competencies required in the workforce. AI can analyze emerging technology, economics, and healthcare trends, enabling the curriculum to be continuously updated in response to these changes (West et al., 2019). For example, the increasing demand for digital literacy and coding skills in various industries may prompt AI systems to integrate relevant content into the curriculum, ensuring that students are equipped with the skills they need for future success. This adaptability is particularly crucial in an era of rapid technological advancements, where the knowledge and skills required by students can shift quickly.

However, the implementation of dynamic curriculum adaptation is not without challenges. One of the key concerns is ensuring that AI systems are used in an ethical and unbiased manner. The algorithms that power AI systems are often based on historical data, which may contain biases that can be perpetuated in the curriculum design. For example, suppose an AI system is trained on data from a particular demographic group. In that case, it may fail to recognize or address the needs of students from different backgrounds or with varying learning needs. It is, therefore, crucial to ensure that AI algorithms are designed to be inclusive and equitable, considering the diversity of student populations and providing opportunities for all students to succeed (West et al., 2019).

Moreover, the successful implementation of dynamic curriculum adaptation requires a robust infrastructure in terms of technology and educator support. Teachers must be trained to effectively use AI tools in the classroom and to interpret the data generated by AI systems. Schools and educational institutions must also ensure they have the necessary resources, such as reliable internet access, sufficient computing power, and ongoing technical support, to implement AI-driven curriculum systems (Luckin et al., 2016). Without these resources, the full potential of dynamic curriculum adaptation cannot be realized.

Dynamic curriculum adaptation enabled by AI represents a significant advancement in educational practice. By offering personalized, flexible, and data-driven approaches to curriculum design, AI can help educators meet the diverse needs of students and ensure that curricula are continuously updated to reflect changing societal and technological demands. While there are challenges to overcome, particularly related to data privacy, equity, and infrastructure, the potential benefits of AI driven dynamic curriculum adaptation are vast. As AI technologies continue to evolve, they promise more personalized, inclusive, and responsive education systems that better prepare students for the complexities of the modern world.

5.1.2. Gamification and AI-Enhanced Learning Tools

Gamification, applying game-design elements and principles to non-game contexts, has emerged as a powerful strategy to enhance engagement, motivation, and learning outcomes in educational environments. Integrating Artificial Intelligence (AI) into gamified learning systems represents a significant advancement, allowing for more personalized, adaptive, and interactive learning experiences. By combining the intrinsic motivation fostered through game mechanics with the data-driven capabilities of AI, these AI-enhanced learning tools can create more dynamic, student-centered educational experiences that foster deep learning and sustained engagement.

One of the key benefits of gamification is its ability to transform traditional educational content into interactive, enjoyable, and goal-oriented activities. In the classroom, gamified systems encourage students to actively participate by incorporating elements such as points, badges, leaderboards, levels, and challenges (Deterding et al., 2011). These game elements tap into the human desire for achievement, competition, and social recognition, motivating students to engage with content more deeply. When integrated with AI, gamified systems can further personalize these experiences, tailoring challenges and rewards to individual students based on their unique learning needs, preferences, and progress (Anderson, 2018). For instance, AI algorithms can analyze a student's interactions with the game and adjust the difficulty level of tasks to match their current skills, ensuring that they remain challenged without feeling overwhelmed.

AI-enhanced gamified tools can also provide real-time feedback, an essential feature for improving learning outcomes. In traditional learning environments, feedback is often delayed or generalized, hindering students' understanding of where they went wrong and how to improve. AI-powered gamification, on the other hand, can provide instantaneous feedback on a student's performance, offering tailored suggestions and resources to guide their learning process. For example, suppose a student answers a quiz question incorrectly in a gamified learning environment. In that case, the AI system can provide hints or alternative explanations to help the student understand the correct answer (Luckin et al., 2016). This immediate feedback loop fosters a more supportive learning environment, where students can correct misconceptions and refine their understanding in real-time.

Moreover, AI can help gamified learning platforms adapt to the individual's learning trajectory, ensuring a personalized experience that accommodates diverse learning paces and styles. In traditional educational settings, students often follow a linear, one-size-fits-all curriculum, which may not align with their personal learning needs. AI, however, allows gamified systems to continuously assess a student's performance and adjust the content to fit their evolving capabilities better. For example, if a student progresses quickly through a particular subject area, the AI system can introduce more complex challenges, keeping the student engaged and intellectually stimulated. Conversely, if a student struggles, the system can adjust the difficulty level or provide additional learning materials to reinforce concepts before moving on (Holmes et al., 2019). This adaptive nature of AI-enhanced gamified tools ensures that students remain engaged while promoting a deeper understanding of the material.

In addition to personalizing the learning experience, AI-enhanced gamified tools offer unique collaboration and social learning opportunities. Many gamified learning environments feature cooperative challenges and multiplayer modes that encourage students to work together to solve problems or achieve goals (Gee, 2003). AI can analyze the interactions between students in these collaborative scenarios, identifying patterns of teamwork, communication, and problem-solving. This data can then be used to adjust the game dynamics, such as forming teams based on complementary skills or introducing new collaborative tasks that foster social interaction and peer learning. By facilitating collaboration in a gamified context, AI-powered tools can help students develop crucial skills such as teamwork, communication, and conflict resolution, which are essential for success in both academic and professional settings.

However, while gamification and AI-enhanced learning tools offer significant benefits, some challenges must be addressed. One concern is the potential for over-reliance on extrinsic rewards, such as points and badges, which may undermine intrinsic motivation if not properly balanced (Deci et al., 1991). Research has shown that when students are primarily motivated by external rewards, they may lose interest in learning for the sake of learning itself. To mitigate this, AI-enhanced gamified systems must be carefully designed to balance extrinsic rewards and intrinsic motivation. For example, the AI system could focus on offering meaningful challenges and fostering a sense of accomplishment rather than relying solely on superficial rewards (Ryan & Deci, 2000).

Another challenge is ensuring equitable access to AI-enhanced gamified tools. As with many technological innovations, there is the risk that students from disadvantaged backgrounds may not have the resources or opportunities to benefit from AI-driven gamification. Issues such as limited access to devices, reliable internet connectivity, and technological literacy may prevent some students from fully participating in these educational experiences (West et al., 2019). It is, therefore, crucial to design AI-enhanced gamified tools in a way accessible to all students, regardless of their socioeconomic status or technological proficiency. This may involve providing offline capabilities, low-cost devices, and comprehensive support for both students and teachers to navigate the technology effectively.

In conclusion, gamification and AI-enhanced learning tools represent a promising fusion of technology and education, offering the potential to transform how students engage with and learn from educational content. By integrating game mechanics with AI's adaptive, data-driven capabilities, these tools create personalized, interactive, and motivating learning environments that cater to the unique needs of individual students. However, careful consideration must be given to the design and implementation of these systems to ensure that they balance extrinsic and intrinsic motivation and are accessible to all learners. With the right approach, AI-enhanced gamification can significantly enhance learning outcomes and foster a more engaging, inclusive, and dynamic educational experience.

References

Anderson, C. A. (2018). The influence of video games on youth: Implications for learning and education. In P. R. Green (Ed.), *The Routledge Handbook of Education and Technology* (pp. 136-147). Routledge.

Deci, E. L., Vallerand, R. J., & Ryan, R. M. (1991). Motivation and education: The self-determination perspective. *Educational psychologist*, 26(3-4), 325-346.

Gee, J. P. (2003). What video games have to teach us about learning and literacy. *Computers in Entertainment* (CIE), 1(1), 20-20.

Holmes, W., Bialik, M., & Fadel, C. (2019). *Artificial Intelligence in Education: Promises and Implications for Teaching and Learning*. Center for Curriculum Redesign.

Luckin, R., Holmes, W., Griffiths, M., & Forcier, L. B. (2016). *Intelligence Unleashed: An Argument for AI in Education.* Pearson Education.

Ryan, R. M., & Deci, E. L. (2000). Self-determination theory and the facilitation of intrinsic motivation, social development, and well-being. *American Psychologist*, 55(1), 68-78.

UNESCO. (2021). Artificial Intelligence and Education: Guidance for Policy-Makers. UNESCO Publishing.

West, S. M., Whittaker, M., & Crawford, K. (2019). *Discriminating Systems: Gender, Race, and Power in AI.* AI Now Institute.

Chapter 6

Bridging Gaps with AI

6.1. Introduction

Artificial Intelligence (AI) is not just a buzzword, but a transformative force that has the potential to revolutionize education. Its applications, particularly in bridging existing gaps related to educational inequality, access to resources, and personalized learning experiences, are promising. By harnessing AI's ability to process large amounts of data, adapt to individual needs, and create scalable solutions, we can address long-standing challenges in education. These capabilities make AI a powerful tool for enhancing equity and empowerment, particularly for marginalized and underserved populations.

One of the primary ways AI bridges gaps in education is through its ability to offer personalized learning experiences. Traditional education systems often struggle to accommodate diverse learning styles and paces, especially in overcrowded classrooms or under-resourced settings. AI-powered tools, such as intelligent tutoring systems and adaptive learning platforms, can analyze individual students' strengths, weaknesses, and learning preferences in real-time, tailoring content and assessments accordingly (Luckin et al., 2016). This level of personalization ensures that students receive the right kind of support at the right time, regardless of their background or initial proficiency level. In environments where teachers may be stretched thin or lack the time to provide individualized attention to each student, AI can fill this gap by offering tailored guidance and feedback, significantly improving learning outcomes (Holmes et al., 2019).

AI has the potential to democratize access to high-quality educational resources, breaking down the barriers posed by geographical location, economic constraints, and lack of access to specialized teachers. In many parts of the world, particularly in remote or rural areas, students may not have access to highly qualified instructors or advanced learning materials. AI-driven educational platforms can bridge this gap by providing universal access to personalized instruction, making high-quality education available to anyone with an internet connection (West et al., 2019). These platforms can offer content in multiple languages, adapt to varying literacy levels, and use multimedia tools to support diverse learning preferences, making learning more inclusive. In addition, AI can help identify learning gaps and provide targeted interventions, ensuring that even students who are falling behind can catch up with their peers.

AI is not just a technological advancement, but a social equalizer in education. It has the potential to enhance inclusivity by providing solutions for learners with disabilities. AI-powered assistive technologies, such as speech recognition software, text-to-speech applications, and real-time language translation tools, can make educational content more accessible to students with hearing impairments, visual impairments, or learning disabilities. By customizing learning experiences to meet the specific needs of students, AI fosters a more inclusive environment where all learners, regardless of their physical or cognitive challenges, can thrive.

AI also plays a critical role in reducing the digital divide by offering scalable and cost-effective solutions. While access to technology remains a significant issue in many parts of the world, AI-based educational tools can be deployed to minimize educational delivery costs. For instance, AI-driven learning management systems (LMS) can streamline administrative tasks, such as grading and feedback, allowing teachers to focus on providing personalized support to students. Furthermore, AI tools can enhance the efficiency and effectiveness of blended learning models, which combine online and in-person instruction, making it easier for schools in under-resourced settings to provide quality education without the need for extensive physical infrastructure or highly specialized staff (Anderson, 2018). This empowerment through technology can bridge the digital gap and provide equal opportunities for all students.

Despite the numerous benefits, implementing AI in education is not without its challenges. One significant issue is the potential for exacerbating existing inequalities if AI technologies are not designed and deployed with equity in mind. For instance, there is a risk that AI algorithms could perpetuate biases related to race, gender, or socioeconomic status, particularly if the data used to train these systems is not diverse or representative of all populations (West et al., 2019). To bridge gaps effectively, it is essential that AI systems are developed with careful attention to fairness, transparency, and inclusivity. This requires urgent collaboration between educators, policymakers, and technologists to ensure that AI tools are designed to serve the needs of all students, not just those in affluent or privileged circumstances. Addressing these ethical challenges is crucial to ensure that AI is a force for good in education.

Additionally, implementing AI in education must consider the ethical implications of data privacy and security. AI systems collect vast amounts of data on students' learning behaviors, performance, and personal information, raising concerns about how this data is used and who has access to it. Ensuring the privacy and security of student data is critical to building trust and ensuring the ethical use of AI in education. As AI technologies continue to evolve, it will be crucial to establish strong policies and frameworks that govern the ethical use of AI in educational contexts, with an emphasis on protecting students' rights and ensuring that AI tools are used to empower rather than exploit (Luckin et al., 2016).

AI has the potential to bridge significant gaps in education by providing personalized learning experiences, democratizing access to resources, supporting students with disabilities, and reducing the digital divide. By tailoring educational content to individual needs and making high-quality education more accessible, AI can enhance learning outcomes and foster greater equity in education. However, to fully realize these benefits, addressing the ethical, social, and technical challenges associated with AI implementation is essential, ensuring that AI systems are inclusive, fair, and transparent. With thoughtful design and careful consideration, AI can be a powerful tool for bridging the gaps historically hindering educational progress for marginalized populations, ultimately contributing to a more equitable and empowered global society.

6.1.1. Accessibility for Special Needs Education: Harnessing AI for Inclusion

Artificial Intelligence (AI) holds significant promise for transforming special needs education by providing tools and systems that enhance accessibility, personalization, and inclusivity for students with disabilities. Traditional educational settings often face challenges when it comes to addressing the diverse needs of students with disabilities, such as physical, sensory, or cognitive impairments. AI can bridge these gaps by offering adaptive technologies and personalized learning experiences that ensure equitable opportunities for all learners, regardless of their abilities. By leveraging AI's capabilities, educational systems can create more inclusive environments that promote the active participation and success of students with special needs.

One of the key areas where AI enhances accessibility in special needs education is through assistive technologies that support students with sensory impairments. AI-powered tools, such as speech recognition software, can help students with hearing impairments by converting spoken language into text in real-time, enabling them to follow lessons more effectively (Luckin et al., 2016). Similarly, AI-driven text-to-speech technologies can aid students with visual impairments by converting written content into audio, allowing them to access textbooks, digital resources, and other learning materials. These assistive tools not only improve accessibility but also encourage greater independence for students who might otherwise rely heavily on human support.

AI also plays a vital role in supporting students with cognitive impairments, such as those with autism spectrum disorder (ASD) or learning disabilities. Personalized learning platforms powered by AI can adapt to individual students' learning styles, preferences, and progress, providing tailored content and feedback that aligns with each learner's unique needs. For example, intelligent tutoring systems (ITS) use AI to analyze a student's responses, learning pace, and areas of struggle, dynamically adjusting the content and difficulty level accordingly (Holmes et al., 2019). This customization helps ensure that students with cognitive challenges are not left behind, as the AI system can provide immediate support, modify the presentation of material, and deliver content in multiple formats, such as visual, auditory, and kinesthetic, to match the student's learning preferences.

AI can offer real-time monitoring of student progress and behavior, which is particularly valuable for teachers working with special needs students. AI systems can track learning progress, identify signs of frustration or disengagement, and provide insights into a student's emotional and cognitive state. This data-driven approach enables educators to intervene promptly and offer targeted support when necessary. For instance, AI can alert educators when a student struggles with a specific task, helping them provide timely interventions or modify teaching strategies to suit the learner's needs better. Additionally, AI can be used to develop personalized learning goals and action plans, ensuring that each student receives the support they need to reach their full potential (West et al., 2019).

AI can assist students with motor impairments by providing alternative methods of interaction. For example, AI-powered eye-tracking systems allow students with limited mobility to control devices and interact with educational content through eye movements. Similarly, voice recognition systems can enable students to use speech commands to operate computers, tablets, or other learning devices. These technologies not only improve accessibility but also empower students with disabilities to engage in educational activities that were previously difficult or impossible. By enabling students to interact with digital content in ways that are tailored to their physical abilities, AI fosters greater inclusivity and ensures that all students can participate in the learning process.

The potential for AI to support students with special needs extends beyond individual learning tools to creating inclusive classrooms and curricula. AI can facilitate the development of universally designed curricula that can be easily customized for learners with different needs and abilities. This dynamic adaptation of curricula ensures that educational content is presented in a way accessible to a diverse student body, promoting equal opportunities for all learners. Additionally, AI tools can support teachers in differentiating instruction by providing insights into students' strengths and weaknesses, guiding them in creating personalized learning pathways for each student. This level of support is fundamental in special needs education, where individualized approaches are often necessary to accommodate different abilities and learning styles.

Despite the promising potential of AI in special needs education, challenges remain, particularly concerning the ethical and practical aspects of its implementation. One concern is ensuring that AI systems are designed to be fair, unbiased, and inclusive. If AI algorithms are trained on data not representative of the diverse populations they aim to serve, there is a risk that the tools will not be effective for all students. For instance, AI systems may inadvertently favor certain learning styles over others or fail to account for cultural or linguistic differences, thus exacerbating existing inequalities (West et al., 2019). To ensure that AI is an effective tool for all students, developers must prioritize inclusivity in the design of AI systems, ensuring that they are responsive to the needs of diverse learners.

Another challenge is the need for professional development and training for educators to integrate AI into special needs education effectively. Teachers must be equipped with the skills to use AI tools effectively, interpret the data generated by these systems, and apply the insights to improve teaching practices. Additionally, schools must ensure that the necessary technological infrastructure is in place to support AI tools, including adequate internet access, hardware, and software. Addressing these barriers is critical to ensuring that AI is used effectively in special needs education and that the benefits are fully realized for students with disabilities.

In conclusion, AI has the potential to revolutionize special needs education by providing personalized, accessible, and inclusive learning experiences for students with disabilities. Through assistive technologies, intelligent tutoring systems, and adaptive curricula, AI can help bridge the gaps that have traditionally hindered educational success for students with special needs. However, careful attention must be given to the ethical and practical challenges associated with AI's implementation, particularly in terms of ensuring fairness, inclusivity, and the development of appropriate training for educators. With thoughtful design and implementation, AI can significantly enhance educational opportunities for all students, fostering a more inclusive and equitable learning environment.

6.1.2. Language Translation and Cross-Cultural Learning: The Role of AI in Global Education

Language barriers have long been a significant obstacle to effective communication and learning in global education systems. Students, educators, and communities worldwide face challenges when accessing resources, collaborating, or exchanging knowledge across linguistic and cultural boundaries. However, advancements in Artificial Intelligence (AI), particularly in the field of language translation and natural language processing (NLP), offer transformative opportunities to bridge these gaps. By enhancing the accessibility and fluidity of cross-cultural interactions, AI can foster more inclusive educational experiences, facilitate global collaboration, and promote a deeper understanding of diverse cultures.

AI-powered language translation systems, such as Google Translate and DeepL, have revolutionized how people worldwide engage with written and spoken languages. These tools use machine learning algorithms and NLP to provide real-time, accurate translations that enable users to access content in multiple languages. In educational settings, AI translation systems break down language barriers by allowing students to use textbooks, research papers, digital resources, and online courses in their preferred languages. For example, international students can use translation tools to understand course materials better, while educators can access research from different linguistic backgrounds to enhance curricula. This accessibility helps to level the playing field, providing equal opportunities for learners from diverse linguistic backgrounds.

In addition to written translation, AI enhances spoken language translation through technologies like real-time speech-to-speech translation. Systems such as Skype Translator and Google's real-time transcription services enable conversations between speakers of different languages, facilitating live communication in academic settings. These tools support collaborative projects, virtual classrooms, and cross-cultural exchanges by allowing students and educators to converse without the need for human interpreters. For instance, in an international research collaboration, AI-powered translation tools can enable seamless dialogue between scholars from different countries, enhancing knowledge sharing and ideas. This immediate translation capability allows for more efficient communication, saving time and reducing the risk of misinterpretation, thereby supporting global learning networks.

Beyond simply translating languages, AI can also support cross-cultural learning by helping students understand the cultural contexts embedded within language. Language is often deeply tied to cultural practices, values, and social norms; translating it without considering these nuances can result in a loss of meaning. AI systems are increasingly capable of recognizing and accounting for these cultural differences, offering more context-aware translations that preserve the intended meaning and tone of the original text. For example, AI models can incorporate contextual learning to interpret idiomatic expressions, regional variations, and culturally specific references like human translators traditionally do. By making these cultural subtleties more accessible, AI helps students develop a deeper appreciation of global perspectives and encourages them to engage more thoughtfully with the content they encounter.

AI-powered translation tools can facilitate language learning itself. Language learning apps like Duolingo, Babbel, and Memrise use AI algorithms to personalize student learning experiences, adapting lessons based on the learner's progress and needs. These platforms often incorporate speech recognition features to help learners with pronunciation, providing immediate feedback on their spoken language skills. Through this personalized approach, AI can enhance the language learning experience by offering adaptive, interactive lessons that help learners build proficiency at their own pace. By combining translation and language acquisition capabilities, AI supports students in accessing content and empowers them to learn new languages and communicate more effectively in a globalized world.

AI can support cross-cultural learning by facilitating virtual exchanges and collaborations among students from different parts of the world. Through AI-enhanced platforms, students can participate in joint projects, discussions, and debates with peers from different countries, gaining firsthand exposure to diverse cultural perspectives. For instance, AI systems can help organize and moderate virtual classrooms where students engage in cross-cultural dialogue and collaborative learning. By connecting learners from different linguistic and cultural backgrounds, AI encourages the development of global competencies, such as cultural sensitivity, empathy, and intercultural communication skills, all essential in today's interconnected world.

AI is being employed to improve the accessibility of educational content for learners with diverse needs, such as those with disabilities. For students with hearing impairments, AI-driven real-time captioning and transcription services enable them to follow conversations and lectures, regardless of spoken language. Similarly, for students with visual impairments, AI-based tools that provide audio descriptions of visual content allow them to engage with educational materials in a more accessible way. By addressing these barriers, AI fosters cross-cultural learning and ensures that students with disabilities can fully participate in the global educational community.

While AI holds great promise in promoting cross-cultural learning and language accessibility, challenges remain in ensuring that these tools are equitable, inclusive, and culturally sensitive. For example, AI models are often trained on data that may not fully represent linguistic or cultural diversity, which could lead to translation biases or misunderstandings of cultural nuances. AI systems must be designed to recognize and respect diverse populations' linguistic and cultural richness. Developers must prioritize inclusivity by training AI models on diverse datasets encompassing various languages, dialects, and cultural contexts. Additionally, it is crucial to ensure that AI translation tools are continuously updated and refined to improve their accuracy and address any biases that may emerge.

In conclusion, AI is increasingly important in breaking down language barriers and promoting cross-cultural learning in global education. By facilitating language translation, real-time communication, and personalized language learning, AI enables students and educators to engage more fully with content and peers worldwide. Moreover, AI fosters cultural understanding by helping learners appreciate the cultural contexts embedded within language. However, to maximize the benefits of AI for cross-cultural learning, developers must ensure these tools are inclusive, equitable, and culturally sensitive. With continued advancements in AI technology and thoughtful implementation, AI has the potential to revolutionize global education by making it more accessible, inclusive, and culturally rich.

References

Anderson, C. A. (2018). The influence of video games on youth: Implications for learning and education. In P. R. Green (Ed.), *The Routledge Handbook of Education and Technology* (pp. 136-147). Routledge.

Holmes, W., Bialik, M., & Fadel, C. (2019). *Artificial Intelligence in Education: Promises and Implications for Teaching and Learning*. Center for Curriculum Redesign.

Luckin, R., Holmes, W., Griffiths, M., & Forcier, L. B. (2016). *Intelligence Unleashed: An Argument for AI in Education*. Pearson Education.

Vlachos, A., & Riedel, S. (2020). *The Role of AI in Language Translation*. Springer.

West, S. M., Whittaker, M., & Crawford, K. (2019). *Discriminating Systems: Gender, Race, and Power in AI*. AI Now Institute.

Part II: Empowerment Through AI-Driven Learning

Introduction

Integrating Artificial Intelligence (AI) into education can fundamentally reshape how individuals learn, thereby fostering empowerment and equipping learners with the skills and knowledge necessary to thrive in an increasingly complex and interconnected world. AI-driven learning uses AI technologies, such as personalized learning systems, intelligent tutoring systems, and data analytics, to enhance and customize educational experiences. By providing tailored instruction, real-time feedback, and continuous support, AI enables learners to take greater ownership of their education, encouraging self-directed learning and fostering a sense of empowerment. This transformation in learning practices can significantly contribute to reducing barriers to access, promoting equity, and supporting lifelong learning, all of which are essential components of empowerment.

One of the primary ways AI can empower learners is through personalized learning systems, which adapt the educational experience to the individual's unique needs, abilities, and interests. Traditional education systems often adopt a one-size-fits-all approach, which can leave many students behind or fail to engage others who may need more advanced challenges. AI-driven systems, on the other hand, provide a more personalized approach by continuously monitoring learners' progress, analyzing their strengths and weaknesses, and adjusting the content and pacing accordingly. This tailored approach allows learners to move at their own pace, fostering a sense of control over their learning process and boosting their confidence in their abilities. Studies have shown that personalized learning systems can lead to improved academic performance, greater student engagement, and enhanced motivation (Holmes et al., 2019; Luckin et al., 2016).

In addition to personalized learning, AI can empower learners by providing continuous, real-time feedback. This feature is particularly important in a learning environment where traditional feedback cycles—such as graded assignments or teacher evaluations—can be delayed and limited. AI systems, particularly intelligent tutoring systems (ITS), provide immediate and actionable feedback, allowing learners to identify areas where they need improvement and make adjustments in real-time. This constant feedback loop not only helps students to stay on track but also builds their confidence by enabling them to see their progress and understand their mistakes in a supportive, non-judgmental way. Such an approach is crucial in fostering a growth mindset, where learners see challenges as opportunities for development rather than as obstacles (Dweck, 2006).

AI also enhances empowerment by promoting autonomy and self-regulated learning. Through AI-enabled tools, learners are encouraged to take control of their learning journey, setting goals, tracking progress, and seeking out resources independently. For example, AI-powered learning platforms such as Coursera and Khan Academy provide learners with the flexibility to choose courses, set learning schedules, and engage in self-directed study. This flexibility is particularly beneficial for adult learners and those engaged in lifelong learning, as it enables them to balance education with personal and professional responsibilities. AI-driven platforms also foster self-efficacy by supporting learners in achieving their individual goals, whether academic, professional, or personal. By placing the learner at the center of the educational experience, AI helps to cultivate a sense of agency and ownership, which are critical elements of empowerment (Zimmerman, 2002).

AI can bridge educational gaps by making learning more accessible to diverse populations, including those with disabilities or individuals from marginalized communities. AI-driven technologies can support inclusive learning environments through features such as speech recognition, real-time captions, and adaptive interfaces for students with visual or hearing impairments. For example, AI tools such as automatic transcription services and voice-to-text applications enable students with hearing disabilities to participate more fully in classroom activities and discussions. Similarly, AI-powered assistive technologies can help students with learning disabilities, such as dyslexia, by providing customized support, including text-to-speech tools and adaptive reading platforms. By catering to the specific needs of learners, AI helps ensure that all individuals, regardless of their background or abilities, have equal access to high-quality education, thereby contributing to greater empowerment (Luckin et al., 2016).

AI's ability to scale educational opportunities is another key factor in promoting empowerment. In regions where access to quality education is limited, AI-driven platforms and virtual learning environments can provide a lifeline. For example, AI-powered MOOCs (Massive Open Online Courses) allow learners from remote or underserved areas to access world-class educational resources, regardless of their geographical location. These platforms often offer courses in multiple languages and can be accessed on various devices, making education more inclusive and equitable. Additionally, AI systems can help overcome resource constraints by providing automated teaching and support, which reduces the dependency on human instructors. This scalability is particularly beneficial in developing countries or areas with limited educational infrastructure, where the availability of skilled educators may be scarce.

Another important aspect of AI-driven learning is its role in fostering skills that are crucial for success in the 21st century, including critical thinking, problem-solving, and digital literacy. As the world becomes more technologically advanced, these skills are becoming increasingly vital for both personal and professional success. AI-based tools encourage students to engage with complex, real-world problems and apply knowledge in innovative ways. For instance, AI-powered platforms can present learners with scenarios or simulations that require them to use analytical skills, think creatively, and collaborate with others to find solutions. These types of learning experiences not only equip students with the skills they need to navigate an AI-driven world but also empower them to become active participants in shaping that future.

However, while AI offers vast potential for empowerment, its integration into education is not without challenges. Concerns about data privacy, algorithmic bias, and unequal access to technology must be addressed to ensure that AI-driven learning tools are used ethically and equitably. For instance, AI systems may inadvertently perpetuate existing biases if they are trained on biased data or lack sufficient diversity in their design. Ensuring that AI tools are transparent, inclusive, and aligned with ethical principles is essential to realizing their full potential for empowering learners. Moreover, educators must be adequately trained to use AI tools effectively and responsibly, ensuring that these technologies are leveraged to support—not replace—human interaction and guidance in the learning process.

In conclusion, AI-driven learning can potentially empower individuals by providing personalized, accessible, and scalable educational experiences. AI fosters autonomy and agency by enabling learners to take control of their educational journey, receive real-time feedback, and engage with complex problems. Furthermore, AI supports inclusivity by catering to diverse learning needs and overcoming barriers to access. As AI continues to evolve, it will play an increasingly central role in promoting lifelong learning, closing educational gaps, and equipping learners with the skills they need to succeed in a rapidly changing world. However, careful consideration of ethical and equity issues is crucial to ensure that AI empowers all learners, regardless of background or ability.

Chapter 7

Skills Development for the Future Workforce

7.1. Introduction

As technological advancements, particularly in Artificial Intelligence (AI), continue to transform the global economy, the future workforce will need to adapt and develop new skills to thrive in an increasingly automated, interconnected, and data-driven world. The rapid pace of technological change, including the rise of AI, robotics, and digital platforms, reshapes industries and redefines the nature of work. In response to these shifts, there is a growing emphasis on equipping workers with the skills required to navigate this evolving landscape, ensuring that they remain competitive, adaptable, and resilient in the face of change. The future workforce will require a combination of technical, cognitive, and socio-emotional skills that enable individuals to harness the opportunities presented by emerging technologies and contribute to developing a sustainable and inclusive economy.

A key aspect of skills development for the future workforce is the need for digital literacy and technical competencies. As AI and automation continue to permeate various sectors, the demand for workers who can understand, operate, and collaborate with advanced technologies is increasing. Digital literacy, which encompasses the ability to use digital tools and platforms effectively, is no longer a luxury but a fundamental requirement for most jobs. This includes proficiency in areas such as data analytics, programming, machine learning, and cybersecurity, which are crucial for understanding and leveraging AI technologies. According to Brynjolfsson and McAfee (2014), workers with these skills will be better positioned to thrive in the digital economy, where the ability to engage with technology is central to job performance. For example, workers in fields like healthcare, education, and manufacturing are increasingly expected to be comfortable with AI-driven tools that assist in decision-making, process optimization, and customer interactions.

In addition to technical skills, the future workforce will require advanced cognitive skills, including critical thinking, problem-solving, and creativity. As AI and automation handle more routine and repetitive tasks, human workers will increasingly be tasked with roles that require higher-level cognitive abilities. The ability to analyze complex problems, generate innovative solutions, and make informed decisions will become more valuable. In this context, fostering creativity and innovation is essential. AI is expected to complement human creativity rather than replace it, as machines excel at processing vast amounts of data but lack the ability to think creatively or understand complex, context-driven scenarios (Shneiderman, 2020). Therefore, cultivating skills that enhance human creativity, such as design thinking and interdisciplinary problem-solving, will be critical for workers to add value in AI-powered environments. As industries move toward more dynamic and knowledge-intensive roles, workers who can think critically and creatively will be better equipped to adapt to new challenges and opportunities.

Equally important for the future workforce is the development of socio-emotional skills, which encompass interpersonal and emotional intelligence. As AI and automation take over more technical and cognitive tasks, human workers will increasingly focus on roles that require collaboration, empathy, and leadership. The capacity to work effectively in teams, communicate clearly, and understand the emotions and needs of others will be essential for success in the workplace. AI, despite its capabilities, lacks the nuanced understanding of human emotions and the ability to navigate complex social dynamics. For this reason, skills such as emotional intelligence, conflict resolution, and negotiation will remain in high demand. In fact, many experts argue that the future workforce will place a premium on human-centered skills that AI cannot replicate, particularly as workplaces become more diverse and globalized (Davenport & Kirby, 2016). These socio-emotional skills will enable workers to collaborate effectively with AI systems, as well as with their human colleagues, ensuring that they remain integral to decision-making processes, leadership, and customer engagement.

Moreover, adaptability and lifelong learning will be critical skills for workers in the future. The rapid pace of technological change means that workers will need to continuously update their knowledge and skills to stay relevant in their fields. This requires a mindset of lifelong learning, where individuals actively seek out opportunities for personal and professional growth, whether through formal education, on-the-job training, or self-directed learning. AI and digital platforms play a central role in facilitating lifelong learning by providing access to a vast array of resources, including online courses, tutorials, and virtual learning environments. Platforms like Coursera, edX, and LinkedIn Learning have already begun to democratize education, enabling individuals to learn at their own pace and according to their specific interests and career goals. According to the World Economic Forum (2020), workers who are committed to lifelong learning and who have the ability to adapt to new technologies will be better positioned to thrive in the future economy, where change is constant and rapid.

In terms of organizational implications, businesses will need to invest in training and reskilling programs to ensure that their workforce is equipped with the necessary skills for the future. Organizations must adopt a forward-thinking approach to talent development, offering employees opportunities to learn new skills, including those related to emerging technologies. Reskilling initiatives, which focus on retraining workers in new areas of expertise, will be crucial for workers whose jobs are at risk of being automated. For example, companies in sectors such as manufacturing and retail are increasingly investing in programs to upskill their employees in areas such as AI, robotics, and data science (Brynjolfsson & McAfee, 2014). Governments and educational institutions must also play an active role in supporting skills development by updating curricula to reflect the changing demands of the labor market, promoting inclusive access to education, and providing financial and logistical support for workers seeking to reskill or upskill.

Ultimately, the development of skills for the future workforce is not just about preparing individuals for specific jobs but also about fostering a more adaptable, innovative, and resilient workforce. The future of work will require workers who can collaborate with AI, solve complex problems, lead teams, and continuously learn and adapt to changing circumstances. As AI continues to redefine industries and economies, it will be essential to ensure that workers are equipped with the skills and mindsets that allow them to not only survive but thrive in the AI-driven economy. This vision of a future workforce is one that is empowered, capable, and resilient, with the skills necessary to shape a more sustainable, equitable, and prosperous future.

7.1.1. AI in Vocational Training and Skills Enhancement

Artificial Intelligence (AI) is transforming vocational training and skills enhancement by providing innovative tools to enhance learning, improve efficiency, and tailor educational experiences to the specific needs of learners. The application of AI in vocational education has the potential to bridge the skills gap, enhance workforce preparedness, and increase accessibility to high-quality training for individuals across various sectors. AI-driven solutions in vocational training focus on personalized learning, real-time feedback, and adaptive learning pathways that allow learners to acquire industry-relevant skills at their own pace while also supporting teachers and trainers with valuable insights into learners' progress and areas for improvement.

One of the most significant contributions of AI to vocational training is the development of personalized learning experiences. Unlike traditional one-size-fits-all approaches to education, AI enables tailored instruction by assessing an individual's prior knowledge, learning preferences, and progress. For instance, AI algorithms can analyze learners' interactions with digital platforms and identify patterns in their learning behavior, offering customized content and suggestions to reinforce weak areas. This personalized approach ensures that each learner receives targeted instruction that matches their learning style, ultimately leading to more efficient and effective skill acquisition (Luckin et al., 2016). Such systems are particularly beneficial in vocational training, where practical, hands-on experience is crucial, and learners may have varying levels of prior knowledge or experience. For example, AI-powered systems can assist trainees in fields such as automotive repair, construction, or healthcare by adjusting the difficulty of tasks, recommending supplemental materials, or providing interactive simulations based on individual performance.

Another key benefit of AI in vocational education is enhancing real-time feedback and assessment. Traditionally, vocational training has relied on human instructors to evaluate learners' skills, often resulting in delayed feedback or subjective assessments. AI systems can provide immediate, data-driven feedback, enabling learners to understand their strengths and weaknesses as they progress through training. For example, AI-powered simulators in fields like nursing or welding can instantly assess the accuracy of a learner's technique, highlighting areas for improvement and offering corrective suggestions. This accelerates the learning process and allows learners to refine their skills continuously without waiting for the next formal assessment or instructor feedback (West et al., 2019). In addition, AI can track performance over time, allowing both learners and instructors to identify trends in progress and tailor future training efforts accordingly.

Furthermore, AI can be used to create adaptive learning pathways in vocational training. Adaptive learning systems use AI to monitor learner performance and adjust instructional content and difficulty in real-time. This ensures that learners are constantly challenged appropriately, preventing boredom from too-easy content or frustration from material that is too difficult. For example, an AI-based learning management system might recognize that a student is struggling with certain technical concepts in a construction course, and it will provide additional learning resources or modified exercises to help the learner gain mastery in that area. Over time, this results in more effective and efficient learning, as the learner is guided through the training content in a way that best suits their needs (Luckin et al., 2016). By offering personalized, adaptive pathways, AI enables vocational training programs to accommodate a diverse range of learners, from novices to experienced professionals seeking to upskill or reskill.

Moreover, AI can support immersive learning environments through technologies such as virtual reality (VR) and augmented reality (AR), which offer learners hands-on practice in realistic, simulated settings. These immersive experiences allow learners to practice skills in a risk-free environment, with AI tracking their actions and providing immediate feedback. In fields like healthcare, aviation, and engineering, VR and AR simulations powered by AI can replicate real-world scenarios, enabling learners to gain practical experience before they enter the workplace. This is especially important in vocational education, where gaining hands-on experience is often difficult due to resource limitations, safety concerns, or the complexity of certain tasks. For example, AI-driven VR simulations can train healthcare workers in emergency medical procedures or train automotive technicians to diagnose engine issues without the need for physical equipment or real-world risks (Holmes et al., 2019). As these AI-powered systems improve in sophistication, the possibilities for immersive learning in vocational training will continue to expand, allowing learners to gain practical skills in any environment.

AI also plays a critical role in skills forecasting and workforce development. By analyzing data from various sources—such as labor market trends, employer needs, and technological advancements—AI can predict future skill requirements across industries. This allows vocational training programs to remain responsive and aligned with the evolving demands of the job market. For example, AI can identify emerging sectors that require specific technical expertise, such as renewable energy, data analytics, or cybersecurity, and help design training programs that equip workers with the skills needed to meet these demands. In this way, AI serves as a tool for workforce development, ensuring that vocational training programs remain relevant and that workers are prepared for future job opportunities (West et al., 2019). Additionally, AI can assist employers in identifying skills gaps within their current workforce, helping to create targeted training initiatives to reskill employees and improve job performance.

Despite these advances, integrating AI in vocational training also presents challenges, such as data privacy concerns, algorithms bias, and the digital divide. As AI systems collect and analyze data about learners' behaviors and progress, robust safeguards must be in place to protect individuals' privacy. Furthermore, AI algorithms can perpetuate existing biases if not carefully designed, potentially leading to unequal learning experiences or biased assessments. For example, if an AI system is trained on data that reflects existing inequalities in the workforce, it may inadvertently favor certain groups over others. To mitigate these risks, AI systems used in vocational training must be designed to be fair, transparent, and accountable, with clear guidelines on data usage and algorithmic fairness (West et al., 2019).

AI holds great promise for transforming vocational training and skills enhancement by providing personalized, adaptive, and immersive learning experiences closely aligned with the workforce's needs. As industries evolve and technology reshapes the job market, AI will be essential in preparing workers with the skills they need to succeed in an increasingly complex, automated world. By integrating AI into vocational education, we can ensure that workers are better equipped to meet future challenges, contributing to more efficient, productive, and equitable labor markets worldwide.

7.1.2. Preparing Students for AI-Driven Careers

As artificial intelligence (AI) continues to reshape industries and drive innovation, preparing students for careers in an increasingly AI-driven world has become essential. Integrating AI into various sectors, such as healthcare, finance, manufacturing, transportation, and education, presents exciting opportunities and challenges. To ensure that students are ready for these opportunities, education systems must equip them with the necessary knowledge, skills, and competencies to thrive in a future shaped by AI technologies. This preparation involves understanding the fundamentals of AI and developing interdisciplinary skills, fostering creativity and problem-solving abilities, and preparing students for lifelong learning in an ever-evolving job market.

7.1.2.1. Developing Foundational AI Knowledge

One of the first steps in preparing students for AI-driven careers is ensuring that they acquire a strong foundational understanding of AI and its applications. As AI technologies permeate various fields, students need to grasp the basic principles of AI, including machine learning, natural language processing, robotics, and data analytics. Early exposure to AI concepts can help demystify technology and encourage students to pursue careers in fields related to AI development, research, and application.

Incorporating AI-related courses into K-12 and higher education curricula is one way to introduce students to the field. For example, high school students can be taught the basics of coding, algorithms, and machine learning through accessible programming tools like Scratch or Python, which provide interactive and engaging ways to understand AI concepts. At the higher education level, computer science, engineering, and business students should be exposed to more advanced AI topics, such as neural networks, deep learning, and AI ethics. These foundational courses will prepare students for technical roles and interdisciplinary careers where AI is applied to solving real-world problems (Brynjolfsson & McAfee, 2014).

7.1.2.2. Fostering Interdisciplinary Skills

AI is not limited to technology; its applications are widespread across healthcare, finance, law, and education. As such, students must be equipped with the interdisciplinary skills needed to understand how AI can be applied in diverse contexts. Encouraging students to pursue AI knowledge and domain-specific expertise can open career opportunities in AI-powered healthcare diagnostics, AI-driven financial analysis, and intelligent legal systems.

For instance, a student interested in AI and healthcare might study AI principles alongside medical sciences to understand how AI can improve diagnostics, treatment planning, and patient care. Similarly, students studying AI in finance could focus on how AI is used in risk assessment, algorithmic trading, and fraud detection. By encouraging students to combine AI with domain-specific knowledge, they will be better prepared to address industry-specific challenges and contribute to developing innovative AI solutions relevant to the field's needs (Chui et al., 2016).

7.1.2.3. Enhancing Problem-Solving and Creativity

While technical skills are critical for AI-related careers, it is equally important to cultivate problem-solving and creativity in students. AI is fundamentally a tool for solving complex problems, and the ability to think critically and creatively is essential for students to leverage AI effectively. AI professionals often work on novel challenges, from designing new algorithms to solving ethical dilemmas related to AI applications. To prepare students for these tasks, education systems should encourage collaborative projects, design thinking, and problem-based learning approaches.

Project-based learning, where students work on real-world problems and create AI-driven solutions, provides an excellent opportunity for developing these skills. For example, students might be tasked with creating an AI tool that improves access to healthcare in underserved regions, addressing language barriers or lack of infrastructure. Such projects expose students to the technical aspects of AI and teach them how to approach problems from different angles, consider ethical implications, and develop innovative solutions (Resnick et al., 2009). Furthermore, fostering a mindset of creativity and adaptability will help students stay ahead of rapid technological changes and continue to thrive as AI evolves.

7.1.2.4. Preparing for Lifelong Learning

AI technologies evolve quickly, and the careers of tomorrow will likely require continuous adaptation and learning. Preparing students for AI-driven careers involves instilling a mindset of lifelong learning. As AI tools, techniques, and applications continue to develop, workers must stay updated on new developments, trends, and best practices. Encouraging students to engage with ongoing learning opportunities—such as online courses, workshops, and certifications—can help them maintain their skills and stay competitive in the job market.

Moreover, promoting a growth mindset, where students are encouraged to see challenges as opportunities for growth, can increase their resilience and adaptability in the face of technological advancements. This mindset is particularly important for students entering AI-driven fields, as they must continuously adapt to new tools, frameworks, and technologies throughout their careers (Dweck, 2006). Offering resources for self-directed learning, such as access to open-source AI libraries, online platforms like Coursera and edX, and mentorship opportunities, will also help students stay current and prepared for the future.

7.1.2.5. Collaboration Between Industry and Education

Educational institutions must collaborate closely with industry partners to effectively prepare students for AI-driven careers. These collaborations can help ensure that the skills taught in classrooms align with the job market's needs. Industry professionals can provide insights into the skills and knowledge most valuable in AI-related roles, allowing educational institutions to update their curricula to reflect the latest trends and technologies.

For example, partnerships between universities and AI companies can lead to internships, mentorship programs, and hands-on research opportunities that give students practical experience in the field. Additionally, industry experts can contribute to course design and teaching, helping to ensure that students are exposed to cutting-edge practices and real-world applications of AI. By fostering strong ties between education and industry, students will be better prepared to transition from academia to the workforce and make meaningful contributions to AI-driven innovations (Frey & Osborne, 2017).

Preparing students for AI-driven careers requires a multifaceted approach that includes foundational AI knowledge, interdisciplinary learning, problem-solving skills, and a commitment to lifelong learning. As AI continues to transform industries and create new career opportunities, education systems must evolve to ensure that students are equipped to succeed in this rapidly changing landscape. By combining technical expertise with creative thinking, practical experience, and industry collaboration, students can be empowered to thrive in an AI-powered world and contribute to the development of innovative solutions that shape the future of work.

References

Brynjolfsson, E., & McAfee, A. (2014). *The Second Machine Age: Work, Progress, and Prosperity in a Time of Brilliant Technologies*. W. W. Norton & Company.

Chui, M., Manyika, J., & Miremadi, M. (2016). *Where machines could replace humans—and where they cannot (yet)*. McKinsey Quarterly.

Davenport, T. H., & Kirby, J. (2016). *Only Humans Need Apply: Winners and Losers in the Age of Smart Machines*. Harper Business.

Dweck, C. S. (2006). *Mindset: The New Psychology of Success*. Random House.

Frey, C. B., & Osborne, M. A. (2017). The future of employment: How susceptible are jobs to computerization? *Technological Forecasting and Social Change*, 114, 254-280.

Holmes, W., Bialik, M., & Fadel, C. (2019). *Artificial Intelligence in Education: Promises and Implications for Teaching and Learning*. Center for Curriculum Redesign.

Luckin, R., Holmes, W., Griffiths, M., & Forcier, L. B. (2016). *Intelligence Unleashed: An Argument for AI in Education*. Pearson Education.

Resnick, M., et al. (2009). *Scratch: Programming for All*. *Communications of the ACM*, 52(11), 60-67.

Shneiderman, B. (2020). *Human-Centered AI: A New Approach to Building Artificial Intelligence*. Oxford University Press.

West, S. M., Whittaker, M., & Crawford, K. (2019). *Discriminating Systems: Gender, Race, and Power in AI*. AI Now Institute.

World Economic Forum. (2020). *The Future of Jobs Report 2020*. World Economic Forum.

Zimmerman, B. J. (2002). Becoming a Self-Regulated Learner: An Overview. *Theory into Practice*, 41(2), 64-70.

Chapter 8

AI and Lifelong Learning

8.1. Introduction

Lifelong learning is a cornerstone of personal and professional development in today's rapidly changing world. As the global workforce continues to evolve, the demand for continuous skill development and adaptation becomes ever more critical. Artificial Intelligence (AI) plays a transformative role in supporting lifelong learning by offering personalized learning experiences, enhancing access to resources, and facilitating continuous skills development throughout an individual's life. AI-powered tools and platforms enable learners to pursue education at their own pace and according to their unique needs, thus reshaping traditional learning paradigms.

8.1.1. Personalized Learning and Adaptation

AI enhances lifelong learning by providing personalized educational experiences tailored to the needs of individual learners. However, it's important to note that traditional education models often take a "one-size-fits-all" approach, which may not meet the diverse needs of learners at different stages of their lives. In contrast, AI can analyze data from learners' previous interactions and performance to create customized learning paths, adjust difficulty levels, and recommend resources that best fit their learning style and pace (Baker, 2016). Yet, the reliance on algorithms and machine learning models can also lead to potential biases and the loss of human touch in the learning process. This ability to personalize learning makes education more efficient and effective, enabling individuals to focus on areas where they need the most improvement and providing them with the appropriate challenges to foster growth.

AI-powered platforms such as intelligent tutoring systems like Duolingo and adaptive learning technologies like Khan Academy can help students of all ages learn more effectively by providing immediate feedback and support (VanLehn, 2011). For example, an AI system like Coursera might recommend specific resources or exercises based on a learner's progress, enabling them to acquire new skills more quickly. These systems can even detect when learners are struggling with concepts and offer additional help or adjust the material to ensure mastery before progressing. This level of personalization makes AI a key enabler of lifelong learning, providing tailored support that was previously difficult to achieve in traditional educational settings.

8.1.2. Expanding Access to Education

AI plays a vital role in expanding access to lifelong learning opportunities. With the rise of digital education platforms, AI makes accessing quality learning resources easier for people from various socio-economic backgrounds, geographical locations, and educational levels. Online courses, AI-powered tutors, and virtual classrooms are breaking down barriers to education, making learning more inclusive and accessible. AI tools can translate educational materials into multiple languages, making learning more accessible to non-native speakers and individuals with disabilities (Luckin et al., 2016).

Moreover, AI-driven platforms can offer a wide range of educational content, from foundational courses to specialized training, thus catering to a broad spectrum of learners. People who may not have access to traditional education institutions due to financial constraints, distance, or other barriers can now learn online, improving their skills and career prospects. This democratization of education is particularly important in a world where access to education is often unequal, and AI serves as a powerful tool in bridging the gap between privileged and underserved populations (Holmes et al., 2019).

8.1.3. Facilitating Skill Development for the Future Workforce

The future workforce will demand skills that are relevant to current industries and adaptable to the changing demands of emerging technologies such as AI. Lifelong learning ensures that individuals can keep up with new developments, acquire new skills, and remain competitive in an evolving job market. AI-powered tools assist in identifying emerging skills and providing relevant training opportunities, thereby preparing workers for the careers of tomorrow.

For example, AI platforms can track the development of industry-specific skills, analyze labor market trends, and identify gaps in workforce capabilities.

With this data, individuals can engage in targeted learning activities to acquire in-demand skills. Moreover, AI can support microlearning, a method where individuals engage with small, focused learning modules that can be completed in short time frames, making it easier to fit learning into busy schedules. This approach allows workers to continuously update their skills without taking extended time away from their jobs (Culp, 2020).

The rise of AI technologies in industries such as healthcare, finance, and engineering means that workers in these fields must continuously update their knowledge and skills. AI-enabled platforms can provide on-the-job learning opportunities, offer real-time performance feedback, and suggest new areas for development, empowering workers to take control of their professional growth. This approach helps individuals remain adaptable and prepared for future job market transformations as AI evolves and reshapes industries.

8.1.4. Fostering Lifelong Learners Through AI

Beyond skills acquisition, AI also contributes to fostering a culture of lifelong learning by supporting self-directed learning and personal growth. AI-powered systems empower learners to take ownership of their learning journeys by offering autonomy in choosing learning paths and content. This personalization empowers individuals to pursue learning aligned with their interests, passions, and career aspirations, promoting intrinsic motivation and long-term engagement with education (Kukulska-Hulme, 2020).

Furthermore, AI's capacity to deliver real-time feedback and track progress over time supports a learner's ability to set and achieve personalized goals. AI systems can identify strengths and areas for improvement, providing targeted suggestions and guiding learners to continue advancing. This ongoing interaction helps learners stay motivated, as they receive encouragement and recognition for their achievements. The integration of AI into the learning process fosters a growth mindset, where learners view challenges as opportunities for growth and are continuously motivated to expand their knowledge and abilities (Dweck, 2006).

AI has immense potential to transform lifelong learning by making education more personalized, accessible, and adaptable to the needs of individual learners. By integrating AI into learning environments, individuals can acquire new skills, continuously adapt to changes in the workforce, and remain competitive in an increasingly AI-driven world. Furthermore, AI supports the development of a culture of self-directed, lifelong learning, empowering individuals to take ownership of their educational journeys and continuously grow. As the workforce evolves and new opportunities arise, AI will continue to play a key role in ensuring that individuals are prepared to meet future demands, thus enabling a more knowledgeable, skilled, and resilient global society.

8.1.5. Continuous Learning Systems: Embracing Lifelong Education with AI

In today's rapidly evolving world, continuous learning is necessary for personal and professional growth. With the constant advancements in technology, shifts in industries, and changes in global economies, individuals must adapt and develop new skills throughout their lives. Artificial Intelligence (AI) is transformative in facilitating continuous learning systems, enabling individuals to engage in flexible, personalized, and adaptive learning experiences that cater to their evolving needs. These AI-driven systems make learning more accessible, efficient, and aligned with real-world applications, ensuring learners can stay relevant in changing job markets and societal demands.

8.1.5.1. Personalized Learning Journeys

One of the key features of continuous learning systems powered by AI is their ability to personalize learning pathways for individuals. Traditional educational models often rely on standardized curriculums that do not account for all students' diverse needs, backgrounds, or learning preferences. In contrast, AI systems can collect data on learners' interactions, performance, and progress, allowing them to adapt content and delivery methods to fit each learner's unique needs (Luckin et al., 2016). This personalization enables learners to move through the material at their own pace, focus on areas where they need improvement, and skip content they have already mastered.

AI-powered platforms, such as adaptive learning technologies, create dynamic learning environments that adjust in real time based on a learner's responses and performance. These systems can also incorporate diverse learning styles, ensuring that auditory, visual, and kinesthetic learners benefit from the educational experience. For example, platforms like Coursera and Duolingo use AI to analyze learner behavior, recommend courses, and personalize learning paths. This personalization enhances engagement, motivation, and learning outcomes, making continuous learning more effective and accessible for everyone (Baker, 2016).

8.1.5.2. Real-Time Feedback and Assessment

Continuous learning systems powered by AI offer learners the benefit of real-time feedback, a key factor in effective learning. Traditionally, learners would have to wait for assignments, exams, or formal evaluations to receive feedback, which can be a delayed and less effective improvement method. On the other hand, AI-driven systems provide immediate feedback, allowing learners to identify mistakes, misunderstandings, or areas where they need further attention. For example, intelligent tutoring systems can evaluate learners' responses to exercises, detect patterns in their mistakes, and suggest corrective actions or additional practice problems (VanLehn, 2011).

In addition to offering feedback, AI systems can perform ongoing assessments of learners' progress, tracking their achievements and challenges over time. This enables learners to visualize their development, set meaningful goals, and stay motivated. Furthermore, AI can tailor the difficulty of tasks based on a learner's proficiency level, providing a continuously appropriate challenge. This type of adaptive assessment is essential in a lifelong learning context, where learners must acquire new skills regularly, stay updated on trends, and ensure their competencies align with changing market needs (Holmes et al., 2019).

8.1.5.3. Lifelong Learning and Career Development

AI is particularly well-suited for supporting lifelong learning, which is increasingly essential for career advancement and personal development. In many industries, rapid technological changes mean that workers must continually update their skills to remain relevant. AI-powered continuous learning systems can assist learners in staying ahead by providing up-to-date information, resources, and courses relevant to their field or desired career path. For example, platforms like LinkedIn Learning and edX offer learners access to courses that align with industry trends, helping them acquire new competencies and credentials without interrupting their professional lives.

AI can also help in career development by identifying skill gaps in the workforce and recommending training programs to address these needs. By analyzing labor market data, AI systems can predict the skills that will be in demand in the future and suggest courses that will help individuals meet these demands. This ensures that learners are keeping up with current trends and preparing for future opportunities. Additionally, AI-powered platforms can assist learners in building personalized portfolios, showcasing their achievements and skills, and connecting them with employers or mentors, further enhancing their professional growth (Culp, 2020).

8.1.5.4. Scalability and Accessibility

One of the greatest advantages of AI-powered continuous learning systems is their scalability and accessibility. Traditional education models often face geography, cost, and resource limitations. In contrast, AI-driven platforms can serve a global audience, offering high-quality education to people from diverse backgrounds and regions. AI systems provide individuals in underserved areas access to the same learning opportunities as those in more privileged locations. Moreover, AI can break down barriers related to language, disability, and learning styles, ensuring that more people can engage in continuous learning regardless of their challenges.

AI can also democratize education by offering flexible learning schedules and formats. Learners can engage with content at their own pace during times that fit their schedules. This flexibility is crucial for people balancing work, family responsibilities, or other commitments, making it easier for them to continue learning throughout their lives. Furthermore, AI systems can support self-directed learning, where individuals take charge of their educational journeys, choosing when and what to study based on their interests, goals, and career aspirations (Holmes et al., 2019).

8.1.5.5. Supporting Diverse Learning Needs

AI-powered continuous learning systems are also crucial in supporting diverse learning needs. With the help of AI, personalized learning paths can be created for learners with different abilities and challenges. For example, AI technologies can help learners with disabilities by providing customized learning experiences that accommodate their specific requirements. Speech recognition, text-to-speech, and real-time translation tools can help learners with hearing, visual, or language challenges, ensuring everyone has an equal opportunity to succeed (Luckin et al., 2016).

Moreover, AI can adapt to cultural, linguistic, and socio-economic differences, offering more inclusive learning opportunities. AI systems can translate materials into multiple languages and even tailor educational content to suit cultural contexts, enhancing the learning experience for a diverse global audience. By supporting diverse learners, AI enables a more inclusive approach to education, where everyone can develop the skills necessary for lifelong learning and success (Baker, 2016).

AI-powered continuous learning systems represent a significant shift in how education and skill development are approached. By offering personalized learning experiences, real-time feedback, and scalable accessibility, these systems make lifelong learning more efficient and adaptable to individual needs. As the global job market evolves, AI enables learners to acquire new skills, stay competitive, and navigate career changes. Furthermore, AI fosters an inclusive learning environment, breaking down barriers related to geography, language, and disability. Integrating AI into lifelong learning systems is not just enhancing educational opportunities; it is reshaping the future of work and personal development.

8.1.6. Transformative Learning Models with AI

Transformative learning is a profound, structural shift in how individuals make sense of their experiences and the world around them. It is a process of critically analyzing one's assumptions and perspectives, challenging these preconceptions, and ultimately adopting new ways of thinking and acting (Mezirow, 1991). In the context of education, transformative learning models focus on encouraging students to reflect on their experiences, engage in critical thinking, and develop new, more inclusive perspectives. Artificial Intelligence (AI) has transformative potential in this regard, as it enhances traditional learning models and supports learners in the deep cognitive processes involved in transformation. AI can facilitate personalized, reflective, and experiential learning environments that foster profound changes in how individuals view themselves, others, and their place in the world.

8.1.6.1. AI in Facilitating Reflective Practice

Reflective practice is central to transformative learning, as it encourages learners to assess their beliefs, values, and behaviors critically. AI plays a significant role in creating platforms for reflective learning, enabling learners to interact with content in ways that provoke deep self-reflection. AI-driven learning systems can analyze learners' responses and track their engagement with specific content or tasks, offering real-time insights and feedback. By analyzing learners' answers, emotional states, and behavior patterns, AI can offer targeted suggestions to help learners engage in reflection, asking probing questions or providing resources that challenge their existing assumptions (Holmes et al., 2019).

For example, AI can facilitate reflective journaling, where learners record their thoughts, feelings, and responses to different experiences. Natural language processing (NLP) algorithms can analyze these journal entries to identify key themes, areas of confusion, or cognitive dissonance, prompting learners to explore these topics further. This process helps learners become more aware of their cognitive and emotional responses, encouraging a deeper engagement with their personal learning process and enhancing their ability to make meaningful connections between new and prior knowledge (DeMott, 2020).

8.1.6.2. Personalization and Adaptivity in Transformative Learning

One of the key aspects of transformative learning is that it requires learners to engage with content in personally relevant and meaningful ways. AI enhances this by offering highly personalized and adaptive learning experiences that align with an individual's learning needs, preferences, and goals. AI-driven learning systems analyze data from learners' interactions to tailor content, pace, and difficulty levels to match their evolving needs, ensuring that the learning process remains challenging and engaging. These personalized experiences can help learners challenge their existing paradigms in authentic and impactful ways, as they are exposed to new perspectives and ideas that directly relate to their personal experiences (Luckin et al., 2016).

AI-powered systems, such as intelligent tutoring systems (ITS) and adaptive learning platforms, can dynamically adjust learning content based on learners' progress and comprehension levels. These systems ensure that learners are not overwhelmed by material that is too difficult, nor do they spend excessive time on too easy content. By providing appropriate challenges at the right time, AI encourages learners to reflect on their assumptions and rethink their understanding of concepts in deeper ways. This form of individualized learning is especially beneficial in transformative education, as it nurtures critical thinking and self-reflection, essential components of the transformative learning process (Baker, 2016).

8.1.6.3. AI-Enhanced Collaboration and Community Learning

Transformative learning models also emphasize the importance of dialogue and collaboration, as interactions with peers and mentors help challenge existing perspectives and broaden understanding. AI technologies can facilitate collaborative learning by connecting learners with diverse groups of people and resources, fostering an environment where new ideas can be shared and critically discussed. Social learning platforms powered by AI can recommend relevant learning communities, discussion groups, or virtual learning environments where learners can interact with peers who offer different perspectives, encouraging deep reflection on complex issues.

AI can also support collaborative problem-solving, which is a key aspect of transformative learning. By simulating real-world scenarios and presenting learners with complex, open-ended problems, AI systems encourage learners to work together to analyze the situation, exchange ideas, and find creative solutions. These types of collaborative learning environments promote critical dialogue and reflection, helping learners examine their assumptions and develop new, more complex understandings of the world (Holmes et al., 2019). AI's ability to track learner interactions and contributions allows it to provide targeted feedback that supports individual and group learning development, ensuring that all learners are equally engaged in the process.

8.1.6.4. Supporting Emotional and Psychological Growth

AI in transformative learning models also plays an important role in supporting the emotional and psychological aspects of learning. Transformative learning is not just a cognitive process. However, it is also deeply connected to emotions, as learners often experience discomfort or cognitive dissonance when confronted with ideas that challenge their current worldview. AI can facilitate emotional support during this process by detecting emotional cues through facial recognition, voice tone analysis, or natural language processing. By understanding learners' emotional states, AI can offer tailored interventions, such as mindfulness exercises, supportive messages, or encouragement, to help learners navigate difficult emotional experiences.

Furthermore, AI systems can detect when learners struggle with specific emotional or psychological barriers, such as anxiety or self-doubt, and provide resources or prompts that encourage learners to persist in facing challenges. In doing so, AI can help create a supportive and empathetic learning environment where emotional growth is nurtured alongside intellectual development. This balance is essential for transformative learning, as learners are more likely to engage in profound cognitive shifts when they feel psychologically supported throughout their educational journey (Baker, 2016).

8.1.7. AI for Lifelong Transformative Learning

Transformative learning is not limited to formal education; it extends throughout life as individuals continue to reflect and re-evaluate their beliefs and experiences critically. AI plays a pivotal role in supporting lifelong transformative learning by providing learners with the tools and resources necessary to continue evolving their understanding throughout their lives. Through AI-driven continuous learning systems, individuals can access learning experiences tailored to their unique developmental stages, goals, and evolving interests, ensuring they continue to grow intellectually and emotionally.

For example, AI-powered platforms that offer personalized learning recommendations can help individuals navigate career changes, deepen their expertise in particular areas, or explore entirely new fields of study. By providing ongoing opportunities for learning and reflection, AI ensures that transformative education is an ongoing process, helping individuals adapt to the world's ever-changing demands (Holmes et al., 2019). This capacity for lifelong learning is essential in an era where individuals must continuously adapt to new technologies, industries, and global challenges.

AI has significant potential to enhance transformative learning models by providing personalized, adaptive, and supportive learning environments. Through AI-powered platforms, learners can engage in reflective practice, challenge their existing assumptions, collaborate with diverse peers, and receive emotional and psychological support as they navigate the transformative process. By fostering continuous learning and providing lifelong opportunities for growth, AI helps individuals engage in deeper levels of critical thinking and personal transformation, ensuring that education remains relevant and empowering throughout one's life.

References

Baker, R. S. (2016). *Big Data and Education: Data-Driven Teaching and Learning*. Springer.

Culp, K. (2020). *AI and the Future of Education*. Springer.

DeMott, J. (2020). The Role of AI in Transformative Learning: Enhancing Reflection and Personal Growth. *Journal of Educational Technology*, 32(2), 121-136.

Dweck, C. S. (2006). *Mindset: The New Psychology of Success*. Random House.

Holmes, W., Bialik, M., & Fadel, C. (2019). *Artificial Intelligence in Education: Promises and Implications for Teaching and Learning*. Center for Curriculum Redesign.

Kukulska-Hulme, A. (2020). *Mobile Learning and Lifelong Learning: Making It Happen*. Springer.

Luckin, R., Holmes, W., Griffiths, M., & Forcier, L. B. (2016). *Intelligence Unleashed: An Argument for AI in Education.* Pearson Education.

Mezirow, J. (1991). *Transformative Dimensions of Adult Learning*. Jossey-Bass.

VanLehn, K. (2011). The Relative Effectiveness of Human Tutoring, Intelligent Tutoring Systems, and Other Tutoring Systems. *Educational Psychologist*, 46(4), 197-221.

Chapter 9

Empowering Underserved Communities

9.1. Introduction

Empowering underserved communities has become a critical global goal, particularly in education, healthcare, economic development, and social equity. Underserved communities often face systemic barriers to accessing resources, services, and opportunities that would enable them to thrive. These barriers are usually rooted in socioeconomic inequality, lack of infrastructure, and limited access to information and technology. However, with the rapid advancement of Artificial Intelligence (AI), there is a growing opportunity to bridge these gaps and create pathways for empowerment in these communities. AI has the potential to transform the lives of individuals in underserved communities by providing tailored educational resources, improving healthcare access, fostering economic opportunities, and enabling civic engagement.

9.1.1. Education as a Key Tool for Empowerment

Education is a fundamental driver of empowerment, offering individuals the skills and knowledge needed to overcome systemic barriers and improve their socio-economic conditions. However, in many underserved communities, access to quality education remains a challenge due to factors such as under-resourced schools, a shortage of qualified teachers, and limited access to learning materials. The transformative potential of AI in education is immense. AI-powered personalized learning platforms can offer tailored educational content to meet the diverse needs of students, regardless of their location or socio-economic status. These platforms can adapt to individual learning styles, identify gaps in knowledge, and provide targeted support, thus enabling underserved learners to receive a more equitable and effective education (Holmes, Bialik, & Fadel, 2019).

Moreover, AI is not just transforming education; it's democratizing it. By providing access to high-quality resources that would otherwise be unavailable in resource-poor settings, AI is becoming a tool for social justice and equality. For example, AI-driven virtual tutors or intelligent tutoring systems (ITS) can assist students with homework, practice exercises, and personalized feedback without requiring the physical presence of a teacher. This flexibility is particularly valuable in rural or remote areas where qualified teachers may be scarce. Furthermore, AI can help overcome language barriers, which is particularly important in multilingual societies or communities with diverse linguistic backgrounds. Through natural language processing (NLP) technologies, AI systems can provide translation services, ensuring students in underserved communities can access educational content in their native languages (Luckin et al., 2016).

9.1.2. Healthcare Access and AI Solutions

In addition to education, healthcare is another crucial area where underserved communities face significant challenges. In many low-income and rural areas, access to healthcare services is limited due to a lack of healthcare infrastructure, shortages of medical professionals, and geographic isolation. AI can enhance healthcare delivery in these communities by improving disease diagnosis, treatment, and management. AI-driven diagnostic tools, such as machine learning algorithms for medical imaging and predictive analytics for disease outbreaks, can provide healthcare workers with more accurate and timely information, allowing them to make informed decisions even in resource-limited settings (Rajpurkar et al., 2017).

Telemedicine, enabled by AI, can also bridge the gap in healthcare access. AI-powered platforms can connect patients in underserved areas with healthcare providers remotely, enabling consultations, diagnostic services, and follow-up care without patients needing to travel long distances. This is particularly important for individuals with chronic conditions or needing specialized care. Additionally, AI can play a role in improving the efficiency of healthcare delivery by automating administrative tasks, freeing healthcare professionals to focus more on patient care. Through these innovations, AI has the potential to address significant disparities in healthcare access and improve health outcomes in underserved communities (West et al., 2019).

9.1.3. Economic Empowerment through AI

Economic empowerment is critical to long-term community development, enabling individuals to achieve financial stability and independence. Underserved communities often face significant barriers to economic opportunities due to a lack of access to financial resources, job training, and employment networks. AI can help create new avenues for economic empowerment by facilitating access to jobs, skills training, and entrepreneurship opportunities. For instance, AI-powered platforms can provide online job training programs, offering individuals in underserved communities the skills needed to participate in the digital economy. These platforms can focus on key skills such as coding, data analysis, and digital marketing, which are in high demand in the modern job market (Brynjolfsson & McAfee, 2014).

AI can also foster entrepreneurship by providing tools and resources for individuals to start and grow their businesses. AI-powered analytics can help entrepreneurs identify market trends, optimize supply chains, and reach customers more effectively. Additionally, AI-driven financial tools, such as credit scoring systems, can help underserved individuals access financial services, including loans and credit, which are often difficult to obtain in low-income communities. These innovations can provide underserved individuals with the resources and opportunities needed to improve their economic circumstances, thereby fostering greater economic equity (Chui et al., 2016).

9.1.4. Promoting Civic Engagement and Social Empowerment

Civic engagement is an essential component of empowerment, as it allows individuals to participate in decision-making processes, influence policy, and advocate for their rights. AI is not just a technological advancement, it's a tool for social change and community empowerment. It can facilitate greater civic participation in underserved communities by providing platforms for individuals to engage with government officials, community leaders, and policymakers. For instance, AI-driven platforms for public opinion analysis and social media monitoring can give underserved communities a voice in local and national issues, ensuring that their concerns are heard and addressed. AI tools can also help to identify and track social issues that disproportionately affect marginalized populations, such as food insecurity, housing instability, or unemployment, and provide actionable insights for policy interventions (Crawford et al., 2019).

Moreover, AI can play a role in promoting social empowerment by enabling individuals to access information about their rights, available services, and support systems. AI-powered chatbots or virtual assistants, such as 'LegalAidBot' or 'CommunityHelp,' can provide instant responses to questions related to legal rights, social services, and community resources, empowering individuals to take informed actions. These chatbots use AI to understand and respond to user queries, providing accurate and timely information. By enhancing access to information and facilitating greater participation in civic life, AI can help strengthen the social fabric of underserved communities, enabling individuals to advocate for themselves and their communities in meaningful ways (West et al., 2019).

Empowering underserved communities through AI presents a unique opportunity to address persistent disparities in education, healthcare, economic opportunities, and civic participation. By leveraging the power of AI, we can create more inclusive, equitable systems that provide underserved individuals with the tools and resources they need to improve their lives and contribute meaningfully to society. AI's ability to personalize education, improve healthcare access, support economic development, and promote civic engagement makes it a powerful tool for fostering empowerment in communities that have long been excluded from the benefits of technology. However, to fully realize AI's potential, it is essential to ensure its implementation is inclusive, ethical, and sensitive to the unique needs and challenges underserved populations face.

9.1.5. AI-Driven Educational Access in Remote Areas

Education is one of the most powerful tools for empowering individuals and communities. However, millions worldwide, especially in remote and rural areas, face significant barriers to accessing quality education. These barriers are often due to inadequate infrastructure, qualified teachers, educational resources, and other systemic challenges. The traditional educational model, which often relies on physical schools and face-to-face interaction with instructors, is limited in these areas. However, Artificial Intelligence (AI) has the potential to revolutionize educational access in remote regions by offering innovative, scalable, and adaptive solutions that can overcome geographical, logistical, and resource-based barriers.

9.1.5.1. AI-Powered Distance Learning Platforms

One of the most prominent applications of AI in remote education is through distance learning platforms. These AI-powered platforms can offer students flexible, scalable, and personalized learning experiences, regardless of their location. AI technologies, such as machine learning algorithms, natural language processing (NLP), and intelligent tutoring systems (ITS), can be used to tailor the learning experience to the specific needs of each student. For instance, AI can identify areas where students are struggling and offer targeted interventions, adapting content and exercises to ensure effective learning outcomes (Holmes et al., 2019). In areas where the physical presence of educators is limited or non-existent, AI-driven platforms can provide real-time assistance, helping students access learning materials and receive personalized feedback.

These platforms also address the problem of teacher shortages in remote areas. By leveraging AI, educational content can be delivered at a scale without the need for many educators. Virtual tutors powered by AI can assist with answering questions, providing explanations, and guiding students through exercises, thus enabling students to receive immediate support and reinforcing the educational process even in the absence of a traditional classroom setting (Luckin et al., 2016). This is particularly important in remote areas where the availability of skilled teachers is often insufficient to meet the demands of the student population.

9.1.5.2. Overcoming Language Barriers through AI

In remote and underserved areas, students often speak languages that may not be represented in traditional educational materials or standardized testing systems. AI can help overcome language barriers through real-time translation and transcription tools. Natural language processing (NLP) technologies enable AI-driven systems to instantly translate educational content into multiple languages, making it accessible to students who might otherwise struggle to understand content in a foreign or non-native language (West et al., 2019). For instance, AI-powered platforms like Google Translate and Duolingo can translate instructional materials, lectures, and assessments, thus enhancing the accessibility of education for students in linguistically diverse regions.

AI can also help create learning content in local languages. By using machine learning techniques, AI can help translate textbooks, learning modules, and other educational resources into languages that are not widely supported, enabling students to access materials in their native tongues. This is especially significant in regions where multilingualism is common and where education systems may only be available in one or two dominant languages and disadvantaged students from different linguistic backgrounds.

9.1.5.3. Mobile Learning and AI Accessibility

The widespread use of mobile phones, even in remote areas, has opened up new avenues for delivering education through mobile learning applications. Mobile phones provide an affordable and ubiquitous platform for AI-powered educational tools, particularly in regions with limited access to computers or internet-connected classrooms. AI-powered mobile learning applications can deliver educational content, quizzes, and interactive learning experiences directly to students' phones, making learning more flexible and accessible.

These AI-driven mobile applications can deliver a wide range of educational services, from basic literacy and numeracy skills to more advanced subjects like mathematics, science, and language arts. Furthermore, AI can help optimize mobile learning applications by tracking students' progress, offering personalized feedback, and adapting the learning experience to individual needs. Mobile-based learning, supported by AI, is a powerful way to bridge educational gaps in remote areas where traditional education delivery methods may be logistically challenging (Crawford et al., 2019).

9.1.5.4. Data-Driven Insights for Education Management

In remote and underserved areas, where resources are often scarce, effective management of educational infrastructure is critical to ensuring that educational services reach those in need. AI can play a crucial role in improving the efficiency and impact of education delivery in these areas through data-driven insights. AI algorithms can analyze large volumes of data to identify trends, such as student performance, resource allocation, and attendance patterns, helping educators and policymakers make informed decisions.

For example, AI-powered systems can track student progress across multiple learning platforms and identify trends in student performance, allowing educators to identify students who may require additional support or intervention quickly. This data-driven approach enables a more targeted and efficient allocation of resources, ensuring that educational opportunities are extended to those who need them the most. In areas where education infrastructure is limited, data-driven insights provided by AI can help prioritize areas for intervention, ensuring that scarce resources are used effectively and strategically (Chui et al., 2016).

9.1.5.5. Collaboration and Community Engagement

AI-driven educational platforms can also foster collaboration and community engagement, which is vital in remote areas. Through virtual classrooms, discussion boards, and peer-to-peer learning networks, students in remote areas can engage with their peers and instructors from other parts of the world. This global collaboration enhances the learning experience and broadens students' perspectives, exposing them to new ideas, cultures, and knowledge systems. AI can facilitate these interactions by recommending relevant learning groups or study materials, helping students connect with others with similar learning goals.

AI can help facilitate local communities' participation in the education process by offering community-based learning initiatives. For example, AI platforms could be used to train local facilitators, who can then deliver lessons or provide support to students, ensuring that educational programs are tailored to the community's specific cultural and social context (Brynjolfsson & McAfee, 2014). When supported by AI technologies, these locally driven efforts can enhance the relevance and effectiveness of educational programs in remote areas.

AI-driven educational access in remote areas can revolutionize how education is delivered and experienced in underserved regions. By leveraging AI, it is possible to overcome many of the barriers that have traditionally hindered educational access, including teacher shortages, lack of resources, language barriers, and geographical isolation. AI-powered learning platforms, mobile applications, and data-driven insights can provide personalized, scalable, and flexible educational opportunities to students in remote areas, empowering them with the knowledge and skills necessary to improve their socio-economic conditions. However, to maximize the benefits of AI in remote education, it is crucial to ensure that these technologies are implemented in an inclusive and equitable manner, taking into account the unique needs of underserved communities.

9.1.6. Reducing Digital and Knowledge Divides Through AI

The digital divide refers to the gap between those with access to modern information and communication technologies (ICT) and those without, while the knowledge divide encompasses disparities in access to and the ability to utilize information for empowerment, learning, and development. Both divides are major barriers to equitable progress, especially in underserved communities, and they exacerbate existing social inequalities. Artificial Intelligence (AI) can potentially be transformative in addressing the digital and knowledge divide by improving access to information, resources, and educational opportunities, regardless of geographic, economic, or social limitations. However, ensuring that AI is accessible and equitable for all requires intentional policies and practices focusing on inclusivity and empowerment.

9.1.6.1. Bridging the Digital Divide with AI

The digital divide, often characterized by unequal access to the internet, devices, and technology, presents significant challenges to education and empowerment in many regions, especially in rural and remote areas. AI can help bridge this gap by creating technology solutions that are more affordable, adaptable, and capable of functioning in low-resource settings. For example, AI-powered mobile platforms offer a feasible solution for delivering education and knowledge to communities without reliable access to traditional, high-tech devices like computers. In many low-income regions, mobile phones are more widespread than desktop computers, and AI-driven mobile learning applications can provide personalized educational experiences tailored to the needs of learners, regardless of their technological infrastructure (Brynjolfsson & McAfee, 2014).

Additionally, AI systems can optimize data usage, enabling more efficient use of limited bandwidth and improving the functionality of educational tools in areas with poor internet connectivity. These systems can adapt to different network conditions, offering offline capabilities and automatic synchronization once a connection is restored, ensuring that learners in remote areas can continue their studies uninterrupted. Furthermore, AI algorithms can be employed to provide targeted solutions for infrastructure challenges, such as optimizing network routing, improving signal coverage, and addressing connectivity issues (West et al., 2019).

9.1.6.2. AI and Knowledge Access for Underserved Communities

Beyond just bridging the digital divide, AI can reduce the knowledge divide by enabling wider and more equitable access to information and learning resources. Many underserved communities face barriers to accessing high-quality educational content due to language, cost, and availability. AI can overcome these challenges by personalizing learning experiences and ensuring that resources are more accessible.

One of the key benefits of AI is its ability to provide adaptive learning experiences that cater to the individual needs of each learner. Through intelligent tutoring systems (ITS) and personalized learning platforms, AI can tailor educational content, exercises, and feedback to students' learning paces and knowledge gaps. This level of customization allows learners in under-resourced areas to receive the support they need to succeed, even when local education infrastructure may be inadequate (Luckin et al., 2016). Moreover, AI can translate content into multiple languages in real time, overcoming linguistic barriers and ensuring that educational materials are accessible to diverse populations. In regions where people speak minority or Indigenous languages, AI-powered language translation tools can help provide inclusive access to information and knowledge that was previously inaccessible (Crawford et al., 2019).

Additionally, AI can aid in creating and distributing open educational resources (OER), reducing the cost barriers that prevent learners from accessing high-quality learning materials. AI technologies can help curate and distribute vast amounts of open content in easily digestible and contextually relevant formats, making education more affordable and accessible for all learners. The proliferation of AI-driven tools, such as open-source educational platforms and digital libraries, ensures that underserved communities can access high-quality content without incurring prohibitive costs (Holmes et al., 2019).

9.1.6.3. AI as a Tool for Lifelong Learning and Skill Development

AI also plays a critical role in addressing the knowledge divide by enabling lifelong learning and skills development, which is essential for empowerment and socio-economic mobility. As the global job market rapidly evolves due to automation, AI, and other technological advances, access to continuous education and skills development becomes increasingly important for people in underserved communities. AI-driven learning platforms can allow people to gain new skills, adapt to technological changes, and enhance their employability, regardless of their initial education level or geographic location (Brynjolfsson & McAfee, 2014).

AI-based platforms can offer flexible, self-paced learning, particularly beneficial for individuals in underserved regions with limited time, resources, or access to formal educational institutions. For instance, mobile-based AI-driven learning systems, which offer microlearning modules, are ideal for learners who can only dedicate small amounts of time to education, such as those who are working or managing family responsibilities. These systems can also offer personalized learning pathways tailored to each individual's unique needs, helping them acquire specific skills for their personal or professional growth.

Moreover, AI can help underserved communities access high-quality vocational training, enabling individuals to acquire marketable skills in technology, healthcare, and business. By providing skills development opportunities, AI ensures that individuals from underserved communities are better equipped to participate in the modern economy, thereby reducing skill-based inequalities and contributing to greater social mobility (West et al., 2019).

9.1.6.4. The Role of AI in Community Empowerment and Knowledge Sharing

In addition to directly improving access to education and skills development, AI can also facilitate community-based empowerment by enabling knowledge sharing and collaboration across regions. AI tools can connect people from diverse backgrounds, allowing them to collectively share knowledge, collaborate on projects, and solve local challenges. By leveraging AI's data processing and knowledge synthesis capabilities, communities can address specific local needs, share solutions, and amplify their impact. For instance, AI-driven platforms can enable farmers in remote areas to access agricultural knowledge, medical professionals to share healthcare insights, or local artisans to promote their crafts to a global audience.

Additionally, AI can assist in identifying local needs and optimizing the use of available resources within a community. AI tools can help local organizations and governments make informed decisions about where to allocate resources most effectively by analyzing data on community health, education, or infrastructure. This approach enhances community development and ensures that interventions are contextually appropriate, equitable, and aligned with the community's priorities (Chui et al., 2016).

AI has significant potential to reduce both the digital and knowledge divide, offering new solutions for ensuring equitable access to education, skills, and knowledge. Through adaptive learning platforms, personalized content delivery, and optimizing learning environments, AI can help bridge the gap for underserved communities, ensuring that individuals can access high-quality education regardless of their location or socio-economic status. Additionally, AI can support lifelong learning and community empowerment, enabling individuals and groups to develop new skills, collaborate, and share knowledge continuously. However, for AI to truly have a transformative impact on reducing these divides, it is crucial to implement inclusive policies that ensure equitable access to AI technologies and that account for the specific needs of underserved communities.

References

Brynjolfsson, E., & McAfee, A. (2014). *The Second Machine Age: Work, Progress, and Prosperity in a Time of Brilliant Technologies*. W. W. Norton & Company.

Chui, M., Manyika, J., & Miremadi, M. (2016). *Where machines could replace humans—and where they cannot (yet).* McKinsey Quarterly.

Crawford, K., Whittaker, M., & West, S. M. (2019). *Discriminating Systems: Gender, Race, and Power in AI.* AI Now Institute.

Holmes, W., Bialik, M., & Fadel, C. (2019). *Artificial Intelligence in Education: Promises and Implications for Teaching and Learning*. Center for Curriculum Redesign.

Holmes, W., Bialik, M., & Fadel, C. (2019). *Artificial Intelligence in Education: Promises and Implications for Teaching and Learning*. Center for Curriculum Redesign.

Holmes, W., Bialik, M., & Fadel, C. (2019). *Artificial Intelligence in Education: Promises and Implications for Teaching and Learning*. Center for Curriculum Redesign.

Luckin, R., Holmes, W., Griffiths, M., & Forcier, L. B. (2016). *Intelligence Unleashed: An Argument for AI in Education.* Pearson Education.

Rajpurkar, P., Irvin, J., et al. (2017). *Deep Learning for Cardiac Image Analysis: A Survey. Journal of the American College of Cardiology*, 69(12), 1516–1528.

West, S. M., Whittaker, M., & Crawford, K. (2019). *Discriminating Systems: Gender, Race, and Power in AI.* AI Now Institute.

Part III: Societal Impacts of AI in Education and Empowerment

Introduction

The rapid evolution of Artificial Intelligence (AI) has prompted a fundamental shift in the educational landscape, with profound implications for empowerment and social progress. AI's potential to revolutionize education lies in its capacity to enhance learning experiences and address entrenched societal issues such as inequality, accessibility, and the skills gap. As AI systems are increasingly integrated into educational settings, they bring opportunities for empowerment and significant challenges that must be addressed. Understanding the societal impacts of AI in education and empowerment requires carefully examining how AI influences learning outcomes, social structures, and individual agency, focusing on promoting equity and inclusion.

Enhancing Educational Access and Equity

One of the most promising impacts of AI in education is its potential to level the playing field by increasing access to quality education for underserved and marginalized communities. AI-powered technologies, such as intelligent tutoring systems and adaptive learning platforms, offer personalized educational experiences that cater to individual learning styles and paces. This personalized approach can be particularly beneficial for students in low-resource settings, as AI can help bridge teacher quality and availability gaps. For instance, in regions with a shortage of trained educators, AI can provide real-time tutoring and feedback, ensuring that students receive the attention and support they need to succeed (Luckin et al., 2016).

Additionally, AI can help mitigate the barriers of cost, geography, and disability that often hinder access to education. Through online platforms and mobile applications, AI enables learners from remote areas or economically disadvantaged backgrounds to access high-quality educational content without the need to travel or incur significant expenses. Moreover, AI can help overcome physical and cognitive barriers to learning by providing tools for students with special needs, such as speech recognition, text-to-speech functionality, and AI-driven accessibility features that tailor learning experiences to the needs of individuals with disabilities (Crawford et al., 2019).

Bridging the Skills Gap and Empowering the Workforce

AI has a transformative role in empowering individuals through skills development, addressing the skills gap in many economies. The demand for workers with advanced technological, analytical, and soft skills continues to grow, and AI-driven learning platforms can provide a more scalable solution to skills development. By offering personalized training in high-demand fields such as data science, artificial intelligence, and digital literacy, AI enables individuals from diverse backgrounds to acquire the skills necessary to thrive in the modern economy. These skills enhance employability and empower individuals to contribute to the economy and society (Brynjolfsson & McAfee, 2014).

Furthermore, AI can assist in identifying emerging job trends and tailoring training programs to equip learners with the skills needed in future job markets. Using data analytics, AI can predict changes in labor market demand and offer real-time updates on the skills required for emerging industries. This enables individuals to adapt proactively and pursue career paths aligned with future workforce needs. This capacity for anticipatory learning is a critical element of the empowerment process, as it provides individuals with the tools to make informed decisions about their education and career trajectories (Chui et al., 2016).

The Role of AI in Fostering Lifelong Learning and Social Mobility

AI can also be critical in promoting lifelong learning, which is essential for social mobility and ongoing personal empowerment. As individuals are required to adapt continuously to the changing demands of the workforce, the ability to engage in lifelong learning becomes crucial. AI-powered educational systems support lifelong learning by offering flexible, self-paced learning opportunities accessible anytime and from anywhere. This allows individuals, regardless of age, socioeconomic status, or location, to pursue learning opportunities throughout their lives, facilitating social mobility and reducing inequalities.

For instance, MOOCs (Massive Open Online Courses) and AI-based platforms can provide access to top-tier educational content, certifications, and degree programs, helping individuals from all walks of life gain qualifications that were previously out of reach. Moreover, AI can foster a culture of continuous learning by offering personalized recommendations for further learning based on an individual's interests, previous achievements, and career aspirations. This dynamic approach ensures that learning is not a one-time event but an ongoing process that supports personal and professional growth (West et al., 2019).

Societal Concerns: Ethical Implications and Bias

While the potential benefits of AI in education and empowerment are vast, it is also essential to acknowledge and address the ethical concerns that arise with its widespread use. One of the most significant challenges is the risk of perpetuating existing biases in AI algorithms. AI systems are only as unbiased as the data they are trained on, and if these systems are trained on biased data sets, they can reinforce stereotypes and discriminatory practices. For example, AI algorithms used in admissions, hiring, and educational assessment may inadvertently disadvantage certain groups based on gender, race, or socioeconomic status (West et al., 2019). As AI becomes more integrated into educational environments, it is crucial to ensure that these technologies are designed with fairness and equity in mind and actively work to counteract bias rather than perpetuate it.

Another concern is the potential for AI to replace human teachers and educators, leading to job displacement and loss of personal connection in learning environments. While AI can undoubtedly enhance teaching and learning by providing personalized support and automating routine tasks, it should complement, rather than replace, the role of educators. Teachers play a vital role in fostering social and emotional learning, providing mentorship, and creating inclusive, supportive learning environments. Therefore, a balanced approach is necessary to ensure that AI enhances, rather than diminishes, the human aspects of education (Brynjolfsson & McAfee, 2014).

A Path Toward Empowerment and Inclusive Growth

In conclusion, the societal impacts of AI in education and empowerment are multifaceted and far-reaching. While AI has the potential to enhance educational access, bridge skills gaps, and promote lifelong learning, it also presents significant challenges related to equity, bias, and the displacement of human workers. To harness the full potential of AI for empowerment, it is crucial to implement policies and practices that prioritize inclusivity, fairness, and ethical considerations. As AI continues to evolve, it must be designed and deployed to empower individuals, promote social mobility, and contribute to a more just and equitable society.

Chapter 10

Ethics and Equity in AI for Education

10.1. Introduction

Integrating Artificial Intelligence (AI) in education has ushered in exciting possibilities for enhancing learning experiences and outcomes. However, the imperative to address AI technologies' ethical concerns comes alongside these advancements. How AI is deployed in educational contexts must consider equity, fairness, and transparency to avoid exacerbating existing disparities or introducing new forms of bias. This section explores the ethical implications and equity challenges of AI in education. It emphasizes the need for careful design and thoughtful implementation to ensure that AI is an inclusive and empowering tool for all learners, regardless of their background.

10.1.1. Bias and Fairness in AI Algorithms

One of the most pressing ethical concerns in using AI for education is the potential for algorithmic bias. AI systems are often trained on large data sets, and if these data sets reflect historical inequalities or biased practices, the AI systems may perpetuate or even amplify these biases. In educational contexts, this could manifest in various ways, such as AI-based admissions systems favoring certain demographic groups over others or automated grading systems unfairly disadvantaging students from marginalized backgrounds. For instance, research has shown that predictive algorithms used in higher education admissions can reinforce inequalities by relying on biased data from previous years, often disadvantaging underrepresented groups such as racial minorities or students from low-income backgrounds (West et al., 2019).

Bias in AI systems is not limited to racial or ethnic disparities; it can also affect gender, socioeconomic status, and disability status. The lack of diversity in the data used to train AI systems is a major contributor to this issue. AI systems that recommend personalized learning resources, for example, may favor content that aligns with the majority culture and exclude resources that are culturally relevant to students from diverse backgrounds. Therefore, it is essential to ensure that AI algorithms are developed and tested with diverse, representative data to mitigate the risk of reinforcing existing inequalities (Holmes et al., 2019).

10.1.2. Transparency and Accountability in AI Systems

As AI becomes more integrated into education, transparency and accountability must be prioritized to ensure ethical decision-making. AI systems often operate as "black boxes," where the decision-making process is not fully visible or understandable to users. This lack of transparency raises concerns, mainly when AI systems are used for decisions such as admissions, grading, or determining students' learning paths. Without a clear understanding of how these systems function, students, teachers, and other stakeholders may be unable to challenge or appeal decisions they perceive as unjust or inaccurate.

To address these concerns, there is a growing call for transparency in developing and deploying AI systems in education. This includes ensuring that the algorithms, data sources, and decision-making processes behind AI systems are open and accessible to scrutiny. Moreover, accountability mechanisms must be implemented to ensure AI systems are regularly evaluated for fairness, accuracy, and bias. Such evaluations should involve diverse stakeholders, including educators, students, and ethicists, to ensure that the system operates in a way that aligns with the values of equity and social justice (UNESCO, 2021).

10.1.3. Privacy and Data Security

In addition to concerns about bias and transparency, the use of AI in education also raises important questions about privacy and data security. AI systems often rely on large amounts of personal data to deliver personalized learning experiences. This data can include sensitive information about students' academic performance, behavior, and health. Protecting this data from unauthorized access, misuse, or exploitation is crucial, particularly when it comes to vulnerable populations such as minors or students with disabilities.

Educational institutions must implement robust data privacy protections to safeguard students' information. Furthermore, students and parents should be informed about how their data will be used and should have control over their information. Ethical AI practices require that data be collected and used to respect students' rights and autonomy while adhering to legal and regulatory frameworks such as the General Data Protection Regulation (GDPR) in the European Union (UNESCO, 2021). Clear guidelines must be established for data usage, ensuring that AI applications do not compromise students' privacy for educational enhancement.

10.1.4. Inclusion and Equity in Access to AI-Driven Education

Equity in access to AI-driven education is another key ethical consideration. While AI can potentially expand educational opportunities, there is a risk that unequal access to technology could exacerbate existing disparities. Students from low-income families, rural areas, or developing countries may not have access to the necessary technology or internet connectivity to benefit from AI-based educational tools. This "digital divide" could further marginalize already disadvantaged groups.

To promote equity in access, governments, educational institutions, and technology providers must work together to ensure that AI-driven educational resources are accessible to all students, regardless of their geographic location or socioeconomic status. This may involve subsidizing access to digital devices, expanding internet infrastructure, and providing affordable or free access to AI-powered learning platforms. Additionally, efforts must ensure that AI tools are designed inclusively, catering to students with diverse learning needs, including those with disabilities or language barriers (Luckin et al., 2016).

10.1.4.1. Ethical AI Design and Human-Centered Approaches

The ethical deployment of AI in education requires a human-centered approach that prioritizes students' well-being and empowerment. This approach involves designing AI systems that support human agencies rather than replacing human educators or making decisions without human oversight. AI should be used to enhance, not replace, the role of educators, helping them better understand their students' needs, personalize instruction, and offer targeted support.

Moreover, AI systems must be designed to promote positive learning outcomes, such as critical thinking, creativity, and collaboration, rather than simply optimizing for efficiency or standardized performance metrics. This requires a holistic understanding of education that goes beyond narrow assessments of academic achievement and considers students' broader social, emotional, and ethical development. By focusing on human-centered design principles, AI in education can empower, support equitable access to quality learning, and foster a more just and inclusive educational system (Crawford et al., 2019).

While AI holds significant promise for transforming education, its integration into educational systems must be approached with careful consideration of ethical principles and equity concerns. Addressing bias, ensuring transparency and accountability, protecting privacy, and promoting equitable access to AI-driven learning are all essential steps in ensuring that AI is a tool for empowerment and social progress. To achieve these goals, policymakers, educators, and technology developers must collaborate to create AI systems that align with the values of fairness, inclusivity, and social justice, ultimately contributing to a more equitable and transformative educational landscape.

10.1.5. Addressing Bias and Inclusivity in AI Algorithms

Artificial Intelligence (AI) algorithms, when used in education and other sectors, can reflect the biases inherent in the data upon which they are trained. These biases can manifest in ways that perpetuate inequalities, marginalizing certain groups while privileging others. Therefore, addressing bias and promoting inclusivity in AI algorithms is crucial to ensure fairness and equity, particularly in contexts like education, where AI decisions can significantly impact individuals' opportunities, access to resources, and outcomes. This section explores how bias arises in AI algorithms, its impact, and strategies for mitigating these biases while promoting inclusivity.

10.1.5.1. The Origins of Bias in AI Algorithms

AI systems learn from vast datasets often derived from historical data or human-generated content. If these datasets reflect societal biases—such as those based on race, gender, socioeconomic status, or geographic location—AI algorithms can inadvertently learn to replicate these biases. For example, if an AI-based admissions system is trained on data from previous years' university applications, and if those applications disproportionately come from certain demographic groups, the AI may "learn" to favor applicants from these groups. This problem, known as "data bias," occurs when the training data does not accurately represent the diversity of the population the AI is meant to serve.

Furthermore, bias can also emerge from the design and implementation of the algorithm itself. Humans create algorithms, and developers' implicit assumptions or choices can unintentionally shape the algorithm's behavior. For example, suppose an AI system is optimized to maximize certain performance metrics, such as standardized test scores. It may unintentionally overlook factors crucial to student success, like creativity, emotional intelligence, or social skills. These factors may be harder to quantify and thus not included in the algorithm's calculations, leading to skewed results that disadvantage students with non-traditional learning styles or marginalized backgrounds (Binns, 2018).

10.1.5.2. Impacts of Bias in AI Algorithms

The impacts of biased AI algorithms are particularly concerning in education, where AI systems are increasingly used for grading, admissions, personalized learning, and career guidance. When AI algorithms are biased, they can result in discriminatory practices that unfairly disadvantage certain groups. For example, a biased grading algorithm might penalize students from underrepresented racial or ethnic groups by misinterpreting their responses or style of communication, resulting in lower grades or feedback that does not reflect their true abilities.

AI bias can exacerbate disparities in admissions by systematically favoring applicants from privileged backgrounds or overemphasizing certain academic metrics while overlooking other important factors such as resilience, extracurricular achievements, or social contributions. In personalized learning, AI systems trained on limited or biased data may fail to provide all students equitable access to high-quality educational resources. As a result, students from marginalized communities may not benefit equally from AI-driven tools, further entrenching existing inequalities (O'Neil, 2016).

10.1.5.3. Strategies for Mitigating Bias in AI Algorithms

To address bias, several strategies can be implemented at different stages of an AI algorithm's lifecycle, from data collection to model development and post-deployment monitoring.

10.1.5.3.1. Diverse and Representative Data

One of the most effective ways to mitigate bias is to ensure that the data used to train AI systems is diverse and representative of the population it serves. This requires careful selection and preprocessing of data to avoid historical biases that might skew results. For example, when developing an AI-based admissions system, it is crucial to incorporate a broad range of data that reflects diverse student experiences, including those of students from various racial, ethnic, socioeconomic, and geographical backgrounds. This ensures that the AI system is not disproportionately influenced by the experiences of any single group (Holmes et al., 2019).

Moreover, efforts should be made to include data that reflects the needs and experiences of students with disabilities, those who speak languages other than the dominant language, and students with non-traditional learning paths. By expanding the data used in training, AI systems can become more inclusive and better able to serve the needs of all learners.

10.1.5.3.2. Algorithmic Transparency and Accountability

Another key approach to addressing bias is to develop and deploy AI algorithms transparently. Transparent AI systems allow stakeholders, including educators, students, and policymakers, to understand how decisions are made and identify potential sources of bias. By making algorithms and their underlying decision-making processes more visible, developers can facilitate better accountability and ensure that AI systems function as intended.

Moreover, regular audits of AI systems can help detect and correct bias before it leads to adverse outcomes. These audits should be conducted by diverse teams of experts, including those with expertise in ethics, law, and social justice, to ensure that the algorithm is fair and aligned with the values of equity and inclusivity. Post-deployment monitoring is also essential, as it helps identify and address any unforeseen biases that may arise after the AI system has been implemented in real-world settings (Binns, 2018).

10.1.5.3.3. Human-in-the-Loop Approaches

One potential solution to the challenges of algorithmic bias is the implementation of human-in-the-loop (HITL) approaches. While AI systems can provide valuable insights and support, human oversight is crucial to ensure that decisions are not made solely by algorithms. Educators and other stakeholders can review AI-generated recommendations and results to identify biases and ensure they align with ethical standards and equitable practices. By keeping humans in the decision-making loop, AI can be used as a tool to augment, rather than replace, human judgment, ensuring that biased decisions do not go unchecked (Holmes et al., 2019).

10.1.5.3.4. Ethical AI Frameworks

Finally, it is essential to adopt ethical AI frameworks that guide the design, deployment, and evaluation of AI systems. These frameworks should prioritize fairness, transparency, inclusivity, and accountability at every stage of development. For example, the European Union's General Data Protection Regulation (GDPR) includes provisions that regulate the use of AI, ensuring that individuals' rights are protected and that AI systems are used responsibly. Similarly, UNESCO's guidelines for AI in education emphasize the importance of ensuring that AI is developed and used to benefit all learners and not exacerbate inequalities (UNESCO, 2021).

10.1.5.3.5. Promoting Inclusivity in AI Design

Ensuring that AI algorithms are inclusive involves more than just addressing bias; it also requires intentional efforts to design AI systems adaptable to diverse learning needs. Inclusivity in AI means designing systems accommodating learners with different abilities, learning styles, and cultural backgrounds. For example, AI-based educational tools should be designed with accessibility features such as text-to-speech, visual aids, and multilingual support to ensure that students with disabilities or those who speak different languages are not excluded.

By designing flexible and adaptable AI systems, developers can ensure that AI empowers all learners, regardless of their background or individual circumstances. This requires a commitment to inclusivity from the earliest stages of AI development, ensuring that diverse perspectives are integrated into the design process (Luckin et al., 2016).

Addressing bias and promoting inclusivity in AI algorithms is an ongoing challenge, but it is critical for ensuring that AI technologies in education benefit all learners equitably. The negative impacts of bias can be mitigated by focusing on diverse data sets, algorithmic transparency, human oversight, and ethical AI frameworks. Ensuring that AI systems are inclusive, adaptable, and fair is essential for creating educational environments that support the success of all students, regardless of their background or abilities. The responsible and ethical use of AI in education has the potential to transform learning and empowerment, but only if the challenges of bias and exclusion are proactively addressed.

10.1.6. Equity in Resource Allocation

Equity in resource allocation is a critical concept in education, development, and broader social systems. It refers to the fair distribution of resources to individuals or communities based on their specific needs and circumstances rather than treating all parties equally. Equitable resource allocation ensures that all students have the tools, opportunities, and support they need to succeed, regardless of their background, socioeconomic status, or geographical location. This approach recognizes that different students face different challenges and that a one-size-fits-all model is insufficient to address the disparities in learning opportunities and outcomes.

10.1.6.1. The Importance of Equity in Education

Education is often seen as the gateway to social mobility and personal empowerment, but this ideal is not always realized in practice. Inequities in the allocation of resources—whether financial, technological, or human—can exacerbate existing disparities, perpetuating cycles of poverty and disadvantage. In many countries, students from marginalized communities, such as those from low-income families, rural areas, or minority ethnic groups, often face significant barriers to accessing quality education. These barriers may include underfunded schools, a lack of qualified teachers, outdated learning materials, and limited access to technology (Sen, 1999).

In contrast, students in wealthier, more privileged communities typically have access to well-resourced schools with modern technologies, highly trained educators, and extracurricular opportunities. This unequal distribution of resources leads to stark educational disparities, affecting future life outcomes, including employment opportunities, health, and social well-being (Nussbaum, 2011). The principles of equity demand that resources be allocated in a way that compensates for these inequities, offering additional support where it is most needed to level the playing field.

10.1.6.2. The Role of AI in Promoting Equity in Resource Allocation

Artificial intelligence (AI) holds significant potential to transform the way resources are allocated in education by enabling more targeted and efficient distribution based on real-time data and individualized needs. AI systems can analyze vast amounts of data to identify areas where resources are most needed and help policymakers, educators, and administrators make more informed decisions about allocating resources. For instance, AI can analyze student performance data to identify learning gaps, predict which students may require additional support, and recommend specific interventions to help them succeed.

AI can also facilitate more personalized learning experiences, tailoring educational content and resources to the needs of individual students. This approach helps bridge gaps for students who may fall behind due to a lack of resources or support. By identifying each student's unique learning style and challenges, AI can ensure that resources, such as tutoring, learning materials, and assistance, are directed where needed most, improving student outcomes (Luckin et al., 2016).

Moreover, AI can assist in resource allocation by automating administrative tasks, allowing educational institutions to redirect saved time and funds toward areas of greater need. For example, AI can optimize scheduling, teacher assignments, and the distribution of learning materials, thereby freeing up resources for targeted interventions. This efficiency is particularly valuable in underfunded schools or regions with limited educational resources, where every dollar and hour spent must be maximized for impact.

10.1.6.3. Challenges in Ensuring Equity in Resource Allocation

While AI can potentially enhance equity in resource allocation, several challenges must be addressed to realize these benefits. First, the data used to train AI systems must be comprehensive, accurate, and representative of all student populations. If the data is skewed toward certain groups—such as those from wealthier, urban areas—AI models may inadvertently reinforce existing inequities by under-serving marginalized groups. Therefore, ensuring that the datasets used in AI training are inclusive is crucial, capturing all students' diverse experiences, needs, and contexts (O'Neil, 2016).

Additionally, there is the risk that AI systems could exacerbate biases in resource allocation if they are not carefully designed and monitored. If algorithms are programmed to prioritize certain types of academic achievements or behaviors that are more commonly associated with privileged groups, students from marginalized communities may be overlooked or underserved. To avoid this, AI systems must be designed with equity and fairness, incorporating mechanisms for identifying and mitigating bias and ensuring all students receive the support they need (Binns, 2018).

Another challenge is the digital divide, which refers to the unequal access to technology and the internet in different regions or communities. In many low-income or rural areas, students may not have access to the devices, internet connectivity, or technical support necessary to benefit fully from AI-driven educational tools. This gap can further widen disparities in educational outcomes if AI-based interventions are not accompanied by efforts to address the broader digital divide (Warschauer, 2011). Therefore, equitable educational resource allocation must focus on digital tools and ensure all students can access the infrastructure to use them effectively.

10.1.6.4. Strategies for Promoting Equity in Resource Allocation

Several strategies can help ensure that resource allocation in education is equitable, particularly in the context of AI. First, it is essential to incorporate principles of equity into the design and implementation of AI systems. This includes using diverse, representative datasets and ensuring that AI models are regularly audited for fairness and inclusivity. Additionally, human oversight remains critical to the decision-making process, with educators and administrators playing a key role in interpreting AI recommendations and ensuring they align with ethical standards of equity and justice (Holmes et al., 2019).

Another important strategy is investing in the infrastructure needed to support AI-driven interventions, such as providing all students with the necessary technology, including devices, high-speed internet, and technical support. This could involve partnerships between governments, educational institutions, and private companies to provide affordable, accessible technology to underserved communities. Furthermore, policies should focus on closing the digital divide, ensuring that students in remote or economically disadvantaged areas are not left behind (OECD, 2021).

Finally, policymakers must ensure that equity is a central goal in allocating funding and resources within educational systems. This may involve directing additional funding toward schools and communities that face the greatest challenges and ensuring that AI technologies supplement rather than replace the critical human elements of teaching and learning, such as teacher-student relationships, mentorship, and emotional support. In this way, AI can be harnessed to enhance equity rather than perpetuate existing inequities in the educational system (UNESCO, 2021).

Equity in resource allocation is essential for ensuring that all students have the opportunity to succeed and thrive, regardless of their background or circumstances. AI offers powerful tools for promoting equity by enabling more personalized, data-driven educational approaches and targeting resources where they are most needed. However, addressing challenges such as biased data, the digital divide, and algorithmic transparency is necessary to achieve equity truly. By designing AI systems with equity in mind, investing in technology infrastructure, and directing resources to where they are most needed, we can move closer to an educational system where all students have equal access to the opportunities and support they need to succeed.

References

Binns, R. (2018). *Fairness in Machine Learning: Lessons from Political Philosophy*. Proceedings of the 2018 CHI Conference on Human Factors in Computing Systems, 1–14.

Brynjolfsson, E., & McAfee, A. (2014). *The Second Machine Age: Work, Progress, and Prosperity in a Time of Brilliant Technologies*. W. W. Norton & Company.

Chui, M., Manyika, J., & Miremadi, M. (2016). *Where machines could replace humans—and where they cannot (yet)*. McKinsey Quarterly.

Crawford, K., Whittaker, M., & West, S. M. (2019). *Discriminating Systems: Gender, Race, and Power in AI*. AI Now Institute.

Holmes, W., Bialik, M., & Fadel, C. (2019). *Artificial Intelligence in Education: Promises and Implications for Teaching and Learning*. Center for Curriculum Redesign.

Luckin, R., Holmes, W., Griffiths, M., & Forcier, L. B. (2016). *Intelligence Unleashed: An Argument for AI in Education*. Pearson Education.

Nussbaum, M. (2011). *Creating Capabilities: The Human Development Approach*. Harvard University Press.

OECD. (2021). *The Digital Divide and the Role of AI in Education*. OECD Publishing.

O'Neil, C. (2016). *Weapons of Math Destruction: How Big Data Increases Inequality and Threatens Democracy*. Crown Publishing Group.

Sen, A. (1999). *Development as Freedom*. Oxford University Press.

UNESCO. (2021). *Artificial Intelligence and Education: Guidance for Policy-Makers*. UNESCO Publishing.

Warschauer, M. (2011). *The Digital Divide: Arguments for and Against Google's New Initiatives*. MIT

West, S. M., Whittaker, M., & Crawford, K. (2019). *Discriminating Systems: Gender, Race, and Power in AI*. AI Now Institute.

Chapter 11

Cultural Sensitivity and Representation in AI Systems

11.1. Introduction

Cultural sensitivity and representation in AI systems are critical concepts that pave the way for artificial intelligence technologies to be designed and implemented in a way that respects and accommodates the diverse cultural contexts, values, and identities of the individuals they serve. AI systems, particularly those used in education, healthcare, marketing, and other sectors, increasingly interact with a global and culturally heterogeneous population. Therefore, AI technologies must be developed with an understanding of cultural nuances to avoid perpetuating stereotypes, reinforcing biases, or exacerbating social inequities. However, the potential of AI to promote cultural diversity is immense, addressing ethical concerns and enhancing the effectiveness and relevance of AI-driven solutions across diverse communities (Dastin, 2018).

Cultural sensitivity in AI refers to the ability of these systems to recognize and respect the cultural values, practices, and norms of the populations they interact with. This includes ensuring that AI algorithms do not promote cultural biases, discrimination, or exclusion. For example, facial recognition systems and language models must be trained on diverse datasets representing different racial, ethnic, and gender groups to avoid misidentification or unfair outcomes (Angwin et al., 2016). When AI systems are culturally sensitive, they can deliver more equitable and inclusive services aligned with all users' values and needs, regardless of their background.

11.1.1. The Importance of Representation in AI Systems

Representation is closely tied to cultural sensitivity and refers to how well different cultural groups, identities, and perspectives are reflected in the data used to train AI models and in the AI systems' design. The lack of adequate representation in AI has been a significant issue, leading to the reinforcement of stereotypes and the marginalization of underrepresented groups. For instance, facial recognition technologies have been shown to have higher error rates for people of color, particularly Black and Asian individuals, due to the underrepresentation of these groups in training datasets (Buolamwini & Gebru, 2018). Similarly, natural language processing (NLP) models, such as chatbots or voice assistants, may struggle to understand and generate responses that reflect global users' linguistic and cultural diversity if they are primarily trained on data from Western or Anglophone contexts.

The underrepresentation of certain cultural groups in AI development leads to technical flaws and perpetuates social inequality. If AI systems are not designed with cultural sensitivity and adequate representation, they risk reinforcing existing power dynamics, marginalizing already disadvantaged groups, and contributing to a cycle of social exclusion. Therefore, it's not enough for AI to be neutral or color-blind. It must actively work to include and empower individuals from all cultural backgrounds. AI developers need to ensure that the voices, experiences, and needs of a diverse range of people are included in the design, data collection, and implementation phases of AI system development. This ensures that the technology actively works to include and empower individuals from all cultural backgrounds (Gershgorn, 2019).

11.1.2. Challenges in Achieving Cultural Sensitivity and Representation

Achieving cultural sensitivity and representation in AI systems is a complex task that involves multiple challenges. One of the primary challenges is the inherent biases in the data used to train AI models. Data collection practices in education, healthcare, or other fields often reflect historical inequalities, stereotypes, and exclusionary practices. As a result, AI models trained on biased data may perpetuate these biases, further entrenching disparities (O'Neil, 2016). Moreover, AI development's dominant narratives and technological standards often stem from Western, predominantly white, and male perspectives, which can overlook other groups' cultural values, languages, and needs (Eubanks, 2018). For example, a voice recognition system trained primarily on American English speakers might fail to understand dialects or non-native speakers accurately, resulting in poor service for a global audience.

Another challenge is the lack of diversity within AI development teams themselves. Research has shown that a lack of diversity among AI practitioners—regardless of gender, race, or cultural background—can lead to developing technologies that do not adequately address the needs of underrepresented groups. Diverse teams, with their varied perspectives and experiences, are better equipped to identify potential biases, design inclusive solutions, and ensure that AI systems are culturally sensitive. However, the tech industry still faces significant challenges related to diversity and inclusion, with women and people of color underrepresented in AI and technology development roles (West et al., 2019). This gap in representation at the level of developers and decision-makers can limit the cultural awareness crucial for building inclusive AI systems.

11.1.3. Strategies for Promoting Cultural Sensitivity and Representation

To promote cultural sensitivity and representation in AI systems, several strategies can be employed. First, ensuring that diverse and representative datasets are used in training AI models is essential. This means collecting data from various cultural, ethnic, and linguistic groups to ensure the AI system recognizes and responds appropriately to diverse users. For example, in language models, it is crucial to include a variety of languages, dialects, and cultural contexts to enable the system to understand better and serve global populations (Blodgett et al., 2020).

Second, AI developers must proactively identify and mitigate biases throughout the development lifecycle. This includes conducting regular audits of AI systems to detect potential cultural biases and implementing strategies to correct these biases before deployment. Algorithms can be designed with fairness constraints, ensuring they do not disproportionately disadvantage certain cultural or demographic groups (Mehrabi et al., 2019). Adopting ethical AI guidelines and prioritizing inclusivity and cultural awareness is essential for guiding AI development and ensuring these technologies serve the public good.

Third, increasing diversity within AI development teams is crucial for fostering cultural sensitivity in AI systems. By incorporating people with different cultural, social, and educational backgrounds into the design and decision-making processes, AI development can become more inclusive and responsive to the needs of diverse users. Initiatives to support underrepresented groups in technology fields, such as mentorship programs, scholarships, and training opportunities, can help address the diversity gap in AI development (Binns, 2018).

Finally, collaboration with cultural experts, community leaders, and stakeholders is crucial. Their insights and perspectives can ensure that AI systems respect cultural norms and values. Engaging with local communities and cultural representatives during the development process can help identify potential issues and ensure that AI systems are aligned with the cultural and ethical standards of the communities they serve (Holmes et al., 2019).

Cultural sensitivity and representation in AI systems are critical for ensuring these technologies serve the diverse and global populations interacting with them. Without cultural awareness and inclusive design, AI systems may perpetuate biases and inequalities, further marginalizing disadvantaged groups. Addressing these challenges requires diverse data collection, inclusive design practices, diverse development teams, and ongoing audits to identify and mitigate biases. By prioritizing cultural sensitivity and representation, AI can become a more equitable and effective tool for promoting social inclusion and empowerment, ultimately contributing to a more just and inclusive society.

11.1.4. Localized Content Development in AI Systems

Localized content development is crucial to artificial intelligence (AI) systems, especially when deployed across diverse geographic regions and cultural contexts. Localized content refers to adapting AI systems, including their language, design, and functionality, to meet a particular region or community's needs, preferences, and cultural norms. This process is essential in ensuring that AI systems are linguistically accurate, culturally relevant, and respectful. As AI technologies, such as chatbots, virtual assistants, and educational platforms, become increasingly integrated into global societies, localized content development becomes a key factor in improving user experience, enhancing accessibility, and promoting inclusivity (Essers et al., 2019).

11.1.4.1. The Importance of Localized Content in AI Systems

The need for localized content in AI systems stems from the diversity of global languages, traditions, values, and practices. AI systems developed without considering local contexts may fail to engage users effectively, leading to misunderstandings, dissatisfaction, and even harm. For example, a voice-activated assistant that functions well in English-speaking countries might struggle with dialects or regional variations in pronunciation in non-Western or non-Anglophone countries. Similarly, cultural differences in humor, social norms, and interaction styles could make AI responses feel out of place or even offensive. Localized content allows AI systems to respond in a way that aligns with local customs and expectations, increasing their relevance and effectiveness (Behrang et al., 2019).

In education, developing localized content is particularly significant, as learning tools must resonate with students from different cultural backgrounds. Educational AI systems that use culturally specific examples, references, and learning materials can enhance student engagement and comprehension. By tailoring content to the cultural context, these systems can also bridge gaps in understanding, making learning more accessible and inclusive. This is especially important in multilingual societies where students may face language barriers or cultural differences in conventional learning materials (Raschka et al., 2020).

11.1.4.2. Challenges in Localized Content Development

Despite its importance, developing localized content for AI systems presents several challenges. One of the main challenges is the availability and quality of local data. AI systems rely heavily on large datasets to train algorithms that accurately represent the target region's language, culture, and social norms. However, for many languages and cultures, especially minority or indigenous ones, the available data may be limited, inaccurate, or biased. This can lead to AI systems that fail to understand or correctly interpret local dialects, idioms, or expressions, diminishing their effectiveness (Gershgorn, 2019). Additionally, there may be challenges in translating AI algorithms into languages with complex grammatical structures or where the written form may not fully capture cultural nuances.

Another challenge is ensuring the content is translated and adapted for cultural relevance. Literal translations are insufficient if they fail to account for cultural differences in humor, values, and behavior. For example, what is considered polite or respectful in one culture may not be viewed differently in another. AI systems must be designed to navigate these cultural differences to avoid misunderstandings or offenses. Developing content that aligns with local ethical norms and societal values is essential, especially in sensitive areas like healthcare, education, and law (Tett, 2020). In some regions, AI systems may also need to be tailored to accommodate varying levels of technological infrastructure or digital literacy, further complicating the localization process.

11.1.4.3. Strategies for Effective Localized Content Development

Developers must take several key steps to develop localized content in AI systems effectively. First, it is essential to collaborate with local experts, linguists, and cultural consultants to ensure the content is culturally relevant and linguistically accurate. By involving local stakeholders in the design and development process, AI systems can better align with local expectations and norms. For example, AI educational tools can incorporate culturally specific scenarios or historical examples that resonate with local learners, enhancing their engagement and learning outcomes (Sengupta et al., 2018).

Second, leveraging community-generated content and user feedback can help improve the localization of AI systems. AI systems that continuously learn from interactions with local users can adapt over time to better meet their needs. This iterative feedback loop can help correct translation errors, improve system responsiveness, and ensure the content remains culturally sensitive. Crowdsourcing data from diverse communities can also contribute to developing more inclusive and representative AI systems, enabling them to understand and interact with various users from different backgrounds (Mitchell et al., 2019).

Third, it is important to prioritize ethical considerations when developing localized content. AI systems must be designed to respect the target communities' cultural values, privacy, and ethical standards. For instance, the content delivered by AI systems in education must not propagate harmful stereotypes or misinformation. Furthermore, ensuring that AI technologies are accessible to all—regardless of socioeconomic status, disability, or geographic location—is key to making the systems equitable and inclusive (West et al., 2019).

Localized content development is essential for the effectiveness, accessibility, and ethical deployment of AI systems across diverse cultural contexts. By ensuring that AI systems are culturally sensitive, linguistically accurate, and relevant to the local environment, developers can create more inclusive technologies that serve the needs of a global population. The challenges associated with localized content, including data availability, cultural adaptation, and ethical concerns, require a thoughtful and collaborative approach involving local stakeholders and ongoing user feedback. AI can better serve diverse communities with these strategies, fostering greater global inclusion and empowerment.

11.1.5. AI's Role in Promoting Cultural Diversity

Artificial Intelligence (AI) has the potential to play a significant role in promoting cultural diversity, fostering inclusivity, and enhancing cross-cultural understanding. AI's ability to process vast amounts of data, adapt to different languages and cultural contexts, and provide personalized interactions opens new opportunities for bridging cultural divides and celebrating diversity. As AI continues to evolve, exploring how these technologies can be harnessed to support, rather than undermine, cultural richness and diversity becomes crucial. Through tailored content, language translation, and the facilitation of cross-cultural exchanges, AI can be a powerful tool for promoting cultural diversity in various sectors, including education, entertainment, healthcare, and communication.

11.1.5.1. Language Translation and Linguistic Inclusivity

One of the most direct ways AI promotes cultural diversity is through advanced language translation technologies. AI-powered translation tools, such as Google Translate and Microsoft Translator, have made it easier for people from different linguistic backgrounds to communicate with one another. These tools translate text and adapt to regional dialects, idioms, and expressions, enabling more prosperous, more accurate cross-cultural communication. In education, AI-driven translation tools allow students who speak different languages to access the same learning materials, bridging the language gap and enhancing educational equity. This capability is particularly valuable in multicultural and multilingual societies, where students from diverse backgrounds can use AI-powered tools to understand lessons and engage with peers (Nawaz et al., 2020).

Moreover, AI systems can also help preserve and revitalize endangered languages. AI can be trained on the phonetic, syntactic, and grammatical features of lesser-known languages through machine learning models, supporting language preservation efforts. By creating digital resources and educational tools in these languages, AI helps sustain cultural heritage and diversity, ensuring that these languages are not lost over time (Cummins, 2017). This application of AI is particularly important for indigenous communities, whose languages often face the threat of extinction due to the dominance of global languages such as English, Mandarin, or Spanish.

11.1.5.2. Personalized Cultural Experiences

AI can also promote cultural diversity by personalizing cultural experiences and providing users with content that resonates with their cultural preferences. In the entertainment industry, for instance, AI-powered recommendation systems on platforms like Netflix or YouTube use algorithms to suggest movies, TV shows, and videos that align with users' cultural backgrounds, preferences, and viewing habits. By analyzing viewing patterns and content preferences, AI systems can introduce users to diverse cultures, expanding their exposure to international media and fostering a broader appreciation for global cultures (Gomez-Uribe & Hunt, 2015).

In education, personalized AI-driven learning platforms can adapt content to students' cultural contexts, ensuring that examples, case studies, and learning materials reflect the students' cultural backgrounds. This personalization enhances engagement and helps students connect more deeply with the content, facilitating better learning outcomes. For example, AI systems can adjust how history, literature, or social studies are taught to reflect students' cultural perspectives, making the learning experience more relevant and meaningful (Luckin et al., 2016).

11.1.5.3. Cross-Cultural Communication and Collaboration

AI tools can also facilitate cross-cultural communication and collaboration, enabling individuals from diverse cultural backgrounds to work together more effectively. In global business environments, AI-powered platforms can bridge cultural gaps by providing real-time translation services and enhancing collaboration among teams across countries and cultures. Furthermore, AI can help businesses navigate cultural differences in marketing strategies, product development, and customer service, ensuring that brands and services are culturally appropriate and sensitive to local customs and values.

AI can enable international collaborations in higher education and research by overcoming language and cultural barriers. Through AI-enhanced communication tools, researchers from different parts of the world can collaborate on projects without being hindered by language or cultural differences. This promotes a more inclusive academic environment where diverse perspectives and ideas are shared and valued, leading to more innovative and globally relevant solutions (West et al., 2019). AI also has the potential to democratize access to educational and research resources, enabling individuals from underrepresented cultures and regions to contribute to global knowledge production.

11.1.5.4. Addressing Cultural Bias in AI Systems

While AI has the potential to promote cultural diversity, it is equally important to recognize and address the challenges posed by cultural bias in AI systems. AI algorithms can inadvertently perpetuate biases if trained on data that is not diverse or representative of different cultural groups. For example, facial recognition technologies have been shown to have higher error rates for people of color, particularly women, due to the underrepresentation of these groups in the datasets used to train these systems (Buolamwini & Gebru, 2018). This can lead to discriminatory outcomes, reinforcing existing societal inequalities.

To ensure that AI contributes positively to cultural diversity, developers must implement inclusive design practices and ensure that AI systems are trained on diverse and representative datasets. This includes including data from different cultural, ethnic, and socioeconomic backgrounds and designing algorithms sensitive to cultural differences in language, behavior, and social norms. Efforts to audit and mitigate bias in AI systems are crucial to prevent these technologies from exacerbating inequalities and to ensure that they serve all cultures fairly and equitably (O'Neil, 2016).

AI has the potential to be a transformative tool for promoting cultural diversity by breaking down language barriers, personalizing cultural experiences, facilitating cross-cultural communication, and supporting the preservation of endangered languages. However, these opportunities come with the responsibility of ensuring that AI systems are designed and deployed in ways that respect cultural differences and avoid reinforcing harmful biases. By prioritizing inclusivity, equity, and cultural sensitivity in the development of AI technologies, we can ensure that AI contributes to a more interconnected and culturally diverse world where all cultures are valued and celebrated.

References

Angwin, J., Larson, J., Mattu, S., & Kirchner, L. (2016). *Machine Bias*. ProPublica.

Behrang, F., Mussa, D. I., & Dastgheib, S. (2019). *Localization and cultural sensitivity in AI applications: A review*. Journal of Computational Intelligence and Technology, 16(4), 8-19.

Binns, R. (2018). *Fairness in Machine Learning: Lessons from Political Philosophy*. Proceedings of the 2018 CHI Conference on Human Factors in Computing Systems, 1–14.

Blodgett, S. L., Barocas, S., Daumé III, H., & Wallach, H. M. (2020). *Language (Technology) is Power: A Critical Survey of "Bias" in NLP*. Proceedings of the 58th Annual Meeting of the Association for Computational Linguistics, 1-11.

Buolamwini, J., & Gebru, T. (2018). *Gender shades: Intersectional accuracy disparities in commercial gender classification*. Proceedings of the 1st Conference on Fairness, Accountability, and Transparency, 77-91.

Cummins, J. (2017). *Language, power, and pedagogy: Bilingual children in the crossfire*. Multilingual Matters.

Dastin, J. (2018). *Amazon Scraps Secret AI Recruiting Tool That Showed Bias Against Women*. Reuters.

Essers, P., Pandey, S., & Raju, S. (2019). *Creating culturally sensitive AI: How to avoid reinforcing stereotypes and biases*. International Journal of Artificial Intelligence, 23(2), 54-66.

Eubanks, V. (2018). *Automating Inequality: How High-Tech Tools Profile, Police, and Punish the Poor*. St. Martin's Press.

Gershgorn, D. (2019). *How the lack of diversity in AI is leading to bad algorithms*. Quartz. Retrieved from https://qz.com/1478703.

Gomez-Uribe, C. A., & Hunt, N. (2015). *The Netflix recommender system: Algorithms, business value, and innovation*. Proceedings of the 21st ACM SIGKDD International Conference on Knowledge Discovery and Data Mining, 2137-2146.

Luckin, R., Holmes, W., Griffiths, M., & Forcier, L. B. (2016). *Intelligence Unleashed: An argument for AI in education*. Pearson Education.

Mehrabi, N., Morstatter, F., Saxena, N., Lerman, K., & Galstyan, A. (2019). *A Survey on Bias and Fairness in Machine Learning*. ACM Computing Surveys, 52(6), 1-35.

Mitchell, M., Wu, S., Zaldivar, A., Barnes, P., & Karami, M. (2019). *Model cards for model reporting*. Proceedings of the 2019 CHI Conference on Human Factors in Computing Systems, 1-13.

Nawaz, S., Khusro, S., & Sher, S. (2020). *AI-powered multilingual translation tools for education: Applications and challenges*. Journal of Educational Technology & Society, 23(3), 1-12.

O'Neil, C. (2016). *Weapons of math destruction: How big data increases inequality and threatens democracy*. Crown Publishing Group.

Raschka, C., Wang, X., & Kumar, M. (2020). *Cultural considerations in AI for education: A case study*. Journal of AI and Education, 10(3), 120-133.

Sengupta, S., Sitaraman, M., & Lee, T. (2018). *Bringing AI into the classroom: How personalized learning is transforming education*. Educational Technology, 58(6), 22-34.

Tett, G. (2020). *The risks of AI bias: Why machine learning needs a cultural overhaul*. Financial Times. Retrieved from https://www.ft.com/content/00f7b3a4.

West, S. M., Whittaker, M., & Crawford, K. (2019). *Discriminating systems: Gender, race, and power in AI*. AI Now Institute.

Chapter 12

Global Collaboration for AI in Education

12.1. Introduction

Global collaboration for Artificial Intelligence (AI) in education is a growing phenomenon where countries, institutions, and organizations work together to harness the potential of AI technologies for transforming teaching and learning systems worldwide. As AI evolves, its impact on education becomes increasingly significant, offering opportunities to improve educational outcomes, address global challenges, and provide equitable access to quality education. However, these benefits can only be fully realized through international collaboration promoting knowledge, resources, and expertise sharing. By engaging in collective efforts, countries and educational institutions can better navigate the complexities of AI integration and ensure its deployment is ethical, inclusive, and aligned with educational goals, prioritizing student learning, teacher support, and broader societal well-being.

12.1.1. Collaborative International Research and Development

One of the primary components of global collaboration for AI in education is international research and development (R&D). Many countries have begun to establish strategic partnerships and networks to facilitate the joint development of AI-powered educational tools, systems, and resources. Collaborative research initiatives allow countries to share data, exchange expertise and collectively tackle global educational challenges such as disparities in access to quality education, teacher shortages, and low learning outcomes. For instance, global partnerships between educational institutions, AI research centers, and technology companies have led to the development of intelligent tutoring systems, personalized learning platforms, and automated assessment tools that can be adapted and scaled for diverse educational contexts (Luckin et al., 2016). These collaborative R&D efforts help ensure that AI innovations in education are more universally applicable and culturally sensitive, considering different regions' varied needs and constraints.

Moreover, global collaboration in AI for education fosters the exchange of best practices. Countries with advanced AI systems in education, such as the United States, China, and Finland, can share their experiences with developing and implementing AI technologies with countries still in the early stages of adopting AI. This sharing of knowledge helps to prevent the duplication of efforts, reduces risks of failure, and accelerates the adoption of effective AI strategies globally. In turn, it encourages the development of AI tools that can serve diverse educational needs, including content delivery, language translation, and special needs education (UNESCO, 2021).

12.1.2. Addressing Global Educational Inequalities

AI-driven educational solutions hold the potential to bridge educational gaps in developed and developing countries. Global collaboration can help scale up the impact of AI in overcoming barriers such as limited access to quality teachers, educational resources, and infrastructure, especially in low-income and rural areas. For instance, AI-powered platforms can offer personalized learning experiences to students who may not have access to high-quality teachers and those facing language or cultural barriers. In such contexts, AI-based learning systems can support differentiated instruction by tailoring educational content to meet the diverse needs of learners across the globe. Through global collaboration, countries can pool resources to develop open-access AI platforms that are accessible to all, ensuring that even the most marginalized communities can benefit from AI-enhanced education (Holmes et al., 2019).

Global collaboration fosters the development of equitable AI solutions by addressing bias and fairness issues. AI systems often reflect the biases present in their training data, which can lead to discriminatory outcomes if not carefully designed. By collaborating internationally, countries and organizations can share insights and methodologies for mitigating bias in AI systems, ensuring that educational tools are inclusive and equitable. This can include the development of guidelines for ethical AI use, the creation of diverse and representative datasets, and the design of systems that are sensitive to cultural differences. Collaborative global efforts can help shape policies that ensure AI is used to reduce, rather than exacerbate, educational inequalities (West et al., 2019).

12.1.3. Policy and Regulatory Frameworks

The widespread adoption of AI in education requires establishing firm policies and regulatory frameworks that can guide the responsible use of these technologies. Global collaboration is essential in developing such frameworks, as it ensures that AI systems in education are deployed to protect student privacy, promote data security, and maintain ethical standards. International organizations like UNESCO, the OECD, and the World Economic Forum are leading initiatives to formulate global guidelines and frameworks for the ethical use of AI in education. These frameworks aim to balance innovation with accountability, ensuring that AI systems are transparent, unbiased, and aligned with human rights principles (UNESCO, 2021).

In addition to ethical considerations, policy collaboration is important for addressing issues such as digital divides and unequal access to AI technologies. Global partnerships can advocate for creating policies that ensure equitable access to AI resources, particularly in low-income and rural areas. Such policies can address infrastructure deficits, providing the necessary connectivity and hardware to support AI integration in schools and ensuring that students in underserved regions are not left behind in the global shift towards AI-enhanced education (Luckin et al., 2016).

12.1.4. Building Capacity and Skills for the AI-Driven Future

Another critical aspect of global collaboration is the development of the human capacity required to implement and manage AI in education effectively. Many countries lack the necessary skills and expertise to develop, deploy, and maintain AI systems. Global collaboration can play a vital role in building capacity by supporting the training of educators, policymakers, and technologists who can design, integrate, and manage AI-based educational systems. Through international partnerships, countries can share training programs, curricula, and professional development opportunities that enable teachers and administrators to understand AI tools better and leverage them effectively in their teaching practices.

Furthermore, global collaborations can facilitate the development of AI literacy programs that equip students with the skills to thrive in an AI-driven world. These programs can help students develop critical thinking, problem-solving, and computational skills, which are increasingly necessary in the future workforce. By promoting AI literacy globally, countries can ensure that their populations are prepared for the job opportunities created by AI and other emerging technologies, thus contributing to economic growth and social mobility (Nawaz et al., 2020).

Global collaboration for AI in education represents a significant opportunity to transform educational systems worldwide by improving access to quality learning, enhancing teaching practices, and addressing educational inequalities. Through international partnerships, the global community can create equitable, ethical, and culturally responsive AI tools that benefit students, educators, and societies as a whole. However, for this potential to be fully realized, collaboration must be accompanied by thoughtful policy development, capacity-building efforts, and a commitment to inclusivity and fairness. As AI continues to shape the future of education, global cooperation will be essential in ensuring that these technologies empower all learners, irrespective of their background or location.

12.1.5. International Partnerships and Knowledge Sharing

International partnerships and knowledge sharing have become crucial in successfully integrating Artificial Intelligence (AI) in education. Given AI's transformative potential, collaborative efforts between countries, organizations, and institutions are essential to ensure that AI technologies in education are designed, implemented, and scaled effectively across diverse global contexts. These partnerships facilitate the exchange of ideas, best practices, and resources, enabling the development of AI tools that can address common educational challenges while respecting cultural, economic, and social differences.

12.1.5.1. Collaborative Research and Innovation

International partnerships foster collaborative research and innovation in AI for education, enabling stakeholders from different regions to pool their expertise and resources in creating AI-driven solutions that meet the needs of diverse populations. For example, AI research projects that combine universities, tech companies, and governments from various countries can produce tools adaptable to different educational systems and contexts. Countries can share data, methodologies, and technology frameworks through global cooperation, accelerating the development of AI tools designed to improve teaching and learning outcomes.

One example is the partnership between the European Union and the United States through initiatives like the EU-U.S. Trade and Technology Council (TTC), which aims to promote cooperation in AI and other digital technologies, including education. These collaborative efforts support research in AI-powered personalized learning, adaptive testing, and educational data analytics, which can help address issues like low student engagement, achievement gaps, and educational inequities. By engaging in these joint research efforts, countries can avoid redundancy, reduce costs, and produce more impactful AI solutions that are globally scalable.

12.1.5.2. Knowledge Sharing and Capacity Building

Knowledge sharing is central to the success of international partnerships in AI for education. Countries and organizations can learn from each other's experiences, successes, and challenges in deploying AI technologies in education. Through conferences, workshops, online platforms, and collaborative research projects, stakeholders can exchange ideas and solutions that have worked in different contexts. For example, educational institutions in high-income countries with advanced AI implementations can share their learnings with countries in low- and middle-income regions, where access to cutting-edge technologies may be more limited.

Capacity building plays a critical role in these knowledge-sharing initiatives. As AI technologies rapidly evolve, there is a growing need for educators, policymakers, and technology developers to stay informed about the latest developments in the field. Through international partnerships, countries can invest in training programs that equip teachers and administrators with the skills needed to use AI tools effectively in the classroom. For instance, organizations like UNESCO have been promoting AI literacy by organizing global workshops and training sessions for educators, policymakers, and students, which enhances the collective ability to adapt to AI's growing role in education (UNESCO, 2021).

Additionally, countries can improve their technical and administrative capacities to manage AI-based educational programs by collaborating with international partners. In countries where AI integration is still in its infancy, sharing knowledge about infrastructure requirements, data management, privacy concerns, and ethical considerations can help streamline the adoption process, ensuring that AI tools are deployed responsibly and effectively.

12.1.5.3. Addressing Global Educational Challenges

International partnerships also help address some of the most pressing global educational challenges, such as inequality in access to quality education, teacher shortages, and disparities in educational outcomes. AI has the potential to bridge educational gaps by providing personalized learning opportunities, offering scalable educational tools, and ensuring that educational resources are available even in remote or underserved regions. Through global collaboration, countries can create AI solutions tailored to the unique needs of disadvantaged students, including those with special needs, language barriers, or limited access to teachers and educational resources.

For example, AI can be used to develop language translation tools that help students in multilingual environments access content in their native language. By collaborating internationally, countries can pool their expertise and develop AI systems capable of supporting a wide range of languages and dialects, making education more inclusive for all learners (Holmes et al., 2019). Furthermore, AI-powered learning platforms can help address the teacher shortage by automating administrative tasks, grading assignments, and providing real-time feedback to students, thus allowing teachers to focus on personalized instruction.

12.1.5.4. Advancing Global Educational Equity

Global collaboration also promotes the equitable distribution of AI technologies in education, ensuring that the benefits of these innovations are shared across countries, regions, and socioeconomic groups. By working together, countries can ensure that AI solutions are not limited to wealthy nations but are accessible to those in low-income and developing regions. This can be achieved by building open-source platforms, offering free access to AI-powered learning resources, and establishing international partnerships that provide funding for AI implementation in resource-poor areas.

Equitable access to AI technologies in education is particularly important for addressing the digital divide, which remains a significant barrier to educational access in many parts of the world. Through collaborative international efforts, countries can work to improve the infrastructure necessary for supporting AI integration, such as high-speed internet access, hardware availability, and digital literacy skills. These efforts can help ensure that students in rural or underserved regions can benefit from AI-enhanced learning, thus reducing global educational inequalities (Luckin et al., 2016).

International partnerships and knowledge sharing are critical for AI's successful and equitable integration in education. Through collaboration, countries and organizations can leverage their collective expertise and resources to develop AI tools that address global educational challenges, improve learning outcomes, and promote inclusivity and equity. The sharing of knowledge and best practices not only accelerates the adoption of AI in education but also helps to ensure that these technologies are used responsibly and ethically. As AI continues to transform the educational landscape, global collaboration will be essential in ensuring that the benefits of AI are accessible to all, regardless of location, socioeconomic status, or educational background.

12.1.6. Case Studies of Successful Implementations of AI in Education

Integrating Artificial Intelligence (AI) in education has shown promising results in various global contexts, demonstrating its potential to enhance teaching, learning, and educational equity. Several case studies highlight successful implementations of AI that have contributed to improving educational outcomes, particularly in terms of personalized learning, accessibility, and teacher support. These examples underscore how AI can address specific educational challenges and achieve broader goals of equity and empowerment.

12.1.6.1. Khan Academy and AI-Driven Personalized Learning

Khan Academy, a well-known online learning platform, has successfully integrated AI to personalize education for millions of students worldwide. The platform uses AI algorithms to assess students' strengths and weaknesses, creating individualized learning paths that adapt as students progress. By providing instant feedback and tailored recommendations, Khan Academy helps students learn at their own pace, fostering a deeper understanding of topics. The AI system also analyzes data from student interactions to identify patterns and predict future learning needs, ensuring that students receive the right content at the right time.

Khan Academy's AI-driven approach has been particularly effective in addressing gaps in education, as it allows students to access high-quality educational resources regardless of their location or socioeconomic background. This approach has proven effective in a variety of educational settings, from K-12 schools to higher education, and has been especially beneficial for students who might struggle in traditional classroom environments. According to a study conducted by the Bill & Melinda Gates Foundation, students using personalized learning platforms like Khan Academy have shown significant improvements in math and reading achievement (Bill & Melinda Gates Foundation, 2013).

12.1.6.2. Squirrel AI in China: Adaptive Learning Systems

Squirrel AI, a Chinese ed-tech company, has developed an adaptive learning system that uses AI to provide personalized education to students in subjects such as mathematics, English, and science. The system leverages machine learning algorithms to identify students' learning needs, diagnose knowledge gaps, and provide customized learning paths. The AI system continuously adapts based on student performance, offering real-time feedback and adjusting the difficulty of tasks as students progress.

The success of Squirrel AI is attributed to its ability to combine the best features of human and AI instruction. While the AI system provides personalized learning and immediate feedback, human teachers can guide students through complex problems and offer support when needed. This hybrid AI and human interaction model has proven to be highly effective in improving student outcomes, particularly in exam preparation. Research on Squirrel AI has shown that students who use the platform outperform their peers in traditional classrooms, significantly improving test scores (Yu, 2020).

12.1.6.3. AI for Special Education: The Use of AI in Supporting Students with Autism

AI has also been successfully integrated into special education settings to support students with disabilities. One such example is the use of AI-powered tools for students with autism. The AI system uses facial recognition and emotion detection to help students understand and express emotions, which can be a challenge for individuals on the autism spectrum. These AI tools can analyze facial expressions, voice tones, and body language, providing real-time feedback to students on their emotional states and helping them improve social interactions.

The AI system's ability to provide personalized and consistent feedback has particularly benefited students with autism, who may struggle with traditional educational methods. One example is the use of AI-powered social skills training tools, which help students practice social interactions in a safe and controlled environment. These tools have been shown to improve social communication skills and increase emotional intelligence in students with autism, ultimately leading to better integration into mainstream classrooms (Huang et al., 2019).

12.1.6.4. AI for Language Learning: Duolingo

Duolingo, a popular language-learning app, utilizes AI to personalize lessons and adapt content to the individual learner's needs. By analyzing user behavior, the app customizes lessons to focus on areas where the user struggles, providing instant feedback and adjusting difficulty levels accordingly. Duolingo's AI algorithms track users' progress, helping them review previously learned material and reinforce weak areas. This personalized approach has made Duolingo one of the most effective language-learning platforms available, with millions of active users worldwide.

Duolingo's success lies in its ability to use AI to make language learning more accessible and engaging. The app has expanded its reach to users in diverse regions, offering courses in over 30 languages. Additionally, the gamification of language learning, powered by AI, has made the process more interactive and enjoyable, increasing user engagement and motivation. Research indicates that learners using Duolingo demonstrate measurable improvements in language proficiency, particularly in vocabulary and grammar acquisition (Vesselinov & Grego, 2012).

12.1.6.5. AI for Teacher Support: IBM's Watson Education

IBM's Watson Education platform is another example of AI's successful application in education, specifically in supporting teachers. Watson uses AI to analyze classroom data and assist educators in developing personalized learning plans for their students. The platform provides teachers with actionable insights into student performance, identifies knowledge gaps, and recommends strategies for improving teaching effectiveness. By automating administrative tasks such as grading and lesson planning, Watson allows teachers to focus more on instruction and individualized student support.

Watson Education has been implemented in several school districts in the United States, where it has helped educators make data-driven decisions and improve student outcomes. In pilot programs, teachers using Watson's AI tools reported increased classroom management efficiency, and students showed improved engagement and academic achievement. IBM's work in education highlights how AI can enhance student learning outcomes and empower educators by reducing their administrative burdens and supporting them in delivering personalized instruction (IBM, 2018).

These case studies demonstrate AI's transformative potential in education, showcasing its ability to personalize learning, support students with diverse needs, enhance language learning, and assist teachers in delivering more effective instruction. While challenges remain, such as ensuring equitable access to AI technologies and addressing ethical concerns, these examples provide evidence of the positive impact that AI can have on educational outcomes. As AI continues to evolve, its role in education will likely expand, offering new opportunities for learners and educators to achieve their full potential.

References

Bill & Melinda Gates Foundation. (2013). *Learning what works: A first look at the research on personalized learning*. Bill & Melinda Gates Foundation.

Holmes, W., Bialik, M., & Fadel, C. (2019). *Artificial Intelligence in Education: Promises and Implications for Teaching and Learning*. Center for Curriculum Redesign.

Huang, W., McQuillan, J., & Rios, J. (2019). *Artificial intelligence in special education: Empowering students with autism and other disabilities*. Journal of Special Education Technology, 34(2), 70-79.

IBM. (2018). *Watson Education: Transforming the classroom with AI*. IBM Corporation.

Luckin, R., Holmes, W., Griffiths, M., & Forcier, L. B. (2016). *Intelligence Unleashed: An Argument for AI in Education*. Pearson Education.

Nawaz, S., Khusro, S., & Sher, S. (2020). *AI-powered multilingual translation tools for education: Applications and challenges*. Journal of Educational Technology & Society, 23(3), 1-12.

UNESCO. (2021). *Artificial Intelligence and Education: Guidance for Policy-Makers*. UNESCO Publishing.

Vesselinov, R., & Grego, J. (2012). *Duolingo effectiveness study*. City University of New York.

West, S. M., Whittaker, M., & Crawford, K. (2019). *Discriminating systems: Gender, race, and power in AI*. AI Now Institute.

Yu, X. (2020). *Squirrel AI and the future of adaptive learning in China*. EdTech Review, 8(5), 34–36.

Part IV: Innovative Applications of AI in Education and Beyond

Introduction

Artificial Intelligence (AI) is revolutionizing numerous sectors, with education being one of the most transformative fields. Beyond traditional applications, AI is being integrated into innovative solutions that have the potential to reshape the entire educational landscape. These applications address persistent challenges such as personalized learning and teacher support and expand into areas like administrative efficiency, global educational access, and lifelong learning. Integrating AI into educational and professional sectors enhances the quality of learning, fosters empowerment, and prepares individuals for the future workforce.

AI-Driven Personalized Learning Systems

One of the most notable applications of AI in education is the creation of personalized learning systems that adapt to individual students' unique needs, strengths, and weaknesses. AI-powered platforms like DreamBox Learning, Smart Sparrow, and Knewton use machine learning algorithms to continuously track student progress and modify learning paths in real time. These systems provide immediate feedback and tailor instructional materials, allowing students to learn independently. Thus, they address the diverse needs of learners in a way that traditional education models have struggled to achieve.

Personalized learning powered by AI promises to enhance engagement and improve academic outcomes by ensuring that each learner receives the right support. Studies have shown that students using AI-driven personalized learning platforms outperform their peers in traditional classroom settings, as these tools offer targeted practice and adjust to students' learning styles (Pane et al., 2015). This approach helps address learning gaps and enables students to explore subjects in greater depth, fostering a more enriching learning experience.

AI in Adaptive Learning and Assessment

AI is also transforming how we assess student progress and provide adaptive support. Traditional assessment methods, such as standardized testing, often fail to capture the nuances of student learning and may not offer immediate feedback to guide improvement. However, AI-driven tools like intelligent tutoring systems (ITS) and adaptive learning platforms continuously monitor student interactions, analyze performance, and adjust lessons based on individual needs.

For example, platforms like Carnegie Learning and Squirrel AI provide students with adaptive assessments that respond to their abilities in real time, offering a tailored learning journey. AI-enabled formative assessments allow for continuous evaluation, ensuring educators can provide timely interventions. AI also assists in reducing the teacher's workload by automating grading and assessment tasks (VanLehn, 2011). These systems have been particularly effective in high-stakes subjects like mathematics and science, where early intervention is crucial for improving long-term outcomes.

AI-Powered Teacher Support Tools

AI is also being employed to support educators, not only in enhancing teaching practices but also in reducing administrative burdens. AI tools like IBM's Watson Education and Google's Classroom use machine learning to streamline tasks such as grading, planning lessons, and providing student feedback. These tools analyze student performance data to suggest specific areas where intervention is needed, empowering teachers to focus on their pedagogical roles.

For instance, AI can automate routine tasks like grading essays or multiple-choice questions, thus giving teachers more time to engage with students and provide personalized instruction. Furthermore, AI is being used to offer real-time recommendations for teachers, identify potential learning gaps in their classrooms, and offer resources tailored to students' needs (Baker et al., 2019). This dual benefit of supporting both teachers and students enables a more dynamic and efficient classroom environment.

AI in Educational Accessibility

AI has shown considerable promise in improving accessibility for students with disabilities. AI-powered assistive technologies, such as voice recognition systems, text-to-speech tools, and real-time captioning, make learning more inclusive. Technologies like Microsoft Learning Tools and Read&Write provide students with dyslexia or other learning challenges with tools to help them access and engage with the curriculum more effectively. Furthermore, AI systems can create customized content that adjusts to the sensory needs of students with visual or auditory impairments, ensuring that education becomes more equitable.

Additionally, AI is helping bridge language barriers in education through automatic translation services, enabling students to access content in different languages and making global learning opportunities more accessible. Tools like Google Translate and Microsoft Translator, powered by AI, offer real-time language translation for students who speak diverse languages, enhancing cross-cultural learning and ensuring linguistic diversity does not hinder educational participation (Baker et al., 2019).

AI for Lifelong Learning and Workforce Development

As the nature of work continues to evolve in the age of automation and AI, lifelong learning has become increasingly important for individuals to remain competitive in the workforce. AI supports this shift by offering personalized, adaptive learning tools for adult learners and professionals looking to upgrade their skills. Platforms like Coursera, Udacity, and LinkedIn Learning leverage AI to suggest courses and programs based on users' skills, career goals, and previous learning patterns, ensuring they engage in relevant and timely education.

AI also helps in vocational and technical education, where specific skills are in demand. For instance, AI-driven platforms can provide real-time feedback and simulations in fields like healthcare, manufacturing, and technology, where practical training is essential. AI-powered systems can analyze a learner's progress and provide personalized guidance for improving technical skills, enhancing employability, and preparing individuals for future careers (Brynjolfsson & McAfee, 2014).

AI in Global Education Access and Equity

AI can potentially transform education globally by enhancing access to quality learning resources in underserved and remote areas. AI-powered platforms can provide high-quality education to students without access to qualified teachers or educational resources. For example, AI can deliver content in remote areas through mobile devices, allowing students in rural or underdeveloped regions to access educational material in their native languages, regardless of location.

Furthermore, AI-powered systems can play a critical role in addressing educational inequality by helping to bridge the digital divide. The application of AI to education in low-resource settings has the potential to democratize learning and provide equitable opportunities for students worldwide. As AI tools become more sophisticated and accessible, they offer unprecedented opportunities for students in marginalized communities to receive the education they need to succeed (Luckin et al., 2016).

AI is ushering in a new era of innovation in education, offering transformative applications that extend beyond traditional learning environments. From personalized learning and adaptive assessment to teacher support and lifelong learning, AI is reshaping how education is delivered and experienced. As these technologies continue to evolve, they promise to enhance educational equity, expand access to learning, and prepare individuals for the demands of the future workforce. The potential of AI in education is vast, and its continued development offers exciting opportunities to improve learning outcomes and empower individuals across the globe.

Chapter 13

AI-Powered Educational Platforms

13.1. Introduction

AI-powered educational platforms are rapidly transforming how education is delivered, offering highly personalized and adaptive learning experiences that cater to the unique needs of individual students. These platforms harness the power of artificial intelligence to provide real-time feedback, adaptive learning pathways, and interactive learning environments. By leveraging data analytics, machine learning algorithms, and natural language processing, AI-powered platforms can create dynamic learning experiences that are both engaging and effective. These platforms are revolutionizing both K-12 and higher education by enabling more individualized, efficient, and accessible educational experiences.

13.1.1. Personalized Learning Experiences

One of the most significant advantages of AI-powered educational platforms is their ability to create personalized student learning experiences. Traditional education systems often adopt a one-size-fits-all approach, but AI can address the diverse learning needs of students by tailoring content to their specific strengths and weaknesses. These platforms use machine learning algorithms to track individual progress and adjust the learning material accordingly. For example, platforms like *Knewton* and *DreamBox Learning* analyze students' responses and behaviors in real time to modify lessons, provide targeted practice, and recommend resources based on their learning pace and style. By personalizing the learning journey, AI platforms help students stay engaged and progress at their own pace, ensuring they are challenged but not overwhelmed.

13.1.2. Automated Grading and Feedback

AI-powered platforms can significantly reduce educators' time and effort on administrative tasks, particularly in grading and providing feedback. Automated grading systems use AI to grade assignments, quizzes, and exams, providing instant feedback to students. This allows educators to focus more on teaching and interacting with students rather than spending time on routine grading tasks. AI systems like *Gradescope* and *Socrative* can accurately grade assignments, quizzes, and even written responses, providing students with immediate insights into their performance. Moreover, these platforms offer educators data-driven insights into student performance, helping them identify patterns, track progress, and intervene when necessary.

13.1.3. Intelligent Tutoring Systems

Intelligent tutoring systems (ITS) are another key application of AI in education. These platforms simulate personalized tutoring experiences by providing real-time assistance to students. Unlike traditional learning management systems, ITS platforms use AI to diagnose student misconceptions, offer customized exercises, and guide learners through complex problems. For example, *Carnegie Learning* uses AI to provide students with personalized math tutoring, helping them understand mathematical concepts step-by-step. ITS platforms are designed to emulate the experience of one-on-one tutoring, offering feedback and guidance that would otherwise be unavailable in large, crowded classrooms.

13.1.4. Natural Language Processing for Language Learning

Natural language processing (NLP), a branch of AI focusing on the interaction between computers and human language, is another powerful tool AI-powered educational platforms use. NLP enables platforms to analyze and process text, allowing feedback on real-time writing, grammar, and language use. This has significant implications for language learning. Platforms like *Duolingo* and *Rosetta Stone* use AI and NLP to provide language learners with personalized lessons, corrections, and practice exercises. The AI engine can identify areas where learners struggle and adjust the difficulty level accordingly. Moreover,

AI-driven language platforms allow students to practice speaking and writing in their target language, offering real-time corrections and pronunciation tips.

13.1.5. AI-Driven Collaboration and Communication Tools

AI-powered educational platforms also enhance collaboration and communication between students and teachers. AI can facilitate peer-to-peer learning and group work by matching students with similar interests or complementary skills. Platforms like *Google Classroom* and *Microsoft Teams for Education* integrate AI tools to support group projects, discussions, and collaborative assignments. AI can help teachers monitor group dynamics and assess the effectiveness of collaboration, providing insights into how students work together and where improvements can be made. Additionally, AI tools can facilitate communication by enabling real-time translation, allowing students from different linguistic backgrounds to collaborate seamlessly.

13.1.6. Data Analytics for Performance Tracking and Insights

AI-powered educational platforms collect vast amounts of data on student interactions, engagement, and performance. This data is analyzed to provide actionable insights for both students and educators. For instance, AI systems track how students interact with learning materials, how long they spend on specific tasks, and where they face difficulties. Platforms like *Edmodo* and *Canvas* use data analytics to offer teachers real-time reports on student performance, highlighting areas where students excel or struggle. These insights help teachers adjust their teaching strategies, provide timely interventions, and offer additional resources where needed. Additionally, AI platforms can predict students' future performance, helping educators identify at-risk students early and take proactive measures to support them.

13.1.7. Scalability and Access to Education

One of the most transformative aspects of AI-powered educational platforms is their ability to scale and offer educational opportunities to a wider audience. Traditional education systems often face challenges in reaching students in remote or underserved areas, but AI-powered platforms can overcome these barriers. Through online learning, AI platforms like *Coursera*, *Udacity*, and *Khan Academy* make high-quality educational content accessible to learners worldwide, regardless of their geographic location or socioeconomic background. These platforms provide learners with access to courses from top universities and institutions, offering education to individuals who might otherwise have limited access to quality learning resources.

Moreover, AI systems are highly adaptable to different learning environments, including mobile learning. Many AI-driven educational platforms are designed to be mobile-friendly, enabling learners to access educational content from smartphones and tablets. This increases accessibility, especially for students in regions with limited access to traditional educational infrastructure. By scaling education through AI, these platforms contribute to closing the global education gap and promoting lifelong learning for individuals of all ages.

13.1.8. Challenges and Ethical Considerations

While AI-powered educational platforms offer immense potential, they raise significant ethical and practical challenges. Data privacy and security are major concerns, as these platforms collect vast amounts of sensitive data about students' performance and behavior. There is also the issue of algorithmic bias, where AI systems may inadvertently reinforce existing biases in education, such as gender or racial disparities. Moreover, the widespread adoption of AI in education raises questions about the role of educators and the potential for AI to replace human teaching altogether. Ethical considerations regarding data usage, fairness, and transparency in AI algorithms are critical areas that must be addressed to ensure that these platforms benefit all learners equitably.

AI-powered educational platforms are at the forefront of transforming the educational landscape, offering personalized, efficient, and accessible learning experiences for students worldwide. From intelligent tutoring systems and personalized learning paths to real-time feedback and data analytics, AI is helping educators meet the diverse needs of learners while enhancing the overall learning experience. However, as these technologies continue to evolve, it is essential to address the ethical challenges surrounding data privacy, bias, and access to ensure that AI in education empowers rather than hinders educational progress.

13.2. Examples of Leading AI Learning Tools

AI-powered learning tools are increasingly transforming education by personalizing learning experiences, automating administrative tasks, and enhancing student engagement. These tools leverage artificial intelligence to create adaptive, efficient, scalable learning environments that benefit students and educators. Here are some leading AI learning tools that are at the forefront of transforming education:

13.2.1. Duolingo

Duolingo is a language-learning platform that uses AI to personalize lessons based on individual performance. It incorporates natural language processing (NLP) to help users learn a variety of languages through interactive exercises, quizzes, and speech recognition. AI algorithms assess users' proficiency and adapt the difficulty of tasks to ensure that learners are constantly challenged but not overwhelmed. Duolingo's personalized learning paths help students retain vocabulary and grammar, providing instant feedback and tracking their progress over time. The platform's gamification elements, including points and levels, motivate students to continue learning, making language acquisition an engaging experience.

13.2.2. Knewton

Knewton is a personalized adaptive learning platform that uses AI algorithms to tailor educational content to meet the needs of individual students. By continuously tracking student progress and interactions with learning materials, Knewton adjusts lesson difficulty in real-time, ensuring that learners are appropriately challenged. The platform also collects data on student performance, providing valuable insights for educators to monitor progress and intervene when necessary. Knewton is used in various subjects, including mathematics, science, and language arts, and has been integrated into textbooks and learning management systems to enhance traditional learning environments.

13.2.3. Carnegie Learning

Carnegie Learning offers an AI-powered math tutoring platform that helps students learn mathematics through personalized, one-on-one tutoring experiences. The system uses AI to diagnose individual student needs and deliver targeted practice problems based on real-time data about student performance. Its "MATHia" software provides interactive lessons and step-by-step feedback, guiding students through mathematical problems and concepts. Carnegie Learning's AI-driven platform has been shown to improve student performance by offering a personalized approach that adapts to each student's learning style and pace.

13.2.4. Quizlet

Quizlet is a learning tool that leverages AI to help students study using flashcards and other customizable study tools. The platform uses machine learning algorithms to track learners' progress, providing personalized study plans that adjust based on the learner's strengths and weaknesses. It also includes features like "Quizlet Learn," which uses AI to create personalized quizzes based on the material the student needs to study most. Quizlet offers interactive learning experiences and has integrated features like voice recognition and automatic feedback to aid students in their learning journey.

13.2.5. Smart Sparrow

Smart Sparrow is an adaptive learning platform that allows educators to create personalized learning experiences for their students. The platform uses AI to analyze learner behaviors and performance, then adapts the content in real-time to suit individual needs. Smart Sparrow helps instructors identify learning gaps and intervene with tailored resources by providing insights into how students engage with the material. It is used widely in higher education, particularly in science, engineering, and mathematics courses.

13.2.6. Socratic by Google

Socratic is an AI-powered educational app developed by Google that uses natural language processing and computer vision to help students with homework. The app allows students to take pictures of homework problems, and the AI system processes the images to provide step-by-step solutions. It also offers explanations, videos, and additional resources to deepen students' understanding of the topic. Socratic AI is designed to adapt to the student's learning style and help guide them through challenging problems in various subjects, such as mathematics, science, literature, and history.

13.2.7. Edmentum

Edmentum offers a suite of AI-powered learning tools that cater to students across K-12 and beyond. The platform provides personalized, adaptive learning pathways for students, with real-time data that helps educators tailor content to the needs of individual learners. The AI algorithms analyze student performance across various subjects and provide recommendations for improvement, helping students develop skills at their own pace. Edmentum's platform integrates assessments, virtual tutoring, and multimedia resources to engage learners and support educators in delivering personalized education.

13.2.8. Cognii

Cognii offers an AI-driven interactive and personalized learning platform that uses natural language processing to assess student responses. Unlike traditional multiple-choice tests, Cognii's system evaluates open-ended answers, providing detailed, formative feedback to students. This tool helps students improve critical thinking and writing skills, as the AI offers suggestions for improving the clarity and depth of responses. It is primarily used in higher education for subjects like humanities, business, and social sciences

13.2.9. Khan Academy

Khan Academy, one of the most well-known educational platforms, uses AI to personalize the learning experience for students. The platform provides free online courses in subjects like math, science, history, and economics. Through the use of AI, Khan Academy tailors the pace and difficulty of exercises to the individual student, helping them build skills progressively. The system's algorithms track student performance, suggest lessons, and provide targeted exercises to reinforce learning. Khan Academy's vast content library and adaptive tools make it a widely accessible learning resource for students worldwide.

AI-powered educational tools are reshaping the learning landscape, offering students personalized, adaptive, and engaging learning experiences. These tools help bridge educational gaps by tailoring learning to individual needs, automating administrative tasks, and providing real-time feedback. Whether through intelligent tutoring, personalized learning platforms, or AI-driven assessment, these tools enhance educational access, improve learning outcomes, and prepare students for a rapidly evolving digital world. As AI advances, the potential for these tools to revolutionize education will only grow, ensuring that learning becomes more effective, inclusive, and accessible to all.

13.3. Trends in EdTech Startups

The educational technology (EdTech) sector has rapidly evolved over the past few years, with startups driving much of this transformation. These companies leverage technological advancements to enhance learning experiences, streamline educational processes, and improve accessibility. Several key trends in EdTech startups are shaping the future of education, ranging from AI integration and personalized learning to immersive technologies and blockchain-based credentials.

13.3.1. Artificial Intelligence and Personalized Learning

One of the most significant trends in EdTech startups is integrating artificial intelligence (AI) to create personalized learning experiences. AI enables adaptive learning platforms that tailor educational content to students' individual needs, analyzing their performance and learning styles in real time. Startups are developing AI-powered tutoring systems, chatbots, and learning management systems (LMS) that adjust content delivery based on a student's progress, helping them work at their own pace and overcome specific challenges. Companies like Duolingo and Knewton are pioneers in this space, offering AI-driven tools that personalize the learning experience.

AI is also helping automate administrative tasks, such as grading and assessments, allowing teachers to focus more on student engagement and interactive learning. This trend towards AI-driven education makes learning more efficient and scalable, providing students with targeted interventions previously unavailable in traditional classroom settings.

13.3.2. Gamification and Immersive Learning

EdTech startups increasingly incorporate gamification and immersive learning technologies to make education more engaging. Gamification, which involves the integration of game mechanics such as rewards, levels, and leaderboards into learning processes, has proven to boost student motivation and retention. Companies like Kahoot! and Quizlet have successfully gamified their platforms, making learning fun while encouraging student competition and collaboration.

In addition to gamification, immersive technologies like virtual reality (VR) and augmented reality (AR) are gaining traction in EdTech. These technologies provide students with experiential learning opportunities that simulate real-world environments. Startups such as ClassVR and Labster use VR to create virtual science labs and simulations, allowing students to explore complex concepts safely and interactively. Immersive learning environments are more engaging and enhance experiential learning, making complex subjects more accessible.

13.3.3. Microlearning and Bite Sized Content

Another trend that is becoming more prevalent among EdTech startups is microlearning, which focuses on delivering small, focused lessons that can be consumed in short bursts of time. This approach aligns with the growing demand for just-in-time learning and offers flexibility for busy students or professionals who need to learn in short intervals. Startups like EdApp and Go1 are capitalizing on this trend, offering platforms that deliver short, mobile-friendly courses on specific skills or topics.

Microlearning has been shown to enhance retention and learning outcomes because it provides content in manageable chunks that are easy to process and remember. The trend toward bite-sized content is being driven by the increasing use of mobile devices for learning. These devices allow users to access learning materials anytime, anywhere, making education more accessible and adaptable to modern lifestyles.

13.3.4. Blockchain for Credentialing and Certifications

Startups in the EdTech space are exploring blockchain technology to address challenges related to credentialing and certification. Blockchain can provide a secure and transparent method for verifying academic credentials, reducing fraud, and improving trust in digital certifications. Companies like Learning Machine and CertifID use blockchain to issue digital diplomas and certificates that employers and educational institutions can easily verify.

Blockchain can also facilitate the transfer of educational records across institutions, allowing students to maintain a lifelong, portable academic history. This could revolutionize how academic achievements are tracked and validated, creating a more efficient and reliable system for credentialing in the digital age.

13.3.5. Collaborative Learning Platforms

Startups also focus on collaborative learning tools that facilitate communication, cooperation and shared learning experiences. These platforms help students work together on projects, exchange ideas, and support each other's learning journeys, regardless of their location. Companies like Slack and Microsoft Teams have already established themselves as collaborative tools in the corporate world, and now startups are adapting these technologies to the educational sector.

Platforms like Flipgrid and Padlet allow students to engage in asynchronous discussions, share multimedia content, and provide feedback to their peers, fostering a sense of community and teamwork. Collaborative learning tools enhance social interaction and encourage peer-to-peer learning, essential for developing critical thinking, problem-solving, and communication skills.

13.3.6. Adaptive Learning Platforms

Adaptive learning is a rapidly growing trend in the EdTech sector. Platforms adjust the content and difficulty level in real time based on a student's learning progress. Startups leverage sophisticated algorithms to analyze data and provide customized learning experiences that meet each student's unique needs. Companies like Smart Sparrow and DreamBox Learning are leading the way in adaptive learning, offering platforms that can tailor the pace and level of content based on individual performance.

This approach ensures that students are neither bored with content that is too easy nor overwhelmed with tasks that are too difficult, creating an optimal learning experience. Adaptive learning also allows for continuous assessment, making it possible for educators to track progress and intervene when necessary.

The EdTech startup ecosystem is continuously evolving, with emerging trends focusing on personalizing education, enhancing engagement, and making learning more accessible and flexible. AI, gamification, microlearning, blockchain, collaborative platforms, and adaptive learning provide a more personalized, immersive, and efficient educational experience. As these trends continue to gain momentum, they promise to reshape the future of education, offering students and educators innovative tools to meet the demands of the digital age.

References

Baker, R. S., & Yacef, K. (2009). *The state of educational data mining in 2009: A review and future visions*. Proceedings of the 2nd International Conference on Educational Data Mining, 1 16.

Baker, R. S., D'Mello, S. K., Rodrigo, M. M. T., & Graesser, A. C. (2019). *Better than humans? The potential of AI-driven education tools. Journal of Educational Psychology*, 111(3), 431-451.

Brynjolfsson, E., & McAfee, A. (2014). *The Second Machine Age: Work, Progress, and Prosperity in a Time of Brilliant Technologies*. W. W. Norton & Company.

Gee, J. P. (2003). What video games have to teach us about learning and literacy. *Computers in Entertainment*, 1(1), 20-20.

Gee, J. P. (2003). What video games have to teach us about learning and literacy. *Computers in Entertainment*, 1(1), 20-20.

Hug, T. (2005). Microlearning: A new pedagogical challenge. In H. H. Schmidt (Ed.), *Proceedings of the European Distance Education Network* (EDEN), 49-55.

Hug, T. (2005). Microlearning: A new pedagogical challenge. In H. H. Schmidt (Ed.), *Proceedings of the European Distance Education Network (EDEN),* 49-55.

Johnson, D. W., Johnson, R. T., & Holubec, E. J. (2008). *Cooperation in the classroom. Interaction Book Company.*

Johnson, D. W., Johnson, R. T., & Holubec, E. J. (2008). *Cooperation in the classroom. Interaction Book Company.*

Kerr, R. (2014). Edmentum's approach to personalized learning in K-12 education. *Journal of Online Learning and Teaching*, 10(3), 189-205.

Kerr, R. (2014). Edmentum's approach to personalized learning in K-12 education. *Journal of Online Learning and Teaching*, 10(3), 189-205.

Khan, S. (2012). The One World Schoolhouse: *Education Reimagined.* Twelve.

Kumar, S., & Parikh, S. (2019). Cognii: AI for educational feedback and assessment. *Journal of Educational Technology*, 56(6), 40-50.

Luckin, R., Holmes, W., Griffiths, M., & Forcier, L. B. (2016). *Intelligence Unleashed: An Argument for AI in Education.* Pearson Education.

Mouza, C., & Lavigne, N. (2020). AI in education: The future of personalized learning. *Educational Technology Research and Development*, 68(4), 849-872.

Pane, J. F., Steiner, E. D., Baird, M. D., & Hamilton, L. S. (2015). *Continued Progress: Promising Evidence on Personalized Learning.* RAND Corporation.

Siu, K. W., & Vredenburg, K. (2020). *Socratic by Google: Helping students learn with AI. Interaction Design and Children,* 1-10.

Tapscott, D., & Tapscott, A. (2016). *Blockchain revolution: How the technology behind Bitcoin and other cryptocurrencies is changing the world.* Penguin.

Tapscott, D., & Tapscott, A. (2016). *Blockchain revolution: How the technology behind Bitcoin and other cryptocurrencies is changing the world.* Penguin.

VanLehn, K. (2011). The relative effectiveness of human tutoring, intelligent tutoring systems, and other tutoring systems. *Educational Psychologist*, 46(4), 197-221.

VanLehn, K. (2013). The relative effectiveness of human tutoring, intelligent tutoring systems, and other tutoring systems. *Educational Psychologist*, 46(4), 197-221.

VanLehn, K. (2013). The relative effectiveness of human tutoring, intelligent tutoring systems, and other tutoring systems. *Educational Psychologist*, 46(4), 197-221.

Vesselinov, R., & Grego, J. (2012). *Duolingo effectiveness study.* City University of New York.

Woolf, B. P. (2010). *Building intelligent interactive tutors: Student-centered strategies for learning.* Elsevier.

Woolf, B. P. (2010*). Building intelligent interactive tutors: Student-centered strategies for learning.* Elsevier.

Chapter 14

AI in Research and Knowledge Production

14.1. Introduction

Artificial Intelligence (AI) is not just a tool, but a transformative force that is reshaping the landscape of research and knowledge production. It is facilitating faster, more accurate, and more efficient ways of generating new insights across disciplines. By leveraging machine learning, natural language processing (NLP), data mining, and other AI technologies, researchers can tackle complex problems, analyze large datasets, and connect disparate fields that would have been challenging or time-consuming through traditional methods. The integration of AI into the research process is leading to innovations that are transforming how knowledge is generated, disseminated, and applied in various academic and practical domains.

14.1.1. Enhancing Data Analysis and Big Data Processing

One of the most significant contributions of AI in research is its ability to handle and process vast amounts of data, thereby significantly speeding up the research process. In fields like genomics, climate science, and social sciences, researchers are dealing with large datasets that require sophisticated tools for analysis. Traditional data analysis methods may struggle with such data's scale, complexity, and variability. AI technologies, particularly machine learning algorithms, have proven to be invaluable in extracting patterns, identifying trends, and generating predictive models from large datasets (Jordan & Mitchell, 2015). AI's capacity to automate data processing and identify meaningful insights accelerates the research process, reducing the time needed to make discoveries.

In fields like healthcare and drug discovery, AI-driven algorithms have demonstrated the ability to analyze patient data and biological information much faster than human researchers. For example, AI models can predict disease outbreaks or assist in discovering new treatments by analyzing molecular data. The ability to process complex datasets speeds up research and opens new discoveries that would have been impossible without AI (Aliper et al., 2016).

14.1.2. Natural Language Processing in Knowledge Discovery

Natural Language Processing (NLP) is another area where AI reshapes research and knowledge production. NLP enables computers to understand, interpret, and generate human language, particularly useful for analyzing academic texts, scientific articles, and patents. Researchers can use AI-powered tools to scan large volumes of literature and identify relevant papers, extract key concepts, or even summarize findings. This is particularly useful for systematic reviews, literature surveys, and meta-analyses, which are essential in various research fields (Blei et al., 2003).

AI applications like text mining and sentiment analysis can also detect emerging trends and topics in a given field, facilitating knowledge discovery. These tools can analyze patterns in research publications, highlight underexplored areas, and suggest new directions for inquiry. Furthermore, AI-powered systems like Semantic Scholar and Google Scholar use NLP to make academic papers more discoverable, allowing researchers to quickly find relevant studies and keep up with the latest field advancements (Huang et al., 2018).

14.1.3. Automating Literature Reviews and Synthesis

AI is also enhancing the process of synthesizing and summarizing large volumes of academic literature. Traditionally, literature reviews are time-consuming processes where researchers must manually review, categorize, and summarize existing work. However, AI tools can automate this process by categorizing studies, identifying key themes, and even generating preliminary conclusions (Salton & McGill, 1983). This is particularly useful in multidisciplinary research areas, where reviewing literature across various fields can be overwhelming for researchers. AI-based systems can cross-reference publications, organize research by topic, and even suggest missing links or contradictory findings in existing literature.

In addition to speeding up the literature review process, AI tools are significantly improving its accuracy and comprehensiveness. They can identify publications that might otherwise be overlooked due to human biases or gaps in research. Researchers are already using tools like Rayyan to speed up systematic reviews, particularly in fields like healthcare and social sciences, by employing machine learning algorithms to rank and organize articles based on relevance and quality (Ouzzani et al., 2016). This not only accelerates the research process but also ensures that the research is more accurate and reliable.

14.1.4. AI in Interdisciplinary Research

AI also contributes to advancing interdisciplinary research by making it easier to integrate knowledge across different domains. In fields such as environmental science, AI algorithms can combine data from diverse sources, such as climate models, satellite imagery, and socio-economic data, to generate insights that were previously difficult to achieve with traditional methods. For example, AI models are used in climate science to analyze atmospheric data and predict weather patterns or assess the impact of climate change on biodiversity (Bierwirth et al., 2020).

AI tools can support collaboration in interdisciplinary research projects by identifying knowledge gaps across disciplines, linking relevant research from different fields, and facilitating communication between researchers from diverse backgrounds. Startups and academic institutions are using AI to bridge gaps in knowledge production, fostering collaborations between scientists, technologists, and policymakers to solve complex global challenges.

14.1.5. AI-Driven Peer Review and Academic Publishing

AI is transforming the academic publishing process, particularly in peer review and manuscript evaluation. Traditional peer review is often criticized for being slow, biased, and inconsistent. AI-based systems are now being used to streamline the review process by automating the detection of plagiarism, checking for statistical rigor, and even suggesting reviewers based on the manuscript's subject matter (Harnad, 2003). AI-powered tools can also assist in evaluating the quality of manuscripts by analyzing writing style, ensuring that they meet academic standards and are free from common errors.

Furthermore, AI can assist in identifying trends within published research and provide scholars with insights into how their work fits within the broader academic discourse. This can help researchers refine their hypotheses and improve their contributions to the scientific community.

AI rapidly transforms research and knowledge production by providing powerful tools to analyze large datasets, automate time-consuming processes, and facilitate interdisciplinary collaboration. However, it's important to note that AI is not without its limitations. For instance, AI-powered tools may struggle with understanding the nuances of human language or may introduce biases if not carefully designed. As AI continues to evolve, its role in shaping the future of research and academic discourse will only grow, creating new opportunities for innovation, discovery, and knowledge sharing across disciplines.

14.1.6. Accelerating Academic Research with AI

Artificial Intelligence (AI) is revolutionizing the academic research landscape, accelerating the pace at which new knowledge is discovered and applied across disciplines. AI technologies, including machine learning, natural language processing (NLP), and data mining, enable researchers to process vast datasets, automate repetitive tasks, and uncover patterns that would be challenging to identify using traditional research methods. By reducing the time and effort required for data analysis, literature reviews, and hypothesis generation, AI is accelerating academic research and expanding the potential for groundbreaking discoveries.

14.1.6.1. AI in Data Processing and Analysis

One of the most impactful ways AI accelerates academic research is its ability to handle large volumes of data. In fields such as genomics, climate science, and social sciences, researchers often face complex datasets that would be difficult to process manually. Machine learning algorithms are particularly effective in analyzing big data, detecting trends, and providing insights that may otherwise go unnoticed. For example, AI systems can process genomic sequences or environmental data far beyond human capability, enabling researchers to quickly identify correlations and trends (Jordan & Mitchell, 2015). In areas like drug discovery, AI-driven systems can analyze biological data to identify potential compounds or predict the effectiveness of treatments much faster than traditional methods (Aliper et al., 2016).

Using AI in data processing reduces the time required to generate results and improves the precision of analyses. AI models can also learn from past data, improving their performance over time, which helps refine research findings and predict future outcomes more accurately. In health sciences, for example, AI is used to process patient data, predict disease outbreaks, and assist in personalized treatment plans, all of which contribute to faster advancements in medical research (Esteva et al., 2019).

14.1.6.2. Enhancing Literature Reviews with NLP

AI-powered tools, especially those based on natural language processing (NLP), are streamlining and accelerating the literature review process in academic research. Traditionally, researchers must manually sift through thousands of articles to identify relevant studies, which can be time-consuming and prone to biases. However, AI-powered tools like Rayyan and EndNote, which utilize NLP techniques, allow researchers to automate parts of the literature review process. These systems can identify relevant papers, categorize articles by topic, and highlight important findings based on keyword searches and citation patterns (Ouzzani et al., 2016). Moreover, NLP tools can extract key concepts and summarize large volumes of academic literature, saving researchers considerable time familiarizing themselves with existing research.

By automating the literature review process, AI enables researchers to quickly identify existing knowledge gaps, spot field trends, and generate hypotheses. Furthermore, AI algorithms can track citation patterns and trends over time, allowing researchers to monitor the evolution of research in their area of interest. This accelerates the research cycle, identifying new research opportunities and generating novel ideas (Huang et al., 2018).

14.1.6.3. Automating Hypothesis Generation and Experiment Design

AI enhances the efficiency of data analysis and literature reviews and plays a role in the early stages of research, such as hypothesis generation and experiment design. Machine learning algorithms can analyze existing data to uncover patterns that may suggest new research questions. For instance, AI systems can analyze historical data from clinical trials to identify potential relationships between variables that researchers might not have considered. This assists in hypothesis generation, helping researchers design experiments that are more likely to lead to discoveries (Sutton et al., 2017).

AI also optimizes experimental design by simulating various experimental conditions and predicting outcomes based on previous data. In fields such as material science and chemistry, researchers are using AI to model molecular interactions and predict the behavior of new materials. This significantly reduces the time required to design and test experiments, enabling quicker validation of hypotheses and faster progress toward practical applications (Xie et al., 2018).

14.1.6.4. AI-Driven Collaboration and Interdisciplinary Research

AI also fosters interdisciplinary collaboration, an essential component in accelerating academic research. AI systems can integrate data from various disciplines, allowing researchers from different fields to collaborate more effectively. For example, AI can combine climate science, economics, and sociology data to provide comprehensive insights into global issues such as climate change or economic inequality. By processing and synthesizing information from diverse fields, AI systems enable researchers to see connections and trends they might not have identified independently.

Moreover, AI is enhancing collaboration between academic institutions, research organizations, and industries. AI-powered platforms like ResearchGate and Google Scholar facilitate the exchange of ideas, resources, and data across borders. These platforms enable researchers to access a vast amount of shared knowledge, collaborate on projects, and gain insights from global experts. AI systems also enhance the peer review process, allowing researchers to connect with appropriate reviewers quickly and facilitating a more efficient exchange of ideas and critiques (Harnad, 2003).

14.1.6.5. AI-Enhanced Peer Review and Publishing

AI is also transforming the peer review and academic publishing process. AI tools can help identify appropriate reviewers for manuscripts based on their expertise, reducing the time required to find suitable reviewers and improving the quality of the review process. AI can also be used to check for plagiarism, ensure that manuscripts adhere to submission guidelines, and assess the quality of writing (Swan, 2008). These tools enhance the efficiency of the peer review process, helping to expedite the publication of high-quality research.

Furthermore, AI can assist in tracking research trends and identifying influential publications. By analyzing citation patterns, AI can identify seminal papers in a field and predict future areas of interest. This allows researchers and publishers to stay ahead of emerging trends and focus on groundbreaking research.

AI is a powerful tool that accelerates academic research by automating time-consuming tasks, enhancing data analysis, and fostering collaboration across disciplines. From literature reviews and hypothesis generation to interdisciplinary collaboration and peer review, AI is transforming the research process, enabling faster and more effective knowledge production. As AI advances, its role in academic research will only grow, paving the way for innovations addressing some of the world's most pressing challenges.

14.1.7. Knowledge Graphs and AI-Assisted Insights

Knowledge graphs (KGs) represent a powerful tool for organizing and accessing complex information, and when combined with AI technologies, they offer transformative potential in accelerating academic research and knowledge production. A knowledge graph is a structured representation of knowledge where entities (e.g., people, organizations, concepts) are nodes, and their relationships are edges. These graphs allow for a semantic network of interconnected facts and concepts, making retrieving, inferring, and organizing knowledge easier. When integrated with AI, knowledge graphs can facilitate advanced analytics, uncover hidden relationships, and provide AI-assisted insights that drive research in innovative ways.

14.1.7.1. Knowledge Graphs in Organizing and Structuring Research Data

In the context of academic research, knowledge graphs serve as a critical framework for organizing vast amounts of information. Research papers, datasets, citations, and methodologies can be linked together in a knowledge graph, providing researchers with a map of related knowledge. This enables researchers to identify existing research gaps, trace ideas' evolution, and discover hidden connections between seemingly unrelated topics. For example, in medical research, a knowledge graph can link specific diseases, drug compounds, research studies, clinical trials, and patient outcomes, enabling researchers to gain a deeper understanding of disease mechanisms or treatment efficacy (Soni et al., 2020).

AI systems can enhance the use of knowledge graphs by enabling intelligent search and recommendations based on the graph's structure. By leveraging machine learning techniques, AI can suggest relevant papers, research datasets, or even potential collaborations based on the relationships within the graph, facilitating more efficient knowledge discovery (Zhou et al., 2020). This is particularly valuable in interdisciplinary fields, where researchers may not have the time or expertise to manually search through all available knowledge but can instead rely on AI to suggest relevant connections.

14.1.7.2. AI-Enhanced Inference and Discovery in Research

AI can provide significant value in generating insights from knowledge graphs by applying advanced machine learning techniques to infer new knowledge and discover hidden patterns. AI algorithms, particularly those based on deep learning and natural language processing, can identify patterns and relationships in data that might not be immediately obvious to researchers. For instance, AI can analyze large-scale scientific literature and propose hypotheses by detecting correlations between research papers, data, and existing findings (West, 2019). These AI-assisted insights can guide researchers in refining their research questions, designing experiments, or identifying new areas of investigation.

In domains such as drug discovery, AI-powered knowledge graphs are used to identify potential interactions between compounds and diseases. By mapping known interactions and leveraging AI to extrapolate additional possibilities, researchers can uncover novel therapeutic targets that may have otherwise remained unexplored. AI can also assist in predicting protein structures or in simulating the impact of various compounds on biological systems, accelerating the drug development process (Vamathevan et al., 2019). Through such processes, knowledge graphs enriched with AI facilitate more rapid discovery and foster the development of entirely new research avenues.

14.1.7.3. Improved Knowledge Accessibility with AI-Driven Search

One of the most compelling applications of knowledge graphs combined with AI is improving knowledge accessibility through intelligent search tools. Traditional search engines in academic research often rely on keyword matching, which can miss valuable connections or context. By contrast, AI-enabled search powered by knowledge graphs allows researchers to perform semantic searches, retrieving relevant information based on the meaning of the terms, relationships, and context rather than exact matches.

For example, AI can help researchers query a knowledge graph with a question or topic and find not only the most directly related research papers but also peripheral works that might offer useful perspectives, methodologies, or applications. By leveraging the relationships encoded within the graph, AI systems can deliver more relevant and context-aware results, greatly enhancing the efficiency and scope of literature reviews (Fang et al., 2020). This AI-driven search capability is increasingly being integrated into academic databases such as Google Scholar and Semantic Scholar, which allow researchers to search not just by keywords but also by concepts, citations, and relationships between papers.

14.1.7.4. Supporting Collaboration and Network Building

Another powerful feature of AI-powered knowledge graphs is their ability to foster collaboration and network-building among researchers. By mapping out relationships between concepts and research and between researchers, institutions, and funding bodies, knowledge graphs can reveal who is working on related topics and where potential collaborations might emerge. AI can enhance this process by identifying commonalities in research focus, methodologies, or even geographic locations, suggesting partners for joint research projects or co-authoring opportunities (Liu et al., 2021).

For instance, the AI-driven network analysis of a knowledge graph could identify a researcher in a distant part of the world whose work aligns with a researcher's current project, offering a pathway for international collaboration. Furthermore, AI systems can track the impact of collaborations by analyzing citation patterns, co-authorship networks, and the dissemination of research results, thus fostering a global academic community (Börner et al., 2018).

14.1.7.5. Knowledge Graphs in Policy and Decision-Making

In addition to accelerating academic research, AI-enhanced knowledge graphs can support policymaking and decision-making. By representing a wide range of knowledge sources, including academic research, government reports, and expert opinions, knowledge graphs can help policymakers better understand complex issues, such as climate change, economic inequality, or public health crises. AI can provide insights by analyzing relationships between policies, outcomes, and external factors, enabling more informed and effective decisions (Mayer-Schönberger & Cukier, 2013).

In climate science, for example, AI-enhanced knowledge graphs can link data on emissions, climate models, policy interventions, and economic impacts, enabling decision-makers to simulate the effects of various strategies. Similarly, AI-powered systems can support sustainable development research by connecting environmental data with social and economic indicators, helping identify holistic solutions to global challenges.

The combination of knowledge graphs and AI is reshaping academic research and enhancing knowledge discovery, organization, and analysis. By enabling smarter, more efficient searches, revealing hidden patterns and relationships, and facilitating collaboration, these technologies are accelerating the pace of research across a wide range of disciplines. As AI continues to evolve, integrating knowledge graphs will become even more essential in fostering innovation, streamlining workflows, and enabling researchers to address some of the most pressing global challenges.

References

Aliper, A., Sergey Plis, Artem Artemov et al. (2016). Deep learning applications for predicting pharmacological properties of drugs and drug repurposing. *Journal of Pharmacology and Experimental Therapeutics*, 357(3), 435-443.

Bierwirth, S., et al. (2020). Artificial intelligence in environmental science: A comprehensive review. *Environmental Science and Technology*, 54(9), 5670-5682.

Blei, D. M., Andrew Y. Ng, Michael I. Jordan. (2003). Latent Dirichlet Allocation. *Journal of Machine Learning Research*, 3, 993-1022.

Börner, K., et al. (2018). The impact of collaboration on research productivity: A network science approach. *Science Advances*, 4(7), eaao0241.

Esteva, A., Alexandre Robicquet, Bharath Ramsundar, Volodymyr Kuleshov, et al. (2019). A guide to deep learning in healthcare. *Nature Medicine*, 25(1), 24-29.

Fang, M., et al. (2020). AI-powered search engines for academic research: Improving knowledge discovery with knowledge graphs. *Journal of Information Science*, 46(5), 650-662.

Harnad, S. (2003). The archive: A response to peer review. *Science*, 300(5619), 741-742.

Huang, Z. et al. (2018). Exploring the usage of natural language processing in scientific literature mining. *Journal of Computer Science and Technology*, 33(5), 1059-1074.

Jordan, M. I., & Mitchell, T. M. (2015). Machine learning: Trends, perspectives, and prospects. *Science,* 349(6245), 255-260.

Liu, W., et al. (2021). Building research networks with AI-powered knowledge graphs: A case study in health sciences. *Health Informatics Journal*, 27(3), 356-369.

Mayer-Schönberger, V., & Cukier, K. (2013). *Big data: A revolution that will transform how we live, work, and think*. John Murray.

Ouzzani, M., Hossam Hammady, Zbys Fedorowicz, Ahmed Elmagarmid. (2016). Rayyan – A web and mobile app for systematic reviews. *Systematic Reviews,* 5, 210.

Salton, G., & McGill, M. J. (1983). *Introduction to modern information retrieval*. McGraw-Hill.

Soni, D., Ravi K. Gupta, Vijayakumar V. V., Sandeep G., et al. (2020). Using knowledge graphs in healthcare: Applications, challenges, and opportunities. *Journal of Healthcare Informatics Research*, 4(2), 189-202.

Sutton, R. S., Andrew G. Barto. (2017). *Reinforcement learning: An introduction*. MIT Press.

Swan, A. (2008). *The Open Access Landscape: A Review of the Current Situation*. Ariadne, 55.

Vamathevan, J., Dominic Clark, Paul Czodrowski, Ian Dunham, et al. (2019). Applications of machine learning in drug discovery and development. *Nature Reviews Drug Discovery,* 18(6), 319-337.

West, J. D. (2019). The role of AI and machine learning in academic research: Enhancing discovery through automated knowledge networks. *AI & Society*, 34(2), 317-325.

Xie, L., et al. (2018). Accelerating material discovery by artificial intelligence. *Joule*, 2(7), 1313-1323.

Zhou, Q., et al. (2020). AI-powered knowledge graphs for academic research: A systematic review. *International Journal of Digital Innovation*, 5(3), 45-61.

Chapter 15

AI for Soft Skills and Emotional Intelligence

15.1. Introduction

The integration of Artificial Intelligence (AI) into education and workforce development has revolutionized technical skill acquisition and paved the way for advancements in the cultivation of soft skills and emotional intelligence (EI). Soft skills, which include communication, teamwork, leadership, problem-solving, and adaptability, are essential for personal and professional success, particularly in the evolving landscape of the global workforce. Emotional intelligence, the ability to recognize, understand, and manage emotions in oneself and others, is crucial in fostering interpersonal relationships and effective decision-making in both professional and educational settings.

AI technologies are increasingly being used to support the development of these skills through tailored learning experiences, emotional recognition, and adaptive learning environments. The potential of AI in enhancing soft skills and EI is vast. It offers personalized interventions, data-driven insights, and real-time feedback that can significantly improve the emotional and interpersonal capabilities of learners and professionals, empowering them to grow and excel in their personal and professional lives.

15.1.1. AI-Powered Emotional Recognition and Feedback

AI technologies, particularly those utilizing Natural Language Processing (NLP) and affective computing, can assess and interpret emotional states in real time. This is achieved by analyzing facial expressions, voice tone, body language, and text input, allowing AI systems to recognize emotional cues and provide feedback accordingly (Picard et al., 2001). In educational and professional settings, this technology can be used to monitor and improve interactions, offering users insight into how they come across emotionally in conversations or presentations.

For instance, AI systems can help students or employees refine their communication skills by providing feedback on the emotional tone of their speech, the appropriateness of their expressions, or their ability to manage emotional responses in various scenarios. AI-powered tools such as virtual agents and chatbots can engage in simulated conversations, helping learners practice emotional responses and social interactions in a safe environment, thus improving their ability to navigate complex social situations (Rani et al., 2019).

15.1.2. AI-Enhanced Personalized Learning for Soft Skills Development

AI can tailor learning experiences to the individual, adjusting content and learning pathways based on a learner's progress and emotional state. In the context of soft skills development, AI can provide personalized simulations and role-playing scenarios designed to cultivate specific emotional intelligence competencies, such as empathy, self-regulation, or conflict resolution (D'Mello et al., 2017).

For example, an AI-driven virtual tutor can offer real-time, personalized feedback on students' ability to collaborate in group projects, solve problems, or lead discussions. This AI system serves as a supportive coach, adapting the scenario based on the student's responses and behavior to introduce challenges that will push the learner to grow in specific areas of emotional intelligence or teamwork.

15.1.3. AI for Enhancing Empathy and Social Awareness

Empathy is a critical component of emotional intelligence, and AI can significantly help individuals develop and practice this skill. AI-powered simulations and virtual role-playing scenarios are being used to foster empathy by allowing users to interact with characters in different emotional states or from diverse backgrounds. These interactions enable users to practice recognizing and responding to emotions in others, thereby fostering a sense of social awareness and responsibility.

In professional training, AI systems can simulate challenging interpersonal situations such as customer service interactions, negotiations, or conflict resolution scenarios, where the learner must understand and appropriately respond to the emotions and needs of others. Through these AI-driven experiences, learners can improve their capacity for empathy, which is critical in building strong, collaborative teams and managing interpersonal dynamics in the workplace (Binns et al., 2020).

15.1.4. AI for Leadership Development and Decision-Making

Effective leadership is deeply connected to emotional intelligence, as leaders must manage their emotions while motivating and guiding others. AI has been integrated into leadership training programs to enhance emotional regulation, decision-making, and interpersonal skills required for successful leadership (Goleman, 1998). AI-based tools analyze leaders' actions and decision-making processes to provide insights into their emotional responses, biases, and communication styles.

For example, AI platforms can simulate high-pressure situations where leaders must manage teams, make decisions, and resolve conflicts. AI feedback systems help these leaders develop emotional resilience, assess their emotional responses, and adapt their leadership styles based on the situation's dynamics. Moreover, these systems can also track and improve leaders' ability to read non-verbal cues from team members, enabling them to adjust their approach to motivate better and manage diverse teams (George et al., 2007).

15.1.5. AI for Conflict Resolution and Negotiation

AI tools can also be employed to develop conflict resolution and negotiation skills, which are integral aspects of emotional intelligence. AI simulations of negotiations or disputes can help individuals practice managing their emotions and responding empathetically in high-stakes situations. These tools can analyze a conversation's dynamics, provide emotional tone feedback, suggest alternative strategies for conflict resolution, and even model successful outcomes based on emotionally intelligent responses (Hochschild, 2016). AI-driven systems are increasingly used in corporate training, where employees and managers simulate negotiations, stakeholder engagements, and problem solving discussions. Through these simulated scenarios, users can learn how to manage their emotions, resolve conflicts effectively, and build consensus among diverse stakeholders.

AI-driven systems are increasingly used in corporate training, where employees and managers simulate negotiations, stakeholder engagements, and problem-solving discussions. Through these simulated scenarios, users can learn how to manage emotions, resolve conflicts effectively, and build consensus among diverse stakeholders.

AI holds significant promise for enhancing soft skills and emotional intelligence, essential components of personal and professional success. By providing personalized, adaptive learning experiences, real-time feedback, and simulation-based training, AI tools enable learners to develop empathy, communication, leadership, and conflict-resolution skills. These AI-driven interventions are increasingly being integrated into education and workforce development programs, offering an opportunity to better prepare individuals for the challenges of an interconnected, rapidly changing world. As AI continues to evolve, its role in nurturing emotional intelligence and soft skills will likely expand, contributing to a more emotionally intelligent and collaborative society.

15.1.6. Virtual Reality (VR) and AI for Behavioral Training

The convergence of Virtual Reality (VR) and Artificial Intelligence (AI) opens new frontiers in behavioral training, offering immersive, interactive, and highly personalized learning experiences. These technologies are increasingly utilized across various domains, including education, corporate training, healthcare, and public safety, to enhance behavior modification, social skills development, and emotional intelligence. VR creates lifelike, simulated environments that allow users to engage in real-world scenarios. At the same time, AI provides adaptive, data-driven insights that personalize the experience, making training more effective, engaging, and responsive to individual needs. Together, VR and AI form a powerful duo in shaping behavior, learning processes, and emotional responses in a way that traditional training methods cannot.

15.1.6.1. Immersive Behavioral Training with VR

VR allows learners to practice various behaviors in simulated, lifelike environments, from customer service interactions to leadership skills and conflict resolution. This immersion into realistic scenarios makes VR a powerful tool for behavioral training because it enables users to experience and interact with complex situations in real time. Unlike conventional classroom training or video-based learning, VR provides an interactive space where individuals can physically move, interact, and respond to challenges, closely mirroring real-life experiences (Durlak et al., 2011).

For example, VR is widely used in healthcare training to help medical professionals develop and refine their interpersonal skills, such as delivering bad news or managing patient emotions. In these simulations, the learner can interact with virtual patients or colleagues, receiving real-time feedback based on their responses and behaviors. This hands-on experience significantly improves the retention of soft skills and helps individuals build confidence in handling high-stakes situations (Baños et al., 2013). Similarly, VR has proven beneficial for social skills training, particularly for individuals with autism spectrum disorder (ASD). It allows them to practice social interactions in a safe, controlled, and non-judgmental space (Kandalaft et al., 2013).

15.1.6.2. AI-Driven Personalization in Behavioral Training

AI's ability to analyze vast amounts of data in real time allows it to personalize the VR training experience, making it more effective for each individual. Through AI, VR environments can adapt to the learner's progress, emotional state, and behavior during training, adjusting the complexity and intensity of scenarios based on real-time performance (D'Mello et al., 2017). For example, in leadership training, AI can track the learner's responses in various situational simulations, such as managing team conflicts or motivating employees. Based on their decisions, AI can provide tailored feedback and suggest areas for improvement, such as adjusting communication styles, managing stress, or fostering collaboration (Steinhauer, 2021).

In emotional intelligence, AI algorithms can monitor physiological data, such as heart rate or facial expressions, to assess emotional reactions during VR-based behavioral scenarios. If a learner becomes stressed or frustrated, AI can adjust the scenario, offering calming exercises, additional support, or a pause in the simulation. This level of personalization ensures that each learner receives the guidance they need at their own pace, enhancing the effectiveness of behavioral training programs (Rani et al., 2019).

15.1.6.3. Behavioral Training in High-Risk Environments

One of the most compelling applications of VR and AI in behavioral training is in high-risk industries, such as aviation, military, and emergency response. These sectors require individuals to perform under pressure, manage complex situations, and make critical decisions quickly. Combined with AI, VR-based training provides a safe environment where trainees can experience high-stress scenarios without real-world consequences. For example, AI-powered VR simulations can replicate the psychological stress of a life-threatening emergency, allowing trainees to practice decision-making, teamwork, and leadership under pressure (Salas et al., 2015).

AI can also track trainees' physiological and cognitive responses in these high-stakes scenarios, analyzing how they manage stress and their decision-making process. AI can then adjust the training conditions based on the learner's performance, providing tailored guidance to help improve resilience and emotional regulation in high-pressure environments (Goleman, 1998). These AI-driven adjustments make VR-based behavioral training more effective, helping learners build the necessary skills to excel in real-world crises.

15.1.6.4. AI and VR for Behavioral Health and Therapy

AI and VR have significant potential in behavioral health, particularly for therapy and treatment of mental health conditions such as anxiety, post-traumatic stress disorder (PTSD), and phobias. AI-powered VR applications are being used in exposure therapy, where individuals are gradually exposed to stress-inducing scenarios in a controlled virtual environment. AI can track the user's emotional responses during these scenarios, providing real-time feedback and adjusting the intensity of the exposure based on the user's progress.

This combination of VR and AI benefits individuals who struggle to engage in traditional face-to-face therapy. VR offers a more immersive, less intimidating environment, while AI ensures that the therapy is tailored to each individual's needs, providing personalized interventions and progress tracking (Freeman et al., 2017). By creating realistic and emotionally engaging scenarios, AI and VR can help individuals confront their fears and develop coping mechanisms in a safe and controlled environment.

Integrating Virtual Reality (VR) and Artificial Intelligence (AI) in behavioral training offers a transformative approach to personal development and skill-building. By immersing learners in lifelike scenarios and leveraging AI for personalized feedback, these technologies enable individuals to develop emotional intelligence, manage stress, and enhance communication, leadership, and conflict resolution skills. Whether applied in high-risk industries, therapeutic settings, or corporate environments, VR and AI hold immense potential to create adaptive, scalable, and impactful training solutions. As these technologies evolve, their role in behavioral training is expected to expand, offering more sophisticated, interactive, and individualized learning experiences that prepare individuals for real-world challenges.

15.1.7. AI-Driven Emotional Analytics

AI-driven emotional analytics refers to using artificial intelligence technologies to identify, interpret, and understand human emotions through analyzing various data inputs, such as facial expressions, speech patterns, physiological responses, and behavioral data. This innovative approach leverages machine learning, natural language processing (NLP), computer vision, and other AI techniques to assess emotional states and provide insights that can be used in diverse fields like education, healthcare, marketing, customer service, and personal development. By analyzing these emotional cues, AI systems can offer real-time feedback, identify trends, and predict future emotional states, allowing for more personalized and effective interactions.

15.1.7.1. Foundations of AI-Driven Emotional Analytics

AI-driven emotional analytics relies on several key AI technologies, with machine learning (ML) algorithms central to the process. These algorithms are trained on vast datasets of emotional expressions, speech patterns, and physiological responses to develop models that accurately recognize emotions such as happiness, sadness, anger, fear, and surprise. For example, facial recognition software can analyze microexpressions or changes in facial muscle movements, while speech analysis tools can identify vocal tone, pitch, and pace to infer emotional states (Schaefer et al., 2012). Additionally, AI algorithms monitor and interpret physiological signals such as heart rate, skin conductance, and brainwave patterns to assess emotional arousal and engagement levels (Picard et al., 2011).

Deep learning techniques allow AI systems to continually improve their emotional recognition capabilities over time as they process more data. This makes AI-driven emotional analytics a dynamic and increasingly accurate method for understanding and responding to human emotions.

15.1.7.2. Applications of AI-Driven Emotional Analytics

AI-driven emotional analytics is already used in various sectors to enhance user experience, improve mental health outcomes, and optimize customer interactions. AI tools can assess students' emotional states during learning, enabling educators to respond more effectively to disengagement or frustration. For instance, AI can monitor facial expressions or analyze voice tone to detect stress or confusion, allowing instructors to adapt their teaching methods accordingly (D'Mello & Graesser, 2015). This real-time emotional feedback helps create personalized learning experiences, improving engagement and academic performance.

In mental health care, AI-driven emotional analytics is used in therapeutic settings to monitor patients' emotional states and adjust interventions accordingly. AI can be integrated into virtual therapists or chatbots that assess patients' emotions through text or speech input, providing immediate emotional support or escalating care when necessary. By continually tracking emotional responses, these systems can help detect early signs of mental health issues like depression, anxiety, or PTSD (Fitzpatrick et al., 2017). For example, AI-driven tools like Woebot, a therapeutic chatbot, use natural language processing to assess users' emotional states and provide guided interventions based on cognitive behavioral therapy (CBT) principles (Fitzpatrick et al., 2017).

15.1.7.3. Enhancing Customer Experience and Marketing

AI-driven emotional analytics is also making significant strides in customer experience (CX) and marketing, where it is used to tailor products, services, and advertisements based on emotional engagement. By analyzing customer sentiment, brands can better understand consumer preferences and improve the customer journey. For example, AI tools can track facial expressions, voice tone, and even body language during interactions with customer service agents to determine the customer's emotional state, helping agents respond more empathetically (Homburg et al., 2017). This emotional insight leads to improved customer satisfaction and loyalty.

Moreover, in marketing, AI systems can analyze consumer emotions in response to advertisements, helping marketers craft more effective messaging. By gauging emotional reactions in real time, AI can provide insights into the effectiveness of different campaigns, guiding the creation of content that resonates with specific emotional triggers, such as happiness, nostalgia, or excitement (Liu et al., 2018). Leading brands are increasingly adopting this personalized, emotion-based approach to marketing to drive engagement and conversion rates.

15.1.7.4. Ethical Considerations and Challenges

While AI-driven emotional analytics holds tremendous promise, it raises significant ethical concerns, particularly around privacy, consent, and the potential for misuse. Collecting and analyzing sensitive, emotional data can infringe on individuals' privacy if safeguards are not in place. For instance, emotional data from facial recognition or physiological sensors can reveal personal feelings and psychological conditions that individuals may not wish to disclose. Ethical frameworks must ensure that individuals are fully informed about the data being collected, how it is being used, and how it will be protected.

Moreover, there are concerns about bias in AI systems used for emotional analytics. AI models may be trained on datasets that do not adequately represent diverse demographic groups, leading to inaccurate or biased emotional assessments. For example, facial recognition systems may misinterpret emotional expressions across different cultures or ethnic groups, resulting in flawed analytics (Buolamwini & Gebru, 2018). Addressing these issues requires improving the diversity and inclusivity of training data and developing transparent and accountable AI models.

15.1.7.5. Future Directions and Potential of Emotional Analytics

The future of AI-driven emotional analytics holds great potential for transforming multiple domains. As AI algorithms become more sophisticated and accurate, emotional analytics will be used in more contexts, from personalized learning and healthcare to smart homes and robotics. For example, AI-powered devices could be integrated into daily life to monitor emotional well-being, alerting individuals to potential mental health concerns before they escalate. Furthermore, emotional analytics will likely play a critical role in the future of human-robot interactions, where AI systems could adapt their behavior based on the user's emotional state, creating more empathetic and responsive machines.

In education, AI-driven emotional analytics can continue to evolve, offering more nuanced insights into learners' emotions and providing customized interventions that improve engagement and motivation. Integrating AI with wearable devices and brain-computer interfaces (BCIs) will further enhance the capacity to monitor emotions, allowing for more sophisticated emotional analytics in real-time. By combining these advances with VR and gamification, educational experiences can be more immersive, engaging, and responsive to emotional cues, creating a more supportive learning environment.

AI-driven emotional analytics is revolutionizing how we understand and respond to human emotions. By harnessing the power of machine learning, computer vision, and natural language processing, AI can offer real-time, personalized insights into emotional states, with applications ranging from education and healthcare to marketing and customer service. However, the ethical challenges surrounding privacy, consent, and bias must be carefully considered to ensure the responsible use of these technologies. As AI continues to improve, the potential for emotional analytics to enhance human well-being, interpersonal interactions, and decision-making processes will only expand, marking an exciting frontier in AI development.

References

Baños, R. M., Botella, C., Rubio, G., & Quero, S. (2013). Virtual reality for the assessment and treatment of anxiety and stress. *Journal of Anxiety Disorders, 27*(5), 457–464. https://doi.org/10.1016/j.janxdis.2013.04.002.

Binns, C., Green, S., & Evans, T. (2020). AI and empathy: Leveraging emotional intelligence for better decision-making in team environments. *Journal of Artificial Intelligence in Education, 21*(4), 345–358.

Buolamwini, J., & Gebru, T. (2018). Gender shades: Intersectional accuracy disparities in commercial gender classification. In *Proceedings of the 1st Conference on Fairness, Accountability, and Transparency* (pp. 77–91). PMLR.

D'Mello, S. K., Graesser, A. C., & Picard, R. W. (2017). Affective computing and intelligent interaction: Enhancing educational experiences through AI. *ACM Transactions on Computer-Human Interaction, 24*(3), 1–27. https://doi.org/10.1145/3079602.

D'Mello, S. K., & Graesser, A. C. (2015). Multimodal detection of engagement in learning. In *Proceedings of the 2015 Conference on Artificial Intelligence in Education* (pp. 233–242). Springer. https://doi.org/10.1007/978-3-319-19773-9_24.

Durlak, J. A., Weissberg, R. P., Dymnicki, A. B., Taylor, R. D., & Schellinger, K. B. (2011). The impact of enhancing students' social and emotional learning: A meta-analysis of school-based universal interventions. *Child Development, 82*(1), 405–432. https://doi.org/10.1111/j.1467-8624.2010.01564.x.

Fitzpatrick, K. K., Darcy, A., & Vierhile, M. (2017). Delivering cognitive behavioral therapy to young adults with emotional distress via smartphone: A randomized controlled trial. *Journal of the American Academy of Child & Adolescent Psychiatry, 56*(10), 823–828. https://doi.org/10.1016/j.jaac.2017.07.007.

Freeman, D., Reeve, S., Robinson, A., Ehlers, A., & Clark, D. M. (2017). Virtual reality in the assessment, understanding, and treatment of mental health disorders. *Psychological Medicine, 47*(14), 2393–2400. https://doi.org/10.1017/S003329171700040X.

George, B., King, E. L., & Roberts, J. L. (2007). The impact of emotional intelligence on leadership effectiveness. *Leadership & Organization Development Journal, 28*(2), 74–95. https://doi.org/10.1108/01437730710726865.

Goleman, D. (1998). *Working with emotional intelligence.* Bantam.

Hochschild, A. R. (2016). Emotional labor: A challenge for conflict resolution in the workplace. *Conflict Resolution Quarterly, 34*(2), 210–225. https://doi.org/10.1002/crq.21165.

Homburg, C., Bucerius, F. G., & Hoyer, W. D. (2017). The impact of customer satisfaction and emotional responses on customer loyalty. *Journal of the Academy of Marketing Science, 45*(6), 735–746. https://doi.org/10.1007/s11747-016-0515-8.

Kandalaft, M. R., Didehbani, N., Krawczyk, D. C., & Allen, T. T. (2013). Virtual reality social cognition training for young adults with high-functioning autism. *Journal of Autism and Developmental Disorders, 43*(1), 1–9. https://doi.org/10.1007/s10803-012-1544-6.

Liu, C., Guo, J., & Shen, B. (2018). Emotional intelligence in marketing: A comprehensive review. *Journal of Business Research, 90,* 379–389. https://doi.org/10.1016/j.jbusres.2018.05.043.

Picard, R. W., Sengers, P., & Cooper, D. (2001). *Affective computing.* MIT Press.

Picard, R. W., Pantic, M., & D'Mello, S. K. (2011). *Affective computing and intelligent interaction.* Springer.

Rani, P., Sharma, K., & Kumar, S. (2019). Emotion detection using AI for improving communication and empathy skills. In *Proceedings of the 2019 International Conference on Artificial Intelligence* (pp. 214–223).

Salas, E., Tannenbaum, S. I., Kraiger, K., & Smith-Jentsch, K. A. (2015). The science of training and development in organizations: What matters in practice. *Psychological Science in the Public Interest, 16*(2), 74–101. https://doi.org/10.1177/1529100615565179.

Schaefer, H., Sager, M., & Steinhauer, M. (2012). A survey on emotion recognition using physiological signals. *International Journal of Affective Computing, 3*(1), 1–20.

Steinhauer, S. (2021). The role of AI in personalized soft skills training: Applications in workforce development. *Journal of Educational Technology, 58*(4), 220–234.

Part V: Challenges and Future Directions

Introduction

AI-driven emotional analytics has made significant strides in understanding and interpreting human emotions across various domains, from healthcare to education and customer service. However, as with any emerging technology, numerous challenges must be addressed to realize its potential fully. These challenges include ethical concerns, the accuracy of emotional recognition, cultural biases, privacy issues, and the complexities of integrating emotional data into real-world applications. Looking ahead, future directions for AI-driven emotional analytics will focus on overcoming these obstacles, improving the technology's capabilities, and expanding its applications across different sectors.

Ethical Concerns and Privacy Issues

One of the primary challenges facing AI-driven emotional analytics is ensuring that emotional data is collected and used ethically. Emotional data, including facial expressions, speech patterns, and physiological signals, can reveal deeply personal aspects of an individual's psychological state. The collection of this data raises concerns about privacy and informed consent. If individuals are unaware that their emotions are being monitored or lack control over how their data is used, this can lead to significant ethical issues.

To address these concerns, frameworks must be established to govern the collection, storage, and usage of emotional data. Clear guidelines must be implemented to ensure that individuals are fully informed about the data being collected and how it will be used. Additionally, robust data protection mechanisms should be developed to safeguard individuals' privacy, ensuring that emotional data is not exploited or misused (Solove, 2021).

Bias and Cultural Sensitivity

AI systems are only as good as the data they are trained on, and the datasets used to train emotional analytics systems often contain biases. These biases can manifest in several ways, including inaccurate emotion recognition for specific demographic groups, especially in terms of ethnicity, gender, and age. For instance, AI models trained predominantly on data from Western societies may struggle to interpret emotions in non-Western populations, leading to misinterpretation and potentially harmful outcomes.

To combat this, future research in AI-driven emotional analytics needs to prioritize diverse and representative datasets. Ensuring that these systems are trained on data that reflects the global diversity of emotional expression will help improve their accuracy and fairness. Additionally, AI developers must engage in cultural sensitivity training and consult with cultural experts when designing emotion-recognition models to minimize biases (Buolamwini & Gebru, 2018).

Accuracy and Reliability

Another significant challenge is the accuracy and reliability of emotion recognition systems. Emotions are complex and subjective experiences, often conveyed through a combination of facial expressions, body language, vocal tone, and physiological signals. AI systems must learn to interpret these cues accurately in real-time, which remains a difficult task.

Current AI models still struggle with recognizing nuanced emotional states, such as mixed emotions or subtle emotional shifts that occur over time. For instance, a person may not always display overt facial expressions, making it harder for AI to detect emotional changes based on visual cues alone. To enhance accuracy, future systems will need to integrate multimodal data sources (e.g., combining facial recognition, speech analysis, and physiological data) to form a more comprehensive and accurate understanding of emotional states. Machine learning techniques, such as deep learning and reinforcement learning, will play a crucial role in improving the system's ability to recognize emotions with greater precision over time (Picard et al., 2011).

Integration with Real-World Applications

While AI-driven emotional analytics holds great promise, integrating these systems into real-world applications presents challenges in terms of usability and acceptance. In education, for example, it can be challenging to integrate emotion-monitoring systems into existing learning management systems (LMS) or classrooms. Teachers may need training to interpret AI-generated emotional feedback, and systems must be in place to ensure the technology enhances learning, rather than making students feel uncomfortable or surveilled.

In healthcare, the application of AI-driven emotional analytics in therapeutic settings must be handled delicately. Mental health professionals may need to be cautious when using AI to monitor patients' emotional states, ensuring that the technology complements, rather than replaces, the human element of care. There is also the challenge of ensuring that AI-driven interventions do not perpetuate mental health stigmas or lead to overreliance on technology instead of human counseling.

To overcome these barriers, AI systems must be designed to be user-friendly, transparent, and easily integrated into existing workflows. Additionally, strong collaborations between AI developers, educators, healthcare professionals, and end-users will be necessary to ensure that the technology is effectively implemented in real-world settings (Fitzpatrick et al., 2017).

The Future of AI-Driven Emotional Analytics

Looking ahead, the future of AI-driven emotional analytics is poised to expand significantly, offering more personalized, responsive, and effective interactions across many domains. In education, the use of AI to monitor and respond to students' emotional states will continue to evolve, enabling more tailored and engaging learning experiences. AI tools will be better equipped to understand the nuances of student emotions, adjusting content delivery, pacing, and instructional strategies based on real-time feedback.

In healthcare, AI will play an increasingly important role in mental health, with emotion-monitoring systems becoming integral to both therapeutic interventions and preventative care. AI-driven emotional analytics may also extend to other industries such as marketing, entertainment, and human-robot interaction, offering personalized experiences based on emotional insights.

Moreover, with advancements in multimodal learning, AI systems will become better at recognizing complex emotional cues and predicting emotional responses, enabling deeper human-AI interactions. The future holds great promise for AI-driven emotional analytics to help bridge the gap between human emotional understanding and machine-based analysis, creating a more empathetic, responsive, and personalized technological ecosystem.

AI-driven emotional analytics has the potential to revolutionize numerous sectors by offering deeper insights into human emotions and enhancing interpersonal interactions. However, challenges remain in terms of privacy, bias, accuracy, and integration into real-world applications. As AI continues to evolve, these challenges must be addressed through improved ethical guidelines, diversified datasets, and the development of more robust AI models. By overcoming these hurdles, AI-driven emotional analytics will play an increasingly central role in enhancing human experiences across education, healthcare, customer service, and beyond. The future of this technology is bright, offering opportunities for more personalized, empathetic, and responsive systems that can cater to the diverse emotional needs of individuals in a variety of contexts.

Chapter 16

Barriers to the Adoption of AI in Education

16.1. Introduction

The adoption of Artificial Intelligence (AI) in education holds immense potential for transforming how teaching and learning occur, but its widespread integration faces several barriers. These challenges span technological, financial, ethical, and societal domains and require careful attention to ensure that AI technologies are deployed effectively and equitably in educational settings. The barriers to AI adoption in education can be categorized into issues related to infrastructure, access and equity, ethical concerns, resistance to change, and the need for professional development. Addressing these barriers is crucial for realizing the transformative potential of AI in education.

16.1.1. Technological Infrastructure and Integration Challenges

One of the primary barriers to the adoption of AI in education is the lack of technological infrastructure in many schools, particularly in low-resource environments. AI-based educational tools often require robust computing hardware, reliable internet access, and advanced software platforms. Many educational institutions, especially in developing countries, face challenges in providing the necessary infrastructure, which can make the deployment of AI tools difficult or impossible.

In addition to hardware and connectivity challenges, integrating AI into existing educational systems requires significant updates to software and learning management systems. Schools may need to invest in infrastructure upgrades, including cloud computing, server capabilities, and real-time data processing systems, to ensure smooth AI functionality. The lack of technical expertise to manage and maintain these systems further complicates the integration process (Mouza et al., 2019).

16.1.2. Equity and Access Issues

Another significant barrier to AI adoption in education is inequity in access to resources. The digital divide between students in wealthy and low-income regions or between urban and rural areas exacerbates the challenges of implementing AI-based education tools. Students in underserved communities often lack access to the necessary devices or internet bandwidth required to benefit from AI-enhanced learning experiences fully. This inequality not only limits access to AI-driven tools but also risks exacerbating existing educational disparities, particularly for marginalized groups.

In addition to access to hardware and connectivity, there is also a disparity in access to high-quality AI content. While AI-powered learning platforms may be available in some well-resourced schools, students in underfunded or rural areas may have limited exposure to these tools. Ensuring that AI tools are accessible to all students, regardless of their socioeconomic status, is a key challenge that must be addressed for AI in education to be truly inclusive (Popenici & Kerr, 2017).

16.1.3. Ethical Concerns and Data Privacy

The integration of AI in education raises significant ethical concerns, particularly around issues of data privacy and surveillance. AI-driven systems collect vast amounts of data from students, including behavioral data, emotional responses, and academic performance. This data is critical for personalizing learning experiences, but it also poses risks to student privacy and security. There is a need for clear guidelines on how student data is collected, stored, and used to avoid exploitation or misuse.

Additionally, there are concerns about the potential for AI systems to reinforce biases in educational outcomes. AI algorithms are only as good as the data they are trained on. If these datasets are biased (e.g., reflecting gender, racial, or socioeconomic disparities), the AI tools can perpetuate or even amplify existing inequalities. Educators, policymakers, and AI developers must ensure that AI systems are transparent, fair, and designed with equity in mind (Williamson & Piattoeva, 2021).

16.1.4. Resistance to Change and Lack of Trust

Another barrier to AI adoption in education is resistance from educators and other stakeholders who may be skeptical about the effectiveness or necessity of AI in teaching and learning. Many educators may feel that AI will replace them or undermine their professional expertise, leading to resistance against adopting AI tools. This skepticism can stem from a lack of understanding of how AI can enhance, rather than replace, the teacher's role in the classroom.

Moreover, there is often a lack of trust in AI systems due to concerns about the accuracy of their outputs. For example, if an AI system inaccurately assesses a student's abilities or emotional state, it could lead to inappropriate interventions or personalized learning pathways. The fear of "automation bias" (i.e., trusting AI systems too much) can make educators hesitant to adopt these technologies. To overcome this barrier, AI systems must be designed to be transparent, and educators must be involved in the decision-making process regarding the use of AI in the classroom (Holmes, Bialik, & Fadel, 2019).

16.1.5. Professional Development and Teacher Preparedness

The successful integration of AI in education requires teachers to have the skills and knowledge to use these tools in the classroom effectively. However, many educators lack the necessary training to incorporate AI into their teaching practices. Teacher education programs have not always kept pace with technological advancements, and many educators are not prepared to teach with or about AI.

Professional development opportunities must be expanded to ensure that teachers are equipped with the skills to use AI tools effectively. These programs should not only focus on how to use AI but also address the pedagogical implications of AI integration. Teachers must be trained to understand how AI can enhance their teaching and support their students' learning, as well as how to critically engage with the ethical, social, and cultural implications of AI in education (Luckin et al., 2016).

While AI has the potential to revolutionize education, its adoption faces several significant barriers. These challenges include technological limitations, equity concerns, ethical dilemmas, resistance to change, and the need for professional development. To overcome these barriers, a multi-faceted approach is necessary, one that involves investment in infrastructure, the creation of policies that promote equitable access, a focus on ethical AI design, and comprehensive teacher training. With these efforts in place, AI can be integrated into education systems in ways that enhance learning experiences, improve educational outcomes, and empower both educators and students.

16.2. Infrastructure Challenges in the Adoption of AI in Education

The integration of Artificial Intelligence (AI) in education holds significant promise for enhancing learning experiences, personalizing education, and improving educational outcomes. However, one of the most substantial barriers to the widespread adoption of AI in education is the lack of robust infrastructure. AI technologies require advanced computing systems, reliable internet access, and effective data management frameworks, all of which are often unavailable or underdeveloped in many educational settings, particularly in low-resource environments. This section explores the key infrastructure challenges that hinder the successful implementation of AI in educational institutions.

16.2.1. Limited Access to Computing Devices and Hardware

AI tools in education, such as intelligent tutoring systems, personalized learning platforms, and data-driven assessment tools, often rely on powerful computing devices to function effectively. These tools require not only modern personal computers, but also sophisticated hardware such as high-performance servers, cloud computing services, and advanced sensors for collecting real-time data from students. For many schools, especially those in underserved or rural areas, the absence of sufficient computing devices for both teachers and students represents a significant obstacle to AI adoption.

Inadequate access to these necessary computing devices leads to digital exclusion, meaning that only well-resourced institutions can harness the benefits of AI-driven education. A study by the *International Society for Technology in Education* (2020) highlighted that in many developing countries, schools often lack the infrastructure to support the integration of modern educational technology, limiting the ability to use AI-based tools and platforms (Jhurree, 2005). Consequently, this digital divide can further exacerbate educational inequalities, leaving marginalized students at a disadvantage.

16.2.2. Inadequate Internet Connectivity

Another critical infrastructure challenge is unreliable or inadequate internet connectivity. Many AI-driven educational tools, particularly those that use cloud-based services or require real-time data transmission, depend on stable and high-speed internet connections. In many parts of the world, particularly in rural or remote areas, access to reliable and fast internet is either limited or non-existent. According to the *International Telecommunication Union* (ITU), while global internet penetration has been increasing, approximately 3.7 billion people worldwide still lack access to the internet, with most of them residing in developing regions (ITU, 2020).

This lack of internet access prevents students and educators from fully utilizing AI-powered educational tools. Schools may face difficulties in uploading and downloading educational content, accessing real-time data, and collaborating online. In environments where internet connectivity is inconsistent, AI tools may not perform optimally, leading to disrupted learning experiences and inefficiencies in educational delivery (Bakia et al., 2012).

16.2.3. Data Management and Storage Constraints

AI systems in education often rely on the collection and analysis of large amounts of data. This data may include student performance metrics, learning behaviors, and even emotional responses in some AI tools. However, the effective use of AI in education requires sophisticated data management systems capable of securely storing, processing, and analyzing this information. Unfortunately, many schools lack the necessary data infrastructure to handle this volume of data, especially in low-income or underfunded institutions.

In addition to the sheer volume of data, there are concerns about the security and privacy of student data. Schools must adhere to strict data protection regulations to safeguard students' personal information. Without proper data governance frameworks and storage facilities, educational institutions may be reluctant to adopt AI technologies due to concerns about compliance with data privacy laws and the potential misuse of sensitive data (Williamson & Cummings, 2021).

16.2.4. Teacher Training and Technical Support

AI in education also requires educators to possess specific technical skills to navigate and integrate these tools into their teaching practices effectively. This involves understanding not only how to operate AI tools but also how to interpret the data they provide and adjust teaching strategies accordingly. Without appropriate training, teachers may struggle to make full use of AI tools, and their lack of confidence in using AI could hinder the adoption process.

Moreover, technical support is essential for maintaining and troubleshooting AI systems. Schools and educational institutions often lack the in-house expertise needed to provide ongoing technical support for AI tools, making it difficult to address issues that may arise during implementation. As AI technologies rapidly evolve, continuous professional development for educators and administrators is necessary to keep up with new tools, software updates, and potential system issues. This need for ongoing training and support creates an additional strain on educational budgets and resources (Luckin et al., 2016).

16.2.5. Financial Constraints and Investment Challenges

Building and maintaining the necessary infrastructure for AI in education requires substantial financial investment. For many educational institutions, especially those in low-income or rural areas, the cost of acquiring the required hardware, software, and internet services is prohibitive. Schools must also account for the costs associated with ongoing maintenance and support, including the hiring of technical staff and the development of professional development programs for educators.

Government funding and private-sector investment are crucial for addressing these infrastructure gaps. However, in many cases, AI adoption may not be prioritized in education budgets, especially when competing with other pressing needs such as basic school supplies, teacher salaries, and curriculum development. This financial constraint limits the ability of educational systems to scale AI integration and ensure that all students benefit equally from these technologies (Brynjolfsson & McAfee, 2014).

Infrastructure challenges are among the most significant barriers to the successful integration of AI in education. These challenges include limited access to computing devices, unreliable internet connectivity, inadequate data management systems, a lack of teacher training, and financial constraints. Addressing these barriers requires a concerted effort from governments, educational institutions, and private-sector partners to invest in the necessary infrastructure, ensure equitable access to AI tools, and provide ongoing professional development for educators. Only by overcoming these infrastructure challenges can the full potential of AI in education be realized, leading to more personalized, accessible, and effective learning experiences for students worldwide.

16.3. Data Privacy and Security Concerns in AI for Education

The integration of Artificial Intelligence (AI) in education has the potential to revolutionize teaching and learning by providing personalized, adaptive learning experiences and offering valuable insights into student performance and behavior. However, as educational institutions increasingly adopt AI-driven tools and systems, concerns surrounding data privacy and security have emerged as significant challenges. AI technologies rely heavily on vast amounts of student data, including personal information, academic performance, behavioral patterns, and even emotional responses. This data collection raises several important questions about how student information is stored, used, and protected, highlighting the need for robust security frameworks and privacy protections in AI-enabled education systems.

16.3.1. The Scale and Sensitivity of Data Collected

AI in education relies on the collection and analysis of large volumes of student data to personalize learning, adapt content to individual needs, and provide teachers with insights into student progress. This data can include not only academic records but also behavioral data (such as engagement levels and participation) and, in some cases, more sensitive information, such as emotional or mental health assessments derived from AI-driven tools like sentiment analysis or facial recognition. The scale and sensitivity of the data collected for these systems present significant privacy risks, particularly when data breaches or unauthorized access occur.

In many cases, educational institutions lack the necessary resources or expertise to ensure proper data management and security, putting student data at risk. For instance, in 2020, the *US Department of Education* reported multiple incidents of data breaches involving educational institutions, underscoring the vulnerability of student information to cyberattacks (U.S. Department of Education, 2020). These breaches can result in the exposure of personal information, leading to identity theft, harassment, or other harmful consequences for students.

16.3.2. Regulatory and Compliance Challenges

The collection and processing of student data in educational AI systems are subject to strict regulations aimed at protecting privacy. These regulations, such as the *Family Educational Rights and Privacy Act (FERPA)* in the United States, the *General Data Protection Regulation (GDPR)* in the European Union, and the *Protection of Personal Information Act (POPIA)* in South Africa, impose specific requirements on how personal data should be handled. Educational institutions must comply with these laws to ensure that data collection, storage, and use do not violate students' rights to privacy.

However, compliance with these regulations can be challenging, particularly for smaller institutions or those in regions with less stringent data protection laws. Many educational institutions may lack the technical infrastructure or legal expertise to navigate the complex landscape of data privacy regulations. Furthermore, as AI technologies rapidly evolve, it is often difficult for institutions to keep up with changing legal and ethical standards. This creates a situation where schools may inadvertently violate privacy laws or fail to implement adequate protections for student data, which can lead to legal repercussions, loss of trust, and reputational damage (Williamson & Cummings, 2021).

16.3.3. Lack of Transparency and Accountability in AI Systems

AI algorithms are often described as "black boxes" because they can make decisions or recommendations without providing clear insight into the reasoning behind them. This lack of transparency poses significant challenges in education, where decisions based on AI recommendations may have a profound impact on students' academic trajectories. For example, AI systems used for personalized learning may recommend specific resources or interventions, but students, parents, and educators may not fully understand the basis for these recommendations.

Moreover, AI systems can perpetuate existing biases if they are trained on incomplete, biased, or unrepresentative data sets. For instance, if an AI system used in education is trained predominantly on data from students in affluent, urban areas, it may not provide accurate or equitable recommendations for students from disadvantaged or rural backgrounds. The lack of transparency in how AI systems make decisions, coupled with the potential for algorithmic bias, creates ethical concerns and raises questions about accountability when things go wrong (O'Neil, 2016).

16.3.4. Ethical Concerns in Data Usage

In addition to privacy concerns, there are ethical issues surrounding the use of student data for AI-driven educational purposes. The data collected by AI systems can be used to track students' learning behaviors and predict future outcomes. While this can be useful for providing personalized learning experiences, it also raises questions about consent and the potential for misuse of student data. For example, students may not fully understand what data is being collected, how it is being used, or the potential consequences of its use. Furthermore, in some cases, AI-driven decisions about students' learning paths or academic future may be based on algorithms that prioritize efficiency or standardized metrics over individual learning needs.

Additionally, AI systems could be used to profile students based on their data, potentially reinforcing stereotypes or making assumptions about students' abilities or interests that could limit their opportunities. For instance, students from marginalized backgrounds might be unfairly steered toward lower-level courses or career tracks based on flawed or biased data (Eubanks, 2018). These ethical concerns highlight the need for clear policies around consent, transparency, and the responsible use of student data in AI applications.

16.3.5. Data Security in Cloud-Based AI Solutions

Many AI systems in education are cloud-based, meaning that student data is stored on remote servers rather than locally within educational institutions. While cloud computing offers many advantages, including scalability, flexibility, and lower upfront costs, it also raises significant security concerns. Data stored in the cloud is vulnerable to hacking, data breaches, and unauthorized access, especially if cloud providers do not implement adequate security protocols. In 2017, a significant breach of a cloud-based learning management system (LMS) exposed the personal information of millions of students, underscoring the risks associated with cloud storage (Chesney & Citron, 2019).

Educational institutions must ensure that the cloud providers they work with follow best practices in cybersecurity, including encryption, secure access protocols, and regular security audits. Furthermore, institutions must develop and implement data governance policies that protect student privacy and ensure compliance with relevant regulations.

Data privacy and security are critical concerns in the adoption of AI in education. As educational institutions increasingly rely on AI systems that collect and analyze sensitive student data, they must address a range of challenges, including protecting against data breaches, ensuring compliance with privacy regulations, and maintaining transparency in AI decision-making. Ethical considerations, such as informed consent and the responsible use of student data, must also be central to the development and deployment of AI tools in education. Moving forward, policymakers, educational leaders, and technology providers need to collaborate on developing robust frameworks for data privacy and security that safeguard the interests of students and ensure the ethical use of AI in educational contexts.

References

Brynjolfsson, E., & McAfee, A. (2014). *The Second Machine Age: Work, Progress, and Prosperity in a Time of Brilliant Technologies*. W. W. Norton & Company.

Buolamwini, J., & Gebru, T. (2018). Gender shades: Intersectional accuracy disparities in commercial gender classification. In *Proceedings of the 1st Conference on Fairness, Accountability, and Transparency* (pp. 77–91).

Chesney, R., & Citron, D. K. (2019). The threats of AI-driven education: An analysis of the challenges of data privacy and cybersecurity. *The Journal of Technology and Privacy Law,* 14(3), 256–276.

Eubanks, V. (2018). *Automating inequality: How high-tech tools profile, police, and punish the poor*—St Martin's Press.

Fitzpatrick, K. K., Darcy, A., & Vierhile, M. (2017). Delivering cognitive behavioral therapy to young adults with emotional distress via smartphone: A randomized controlled trial. *Journal of the American Academy of Child and Adolescent Psychiatry*, 56(10), 823–828. https://doi.org/10.1016/j.jaac.2017.07.004.

Holmes, W., Bialik, M., & Fadel, C. (2019). Artificial intelligence in education: Promises and implications for teaching and learning. Center for Curriculum Redesign.

International Telecommunication Union. (2020). Measuring digital development: Facts and figures 2020. ITU. https://www.itu.int/en/ITU-D/Statistics/Documents/facts/FactsFigures2020.pdf.

Jhurree, V. (2005). Technology integration in education in developing countries: Opportunities and challenges. *Educational Technology & Society*, 8(4), 31–42.

Luckin, R., Holmes, W., Griffiths, M., & Forcier, L. B. (2016). *Intelligence unleashed: An argument for AI in education*. Pearson Education.

Mouza, C., Yang, H., Pan, Y. C., Ozden, S. Y., & Pollock, L. (2019). Preparing teachers for digital learning: Challenges and opportunities in the use of technology in education. *Educational Researcher*, 48(4), 211–223. https://doi.org/10.3102/0013189X19856621.

O'Neil, C. (2016). Weapons of math destruction: How big data increases inequality and threatens democracy. Crown Publishing Group.

Picard, R. W., Papert, S., Bender, W., Blumberg, B., Breazeal, C., Cavallo, D., ... & Strohecker, C. (2011). Affective computing and intelligent interaction. In Affective Computing and Intelligent Interaction (pp. 1–16). Springer. https://doi.org/10.1007/978-3-540-25939-6_1.

Popenici, S. A. D., & Kerr, S. (2017). Challenges of artificial intelligence in education: Learners' perspectives. Educational Media International, 54(3), 221–232. https://doi.org/10.1080/09523987.2017.1362810.

Solove, D. J. (2021). Privacy and data protection: Why AI's challenges require new ethical frameworks. *Journal of Information Ethics*, 30(1), 31–47.

U.S. Department of Education. (2020). Annual report on data security incidents in U.S. educational institutions. https://www.ed.gov.

Williamson, B., & Cummings, C. (2021). The governance of AI in education: Challenges and opportunities. *Educational Technology & Society*, 24(3), 134–146.

Williamson, B., & Piattoeva, N. (2021). Education governance and the role of data in shaping policy. Educational Philosophy and Theory, 53(7), 676–687. https://doi.org/10.1080/00131857.2020.1835646.

Chapter 17

Policy and Governance Frameworks

17.1. Policy and Governance Frameworks

The rapid integration of Artificial Intelligence (AI) in education necessitates the establishment of robust policy and governance frameworks. These frameworks ensure that AI technologies are implemented ethically, transparently, and in alignment with the best interests of students, educators, and society. They are vital in addressing the ethical, legal, and social implications of AI in educational contexts, safeguarding privacy, ensuring equitable access, and fostering accountability in AI-driven decisions. Importantly, a well-developed policy and governance structure can help mitigate risks associated with AI while maximizing its potential to enhance learning outcomes, support teachers, and empower students, offering a hopeful future for education.

17.1.1. The Role of Policy in AI Adoption in Education

Policymakers play a pivotal role in shaping the adoption and integration of AI technologies in educational systems. It is their responsibility to create policies that not only guide the ethical use of AI but also set standards for data privacy, security, and accountability. These policies should address concerns such as data collection and usage, algorithmic transparency, and the protection of vulnerable student populations.

A key component of AI policy is the establishment of clear guidelines regarding the use of student data. As AI systems in education rely on large datasets, often involving sensitive personal information, policies must govern how data is collected, stored, and processed. For instance, the *Family Educational Rights and Privacy Act (FERPA)* in the United States and the *General Data Protection Regulation (GDPR)* in the European Union offer frameworks for data privacy, emphasizing informed consent, transparency, and data subject rights. These regulations must be adapted and extended to account for the unique nature of AI systems, ensuring that the data used in AI models is protected and that students' privacy rights are respected.

17.1.2. Establishing Accountability and Transparency in AI Systems

In the realm of AI in education, accountability is a fundamental concern. As AI algorithms become increasingly responsible for making decisions about students' learning paths, assessment results, and even access to educational resources, it is essential that there be clear lines of accountability. Governance frameworks should address who is responsible when AI systems make erroneous decisions, such as misidentifying a student's learning needs or providing biased recommendations. Additionally, ensuring transparency in AI decision-making processes is critical to maintaining trust among students, educators, and parents.

To foster accountability and transparency, governments and educational institutions must prioritize the development of 'explainable AI' (XAI) systems. These systems provide understandable and interpretable reasons for their decisions, which is crucial for maintaining trust among students, educators, and parents. This can be achieved through the implementation of standardized frameworks that require AI providers to document how algorithms are designed, how data is used, and how decisions are made. Educational institutions should also establish mechanisms for auditing AI systems, ensuring that these systems comply with both internal policies and external regulations.

17.1.3. Ethical and Equity Considerations in AI Governance

Integrating AI in education also requires careful consideration of ethical issues, particularly around fairness, bias, and inclusivity. AI systems are susceptible to biases if trained on biased datasets or programmed without attention to diversity and inclusivity. For example, an AI tool designed to assess student performance might disproportionately favor certain groups over others based on underlying biases in the data. This could result in systemic inequality, where the system unfairly disadvantages students from marginalized backgrounds.

Policy frameworks must promote ethical AI practices that ensure fairness, inclusivity, and equity in all AI-driven educational tools. This includes addressing biases in algorithm design, ensuring that AI systems are tested on diverse and representative datasets and that educational institutions actively work to identify and mitigate any harmful consequences of AI deployments. Policymakers must also consider how to bridge the digital divide, ensuring that AI-enhanced educational tools are accessible to students from all socioeconomic backgrounds, including those in rural or underserved communities.

17.1.4. Global Cooperation and Intergovernmental Collaboration

Given the global reach and impact of AI technologies, it is imperative that AI governance in education be shaped by international collaboration. Many aspects of AI in education, such as data privacy, algorithmic transparency, and bias reduction, require coordinated efforts among governments, international organizations, and industry stakeholders. Global cooperation is key to ensuring that AI technologies are developed and deployed in ways that benefit all students, regardless of their geographic location or socioeconomic status.

International organizations like UNESCO, the Organization for Economic Co-operation and Development (OECD), and the International Telecommunication Union (ITU) are already working to establish global guidelines and frameworks for the ethical use of AI in education. By working together, nations can ensure that AI technologies are used to advance universal access to quality education, promote lifelong learning, and reduce inequalities in global education systems.

17.1.5. Promoting Public-Private Partnerships in AI Governance

Public-private partnerships (PPPs) are not just beneficial but crucial for the successful governance of AI in education. These partnerships facilitate the exchange of knowledge, resources, and expertise between governmental bodies, educational institutions, and private-sector companies developing AI technologies. Collaboration with tech companies is not just a luxury but a necessity, providing educational institutions access to cutting-edge AI tools. Governments, in turn, can help ensure that these tools are used ethically and in ways that support educational equity, making them an integral part of the process.

For example, partnerships with AI developers can lead to the creation of AI systems specifically tailored to the needs of diverse educational contexts, ensuring that AI tools are accessible, inclusive, and adaptive. In return, policymakers can help AI developers align their products with ethical standards and ensure their tools comply with data privacy regulations and fairness guidelines.

Developing effective policy and governance frameworks is essential to AI's responsible and equitable integration in education. These frameworks should address key issues such as data privacy, accountability, bias, and equity while promoting transparency and inclusivity. Ethical considerations should be at the forefront of AI governance, with policies designed to ensure that AI tools are used in ways that benefit all students, particularly those from underserved or marginalized communities. Furthermore, global cooperation and public-private partnerships are essential to create AI solutions that can address the challenges faced by education systems worldwide. Through well-crafted policies and governance structures, AI can be harnessed to transform education in ethical, fair, and beneficial ways for all students.

17.1.6. Regulation of AI in Education Systems

As Artificial Intelligence (AI) increasingly integrates into education systems worldwide, clear and effective regulation is paramount. The regulation of AI in education aims to balance innovation with the protection of students' rights, the assurance of fairness, and the promotion of equality in learning outcomes. This complex challenge involves technological considerations and ethical, legal, and societal concerns. Regulatory frameworks for AI in education must address the implications of AI-driven educational tools on data privacy, algorithmic accountability, inclusivity, and transparency while promoting innovation that enhances learning experiences for all students.

17.1.6.1. AI Regulatory Frameworks in Education

The regulation of AI in education requires the establishment of guidelines that clearly define acceptable practices, responsibilities, and standards for AI development, deployment, and use in educational settings. These frameworks should guide the design and implementation of AI systems, ensuring they adhere to ethical principles, safeguard personal data, and contribute to positive learning outcomes. AI regulation must include provisions for data privacy, informed consent, and the protection of sensitive student information, which is especially important given that AI systems rely on vast amounts of data to function effectively.

For instance, data privacy laws, such as the General Data Protection Regulation (GDPR) in the European Union, impose strict guidelines on how personal data can be collected, stored, and processed. In educational contexts, these regulations apply to the data collected from students interacting with AI-powered learning platforms, ensuring that AI systems comply with the highest data protection standards. These frameworks are essential in preventing misuse of personal information, such as student performance or behavioral data, which can be vulnerable to exploitation or discrimination if not handled responsibly.

17.1.6.2. Algorithmic Accountability and Transparency

A critical aspect of regulating AI in education is ensuring algorithmic accountability and transparency. AI systems, particularly those that assess student performance, provide recommendations, or facilitate personalized learning, can make decisions that have significant consequences for students. However, many AI models, particularly black-box algorithms, do not provide clear explanations for their decision-making processes, which makes it difficult for educators, students, and parents to understand how and why specific decisions are made. This lack of transparency can lead to mistrust and reinforce biases in educational contexts.

To mitigate these risks, AI regulations must enforce the use of explainable AI (XAI), ensuring that AI systems are designed to provide clear and understandable explanations of their actions. By doing so, educational stakeholders—teachers, students, and administrators—can better understand how AI-generated recommendations are made and how data is processed. Furthermore, AI regulation should establish standards for ongoing audits and evaluations of AI systems to identify and correct potential biases, ensuring fairness and inclusivity in AI-driven decision-making processes.

17.1.6.3. Inclusion and Equity in AI Regulation

AI education systems can potentially perpetuate or exacerbate existing inequalities if not carefully regulated. For instance, AI tools trained on biased data or designed without attention to cultural or socioeconomic contexts can lead to skewed learning experiences and perpetuate inequalities, particularly for marginalized groups. Regulatory frameworks must ensure that AI systems are designed inclusively, addressing the diverse needs of students, including those with disabilities, those from low-income backgrounds, and those from minority or underrepresented communities.

One key aspect of AI regulation is promoting equity, ensuring that all students have equal access to AI-enhanced learning opportunities. This may include policies that promote the development of AI systems adaptable to various learning styles, support students with special educational needs, and are accessible across different languages and cultures. Regulations should also mandate that AI tools be tested for bias, ensuring that they are equally effective across demographic groups, including race, gender, and socioeconomic status.

17.1.6.4. Ethical Considerations and Governance Models

The ethical use of AI in education is central to its regulation. AI systems can impact academic performance and students' well-being, self-esteem, and future opportunities. Consequently, AI systems should be designed with ethical considerations, ensuring they promote human dignity, autonomy, and fairness. AI regulation in education must ensure that these systems are aligned with moral principles, such as respect for students' rights, autonomy in decision-making, and fairness in evaluating their capabilities.

Governments, educational institutions, and industry stakeholders should work together to establish governance models that ensure AI in education adheres to these ethical standards. This includes creating ethical review boards or committees to evaluate the potential risks of AI tools before they are deployed in classrooms and encouraging continuous monitoring and accountability throughout their lifecycle. These governance structures can help ensure that AI systems remain aligned with ethical guidelines and are responsive to emerging ethical challenges as AI technology evolves.

17.1.6.5. International Standards and Global Cooperation

Given the global nature of AI development, the regulation of AI in education must also consider international collaboration and the creation of global standards. Countries have varying regulation levels and differing cultural norms regarding privacy, data security, and educational practices. To ensure a cohesive approach to AI governance, international bodies such as the United Nations Educational, Scientific and Cultural Organization (UNESCO), the OECD, and the European Union are working on frameworks and guidelines that promote cross-border cooperation in AI education.

International cooperation can facilitate the sharing of best practices, data protection standards, and ethical frameworks across borders, helping countries with less developed regulatory environments benefit from the experiences of others. It can also ensure that AI tools developed in one country are adaptable and usable in other educational contexts, promoting a more equitable global distribution of AI-enhanced learning resources.

The regulation of AI in education is crucial to ensure that these technologies are used responsibly, ethically, and equitably. Clear and comprehensive regulatory frameworks can help protect students' privacy, ensure fairness, and promote inclusivity while fostering innovation that enhances the educational experience. Addressing algorithmic transparency, bias, and ethical considerations and ensuring global cooperation and equity in access will enable AI to transform education practically and ethically. Moving forward, policymakers must collaborate with educators, technology developers, and international bodies to create adaptive, transparent, and inclusive regulations that promote the responsible use of AI in education.

17.1.7. Frameworks for Ethical AI Development

As Artificial Intelligence (AI) continues to transform various sectors, including education, healthcare, finance, and more, the need for ethical frameworks governing AI development has become crucial. These frameworks guide the design, deployment, and use of AI technologies to ensure they align with societal values, human rights, and ethical principles. Ethical AI frameworks aim to minimize harm, ensure fairness, promote transparency, and foster accountability, ensuring AI systems contribute to the greater good without compromising individual rights or societal well-being.

17.1.7.1. The Need for Ethical AI Frameworks

AI technologies have the potential to enhance productivity and innovation greatly, but they also present significant risks, such as exacerbating biases, infringing on privacy, and undermining trust in automated systems. Ethical AI development frameworks are designed to mitigate these risks and ensure that AI systems are aligned with values such as fairness, justice, accountability, and transparency. Without clear ethical guidelines, AI systems could perpetuate and amplify existing inequalities, leading to societal harm. Thus, the establishment of comprehensive frameworks is essential to create systems that are both effective and ethical.

Ethical AI frameworks help organizations and governments establish standards and practices for creating AI that serves humanity responsibly. They guide the design of AI systems that respect privacy, are free from bias, offer equitable outcomes, and do not infringe on fundamental rights. These frameworks are also critical in ensuring AI systems are transparent in their decision-making processes and that developers can explain how their models function, especially when AI systems are involved in decision-making processes that impact people's lives.

17.1.7.2. Key Ethical Principles for AI

Several foundational principles guide ethical AI development, including:

- *Fairness:* AI systems must be designed to treat all individuals fairly, avoiding bias that could lead to discriminatory outcomes. This requires ensuring that diverse, representative data sets are used for training AI systems and that regular audits are conducted to detect and mitigate potential biases.
- *Transparency:* AI systems should be transparent in their operations, enabling users to understand how decisions are made. Transparency also explains the underlying algorithms, data sources, and decision-making processes that guide AI systems, especially in high-stakes environments like healthcare and law enforcement.
- *Accountability:* Developers and organizations that deploy AI systems must be held accountable for the decisions and outcomes that arise from these systems. This includes ensuring a transparent chain of responsibility for AI-driven decisions and addressing any harm from their use.
- *Privacy and Data Protection*: Ethical AI frameworks emphasize protecting individuals' data and respecting their privacy. AI systems should be designed with robust data protection mechanisms, ensuring that data collection, storage, and processing are done securely and transparently.
- *Beneficence:* AI should be designed and used to better society, maximizing benefits while minimizing potential harm. This includes considering AI technologies' social, environmental, and economic impacts and striving to create systems that promote positive societal outcomes.

17.1.7.3. Popular Ethical AI Frameworks

Various governmental and non-governmental organizations have developed frameworks for ethical AI development. Some of the most influential ones include:

- *The OECD Principles on Artificial Intelligence (2019):* These principles promote AI's responsible development and use. They emphasize the importance of fostering inclusive growth, well-being, and sustainable development through AI while ensuring fairness, transparency, and accountability. These principles provide a global perspective on the ethical implications of AI and recommend policy actions for ensuring that AI technologies are aligned with human rights and democratic values.

- *The European Commission's Ethics Guidelines for Trustworthy AI (2019):* This framework ensures that AI systems are trustworthy by focusing on transparency, accountability, fairness, and privacy. It lays out requirements for AI systems, including ensuring that AI is lawful, ethical, and robust. The guidelines emphasize the need for AI systems to be explainable and that the data used is relevant, unbiased, and adequately protected.
- *IEEE Global Initiative on Ethics of Autonomous and Intelligent Systems*: The IEEE initiative provides a set of ethical standards that prioritize individuals' safety, privacy, and dignity while promoting transparency in AI development. This initiative focuses on developing AI systems that align with human values, respect privacy, and mitigate bias.
- *AI Now Institute's Annual Reports*: The AI Now Institute, based at New York University, has been a leading voice in examining the social implications of AI. Their reports focus on the role of AI in policy, labor, and bias, providing comprehensive guidelines for creating socially responsible AI systems that consider a broad range of societal impacts, including issues of race, gender, and inequality.

17.1.7.4. Implementation Challenges of Ethical AI

While the frameworks for ethical AI development provide essential guidance, their practical implementation can be challenging. One major difficulty is ensuring the alignment of AI systems with ethical principles during their design, development, and deployment stages. AI systems are complex and often evolve in ways that are difficult to predict, which complicates the ability to foresee and address ethical concerns in real time.

Moreover, the global nature of AI development means that ethical standards must account for diverse cultural, social, and political contexts. The ethical implications of AI may vary significantly across different countries or regions, requiring a careful balancing of universal principles with local considerations. For example, issues such as privacy expectations, data ownership, and algorithmic transparency are perceived differently depending on regional norms, which can hinder the creation of global standards.

Furthermore, ensuring accountability remains a persistent challenge. AI systems' distributed and often opaque nature makes it difficult to determine who is responsible when AI decisions lead to harmful outcomes. This is particularly critical in high-stakes environments, such as criminal justice, hiring practices, and healthcare, where AI decisions directly impact people's lives.

The future of AI ethics depends on continuous dialogue and collaboration among technologists, ethicists, policymakers, and the public. As AI systems become more integrated into our daily lives, it is crucial to develop adaptive and robust ethical frameworks that can keep pace with technological advancements. This includes addressing issues related to AI's potential for societal impact, ensuring diverse voices are included in AI design, and continuously revising ethical guidelines as new challenges arise.

Ultimately, ethical AI development aims to create systems that enhance human well-being, promote equality, and uphold societal values. By adhering to established ethical frameworks and prioritizing accountability, fairness, and transparency, AI can be developed to contribute positively to society, ensuring that the technology serves humanity rather than harming it.

References

AI Now Institute. (2020). *AI Now 2020 Report*. AI Now Institute.

Binns, R. (2018). On the Importance of Ethical AI. In *Proceedings of the 2018 Conference on Fairness, Accountability, and Transparency*, 56-60.

Bryson, J. J., & Winfield, A. F. (2017). Standardizing Ethical Design for Artificial Intelligence and Autonomous Systems. *Computer,* 50(11), 116-119.

Calo, R. (2017). The Boundaries of Privacy Harm. *Indiana Law Journal*, 86(3), 1131-1162.

Dastin, J. (2018). *Amazon Scraps Secret AI Recruiting Tool That Showed Bias Against Women*. Reuters.

Eubanks, V. (2018). *Automating Inequality: How High-Tech Tools Profile, Police, and Punish the Poor.* St. Martin's Press.

European Commission. (2016). General Data Protection Regulation (GDPR). *Official Journal of the European Union.*

Floridi, L., & Cowls, J. (2019). A Unified Framework of Five Principles for AI in Society. *Harvard Data Science Review*, 1(1), 1-18.

González, G. A., & Turhan, B. (2020). Fairness in Artificial Intelligence Systems: A Review of Ethical Guidelines. *Ethics and Information Technology*, 22(1), 57-68.

Gordon, L., & Kelly, C. (2020). Algorithmic Bias and Equity: A Call for Regulation in AI Education. *Journal of Educational Technology*, 45(4), 15-30.

Hsu, P. S. (2020). AI and Data Privacy in Education: A Global Perspective. *Education Policy Analysis Archives*, 28(39), 1-25.

IEEE. (2019). Ethically Aligned Design: A Vision for Prioritizing Human Well-Being with Autonomous and Intelligent Systems. IEEE Standards Association.

Jobin, A., Ienca, M., & Vayena, E. (2019). *The Global Landscape of AI Ethics Guidelines*. Nature Machine Intelligence, 1(9), 389-399.

Lipton, Z. C. (2016). *The Mythos of Model Interpretability*. Communications of the ACM, 59(10), 36-43.

Liu, S., & Kwan, H. K. (2020). Public-private partnerships for AI development in education: A new model for fostering innovation and equity. Journal of Educational Technology Systems, 48(2), 257-276.

OECD. (2019). OECD Principles on Artificial Intelligence. OECD Publishing. European Commission. (2019). *Ethics Guidelines for Trustworthy AI.* European Commission.

OECD. (2020). Artificial Intelligence in Education: Promises and Implications for Teaching and Learning. OECD Publishing.

O'Neil, C. (2016). *Weapons of Math Destruction: How Big Data Increases Inequality and Threatens Democracy*. Crown Publishing Group.

Taddeo, M., & Floridi, L. (2018). How AI Can Be Ethical: A European Perspective. In *Ethical AI and the Future of Work* (pp. 125-139). Springer.

U.S. Department of Education. (2020). *Annual report on data security incidents in U.S. educational institutions*. U.S. Department of Education.

UNESCO. (2021). AI in Education: A Strategic Framework for Policy Development. UNESCO Publishing.

Veale, M., Van Kleek, M., & Shadbolt, N. (2018). Fairness in AI and the Need for Accountability and Transparency. *Proceedings of the 2018 CHI Conference on Human Factors in Computing Systems*, 1-11.

Williamson, B., & Cummings, C. (2021). The governance of AI in education: Challenges and opportunities. *Educational Technology & Society*, 24(3), 134-146.

Williamson, B., & Piattoeva, N. (2021). Governing educational data and digital platforms in global education markets: The rise of the AI-driven education ecosystem. *Journal of Education Policy,* 36(4), 493-514.

Chapter 18

Future Possibilities: The Next Generation of AI in Education

18.1 Introduction

The landscape of education is rapidly evolving with the advent of Artificial Intelligence (AI). As AI technologies continue to advance, they hold the potential to redefine how education is delivered, experienced, and evaluated. From personalized learning experiences to the automation of administrative tasks, AI's role in education is poised to become increasingly transformative. The next generation of AI in education promises to build on the existing capabilities of AI while introducing novel, more sophisticated applications that will make education more inclusive, adaptive, and responsive to the diverse needs of learners worldwide, ushering in a new era of education.

18.1.1. AI-Enhanced Personalized Learning

Personalized learning, a cornerstone of AI's potential in education, is set to reach new heights as AI technologies advance. Current AI systems already offer adaptive learning tools that adjust the content, pace, and style of delivery based on a student's strengths and weaknesses. In the future, AI could integrate more granular data, such as learning styles, emotional responses, and cognitive load, to create hyper-personalized learning environments.

These AI-driven systems will not only deliver personalized content but also dynamically adjust the learning path to optimize each student's educational journey. For instance, if a student struggles with a particular concept, the AI could offer additional resources or adjust the teaching strategy. This level of personalized attention is difficult to achieve in traditional classrooms due to the limitations of human resources and individualized support. In the future, AI could function as a continuous tutor, helping students progress at their own pace and providing real-time feedback that promotes deep learning.

18.1.2. AI in Global and Cross-Cultural Education

As the world becomes more interconnected, AI has the potential to bridge geographical and cultural gaps in education, opening up exciting new possibilities for global collaboration. AI systems could facilitate cross-cultural learning experiences by providing real-time translation and cultural context to students from diverse backgrounds. This could enhance global collaboration, allowing learners to access high-quality educational resources from anywhere in the world, regardless of language barriers.

Moreover, AI could provide educators with insights into the cultural preferences and learning behaviors of students from different parts of the world, enabling them to tailor teaching approaches accordingly. AI could also help educators understand the impact of cultural factors on learning outcomes, ensuring that curricula are more inclusive and respectful of diverse perspectives. This could lead to a more globalized and culturally aware education system where students have access to a wide range of global learning opportunities.

18.1.3. AI for Lifelong Learning and Continuous Education

As the world faces rapid technological changes, lifelong learning has become a necessity. AI will play a significant role in enabling continuous learning by providing learners with personalized, on-demand educational resources. The future of AI in education will likely see the development of platforms that offer lifelong learning opportunities tailored to individuals' evolving needs and career aspirations. These platforms could analyze a person's learning history, career trajectory, and personal preferences to suggest courses, micro credentials, and skill-building opportunities, helping individuals stay competitive in an ever-changing job market.

AI could also make education more accessible to non-traditional learners, such as adult learners, those seeking career transitions, or individuals living in remote areas. Through automated recommendations and personalized learning paths, AI could provide these learners with opportunities to upskill and reskill at any stage of life. This shift towards lifelong learning could empower individuals to take greater control of their educational and professional development.

18.1.4. AI in Collaborative and Peer-Based Learning

One of the exciting future possibilities for AI in education is the facilitation of more dynamic and effective collaborative learning environments. AI could help foster collaborative learning by connecting students with peers who have complementary knowledge and skills. These AI systems could also track group dynamics, offering suggestions for improving group interaction and supporting more productive teamwork.

In addition, AI could support peer-based learning by helping students form study groups, share resources, and offer feedback to one another. By analyzing students' interactions, AI could recommend ways for learners to engage more effectively with their peers, ensuring that collaborative activities are optimized for learning. This could make peer-to-peer education a more integral and scalable part of the learning experience, especially in digital classrooms.

18.1.5. AI-Driven Assessment and Feedback

AI could revolutionize the way educational assessments are conducted, moving beyond traditional testing methods to more sophisticated, formative assessments. By analyzing students' learning patterns, AI can provide real-time feedback on their progress, helping them identify areas for improvement. This data-driven approach could provide a more accurate and detailed understanding of a student's abilities, not just based on a final exam, but throughout the learning process.

Furthermore, AI systems could help eliminate biases in grading and evaluation by providing objective assessments that rely on data rather than subjective interpretations. These systems could also tailor feedback to individual students, providing specific advice or resources based on their performance. This shift toward continuous, personalized feedback could enhance student engagement and motivation by making learning more responsive to individual needs.

18.1.6. Challenges and Ethical Considerations

Despite the promising possibilities of AI in education, its future development will need to address several challenges, including data privacy, algorithmic bias, and accessibility. As AI systems increasingly rely on data to make decisions, ensuring the protection of students' personal information and maintaining ethical standards in data collection will be essential. Additionally, AI systems must be designed to be inclusive and equitable, ensuring that all students, regardless of background, have access to the same high-quality educational opportunities.

Moreover, the integration of AI in education must be done in a way that complements, rather than replaces, human educators. While AI can augment teaching and learning, human educators play a critical role in providing emotional support, mentorship, and fostering social and emotional learning.

The next generation of AI in education holds immense potential to transform how we teach, learn, and collaborate. By enabling personalized, accessible, and equitable learning experiences, AI could reshape the educational landscape, fostering lifelong learning, cross-cultural exchange, and more effective assessment. However, to fully realize these possibilities, careful consideration of ethical implications, privacy concerns, and human-centered design will be essential. As AI continues to evolve, so will the opportunities to revolutionize education, making it more inclusive, adaptable, and responsive to the needs of all learners.

18.1.7. Emerging Technologies in EdTech

The field of education technology (EdTech) is undergoing a profound transformation due to the rapid development and integration of emerging technologies. These innovations are reshaping how education is delivered, accessed, and experienced. Emerging technologies in EdTech not only enhance traditional teaching methods but also create new possibilities for learning that are more personalized, accessible, and efficient. This section explores several key emerging technologies in EdTech, including artificial intelligence (AI), virtual reality (VR), augmented reality (AR), blockchain, and the Internet of Things (IoT), which are revolutionizing the educational landscape.

18.1.7.1. Artificial Intelligence (AI) in Education

AI is one of the most influential technologies in EdTech, transforming personalized learning, assessment, and administrative processes. AI-powered systems enable customized learning experiences by adapting educational content to the needs, preferences, and progress of individual students. Tools such as intelligent tutoring systems (ITS) offer students real-time feedback, identifying areas of difficulty, and providing tailored support. AI algorithms can also analyze student data to predict performance trends, allowing educators to intervene before problems arise.

Furthermore, AI is being used to automate administrative tasks such as grading, attendance, and even curriculum development, freeing up educators to focus on more critical aspects of teaching. AI chatbots are increasingly common in EdTech, providing students with instant answers to queries, thus enhancing engagement and reducing the burden on educators. AI's potential to scale personalized education makes it an indispensable tool for the future of education.

18.1.7.2. Virtual Reality (VR) and Augmented Reality (AR)

Virtual reality (VR) and augmented reality (AR) are increasingly being integrated into EdTech to create immersive and interactive learning environments. VR allows students to experience simulated environments that would otherwise be inaccessible, such as historical sites, scientific phenomena, or foreign countries. This level of immersion makes learning more engaging and helps students grasp complex concepts by providing experiential learning opportunities.

On the other hand, AR overlays digital content onto the physical world, enhancing real-world learning experiences. For example, AR can be used in science classrooms to visualize molecular structures or in history lessons to bring ancient civilizations to life through interactive 3D models. These technologies are transforming traditional classrooms, making learning more interactive and engaging while fostering deeper comprehension through experiential and visual learning.

18.1.7.3. Blockchain Technology in Education

Blockchain, a decentralized and secure digital ledger technology, is emerging as a powerful tool in EdTech. It has the potential to revolutionize credentialing, record-keeping, and the verification of academic achievements. Blockchain can be used to securely store and verify certificates, diplomas, and transcripts, reducing the risk of fraud and ensuring that credentials are easily accessible to students, employers, and institutions. Furthermore, blockchain could enhance transparency and accountability in educational systems by providing an immutable record of academic progress.

Additionally, blockchain technology has the potential to facilitate micro-credentialing and the creation of digital portfolios, which allow learners to showcase their skills and achievements beyond traditional degrees. This could help address the growing demand for skills-based education and improve lifelong learning opportunities.

18.1.7.4. The Internet of Things (IoT) in Education

The Internet of Things (IoT) refers to the network of interconnected devices that can communicate and share data. In the context of education, IoT is creating more interactive and efficient learning environments. IoT devices such as smartboards, sensors, and wearable technology can gather data on students' behavior, engagement, and performance, providing teachers with real-time insights into their learning needs.

IoT-enabled classrooms allow for more dynamic and personalized learning experiences. For example, smart desks could adjust their height based on the students' preferences or learning requirements, while wearable devices could monitor students' stress levels or cognitive load during lessons. Additionally, IoT can streamline campus management by automating tasks such as energy usage, security, and inventory control, making educational institutions more efficient and responsive.

18.1.7.5. 5G Technology and Education

The rollout of 5G technology is expected to significantly impact EdTech by enabling faster, more reliable, and high-capacity internet access. 5G's ultra-low latency and high-speed connectivity will facilitate seamless online learning experiences, especially in remote and underserved areas. This will enable better access to cloud-based educational resources, real-time video conferencing, and collaborative tools, promoting more interactive and immersive learning experiences.

5G could also enable new applications such as real-time data analytics for personalized learning, the integration of advanced VR/AR experiences, and the expansion of AI-driven educational tools that require high data throughput and minimal lag. As 5G infrastructure becomes more widespread, educational institutions will be able to leverage its capabilities to enhance both in-person and online learning.

18.1.7.6. Adaptive Learning Technologies

Adaptive learning technologies use data and algorithms to adjust the learning experience based on individual student needs. These systems assess a learner's current level of knowledge and adapt the content, pace, and difficulty accordingly. Unlike traditional one-size-fits-all methods, adaptive learning offers a personalized learning experience that improves student engagement and academic performance.

Emerging adaptive learning platforms are designed to integrate AI and machine learning to enhance the customization of learning content. These platforms can deliver personalized lessons, quizzes, and assessments tailored to individual learning paths, enabling a more efficient learning process. Over time, as these technologies become more sophisticated, they could create truly individualized learning environments that enhance educational outcomes.

Emerging technologies in EdTech are driving a paradigm shift in how education is delivered and experienced. AI, VR, AR, blockchain, IoT, and other technologies are not only enhancing the effectiveness and accessibility of education but also making learning more personalized, immersive, and dynamic. As these technologies continue to evolve, their potential to create innovative learning environments will further transform the educational landscape, leading to more equitable, efficient, and engaging learning experiences for students worldwide. However, it is essential to address the challenges related to infrastructure, data privacy, and digital equity to ensure that these technologies benefit all learners and educators.

18.1.8. Vision for AI-Enhanced Global Learning Ecosystems

The vision for AI-enhanced global learning ecosystems revolves around the integration of artificial intelligence (AI) to create a more personalized, accessible, inclusive, and efficient education system. As technology continues to evolve, the potential for AI to transform the way learning takes place is vast, offering opportunities to break down traditional barriers such as geographic location, socio-economic status, and learning styles. In such a vision, AI is not just a tool for individual learning but a key enabler in creating interconnected, adaptive, and responsive global education systems that cater to diverse learning needs and foster lifelong learning.

18.1.8.1. Personalized and Adaptive Learning Environments

AI has the potential to revolutionize the personalization of education, tailoring learning experiences to meet the specific needs, preferences, and learning speeds of individual students. In a global learning ecosystem, AI-driven platforms can offer dynamic learning paths that adapt in real-time, providing customized lessons, feedback, and assessments. This personalization goes beyond academic content, incorporating cognitive and emotional factors to improve engagement, motivation, and retention.

AI systems can continuously assess students' progress, identify strengths and weaknesses, and suggest individualized learning strategies or additional resources. This adaptive learning model ensures that no learner is left behind, regardless of their background or previous knowledge. For instance, AI-powered tutoring systems can provide immediate feedback and personalized support, while intelligent learning environments can curate content based on students' evolving needs. The scalability of AI makes this level of personalization achievable for learners around the globe, from rural communities to urban centers.

18.1.8.2. Access to Education for All

One of the core promises of AI-enhanced global learning ecosystems is the potential to democratize education. AI can help bridge educational gaps, providing underserved and remote communities with access to high-quality learning resources. By using AI-driven platforms and applications, learners from diverse backgrounds can access personalized, on-demand content and instruction, breaking down the traditional barriers imposed by geography, infrastructure, and financial constraints.

AI-powered educational tools can be made available on low-cost devices and smartphones, which are increasingly widespread in developing countries. For example, AI-enabled language translation tools can facilitate access to educational content in multiple languages, overcoming the language barrier that often limits access to knowledge. Furthermore, AI can help provide adaptive learning experiences in remote areas where skilled educators may be scarce, empowering students with the tools they need to succeed.

18.1.8.3. Promoting Lifelong Learning

In a rapidly changing world, the need for lifelong learning has never been more pressing. AI plays a crucial role in facilitating continuous learning throughout individuals' lives. AI-enhanced learning ecosystems allow for adaptive learning across various stages of life, from early childhood education to adult learning and professional development. These systems can support learners in acquiring new skills and knowledge, helping them stay competitive in the workforce, navigate career transitions, and adapt to emerging challenges in various industries.

AI-powered platforms can provide personalized learning experiences that evolve with the learner, offering tailored educational content that reflects changing personal interests, career goals, or skills requirements. Moreover, AI can track learning progress over time, helping individuals reflect on their growth and adjust their learning goals accordingly. The integration of AI into the global learning ecosystem thus encourages a culture of lifelong learning, making it more accessible, flexible, and aligned with the ever-changing demands of the job market.

18.1.8.4. Collaborative Global Learning Networks

AI can help build interconnected global learning ecosystems that foster collaboration across cultures, languages, and educational systems. In such ecosystems, students, educators, and institutions can interact in real-time across borders, share knowledge, and engage in collaborative problem-solving. AI can facilitate cross-cultural communication, enhance collaborative learning experiences, and help students understand and appreciate diverse perspectives, which is essential in an increasingly globalized world.

The integration of AI can allow for the creation of global classrooms, where learners from different parts of the world can collaborate on projects, engage in peer-to-peer learning, and access shared resources. AI can manage and moderate these interactions, ensuring that learning is productive, respectful, and culturally sensitive. Additionally, AI can help identify patterns in global learning data, offering valuable insights into effective teaching methods, curriculum design, and learner engagement on a global scale.

18.1.8.5. Ethical AI for Education

As AI becomes more integrated into education, it is essential to ensure that its development and use align with ethical principles that prioritize equity, inclusivity, and fairness. The future of AI-enhanced global learning ecosystems must focus on addressing biases in AI algorithms, ensuring data privacy, and creating transparent systems that students and educators can trust. Ethical considerations will also need to address the potential for AI to inadvertently reinforce inequalities, such as by providing unequal access to resources or creating discriminatory outcomes in automated assessments.

To achieve this, AI systems must be designed with inclusivity in mind, ensuring they work for all students, regardless of socio-economic background, ability, or location. The global nature of AI in education necessitates the development of international frameworks for AI governance that uphold human rights and promote fairness in educational opportunities worldwide.

The vision for AI-enhanced global learning ecosystems is one where education becomes more personalized, accessible, and collaborative, breaking down traditional barriers to learning and fostering lifelong development for all. As AI technologies continue to evolve, they promise to transform education into a more adaptive, efficient, and equitable process. However, realizing this vision requires careful attention to the ethical implications of AI, ensuring that its benefits are shared equitably and responsibly across the globe. By addressing these challenges, AI has the potential to create a more inclusive, empowered, and connected global educational community.

Chapter 19

Reflections on AI's Role in Shaping the Future of Education

19.1. Introduction

Artificial Intelligence (AI) is increasingly shaping the future of education, offering unprecedented opportunities to enhance learning experiences, improve accessibility, and support individualized educational pathways. As AI technologies continue to evolve, their integration into educational systems is driving transformative changes. However, while AI promises substantial benefits, it raises critical questions about ethics, equity, and the potential risks associated with its widespread use. Reflecting on AI's role in education requires a nuanced understanding of its capabilities, limitations, and the broader societal implications accompanying its deployment.

19.1.1. AI's Potential to Transform Learning Environments

AI has the potential to revolutionize learning environments by making them more personalized, adaptive, and efficient. One of the key strengths of AI in education lies in its ability to tailor educational content to individual learners. AI-driven systems can analyze students' progress, learning styles, and areas of difficulty in real time, adjusting instructional content to optimize engagement and retention. Personalized learning platforms, such as intelligent tutoring systems, provide real-time feedback and support, offering students an experience uniquely suited to their needs (Woolf, 2010). This shift towards individualized learning can ensure that students are neither held back by a one size-fits-all approach nor left behind due to their learning pace, thereby enhancing overall educational outcomes.

Furthermore, AI powered tools can support educators by automating administrative tasks like grading and tracking student progress. This reduces the burden on teachers and allows them to focus more on teaching, mentorship, and the emotional aspects of student development. AI can also assist in identifying students at risk of falling behind, enabling timely interventions that can prevent academic failure and improve student retention (Siemens, 2005). By transforming classrooms into dynamic, adaptive environments, AI holds the potential to make learning more engaging, relevant, and effective.

19.1.2. Enhancing Accessibility and Inclusivity

One of AI's most profound impacts on education is its potential to make learning more accessible, particularly for underserved communities. AI can bridge gaps in access to quality education by providing learning tools and resources to students in remote or marginalized areas. AI-driven platforms that offer real-time language translation, adaptive learning content, and scalable instructional delivery can reach students who otherwise might not have access to formal education or well-trained educators (UNESCO, 2020).

AI can also be transformative for students with disabilities. Assistive technologies powered by AI, such as speech-to-text tools, personalized learning environments, and real-time sign language recognition, can remove barriers for students with visual, auditory, or cognitive disabilities. These AI innovations can ensure that students with diverse learning needs receive the same high-quality education as their peers, fostering greater inclusivity and reducing educational disparities (Punie & Cabrera, 2009).

19.1.3. Lifelong Learning and Workforce Development

The rapid pace of technological change and the evolving demands of the global workforce necessitate continuous learning. AI in education plays a crucial role in fostering lifelong learning by providing learners the tools to develop new skills and knowledge throughout their lives. AI-powered platforms can help individuals engage in self-directed learning, offering resources and personalized recommendations for skill development (Schneider & Shaffer, 2018). Moreover, AI can guide learners through career pathways, providing feedback on skill gaps and suggesting learning opportunities that align with emerging job markets.

For workforce development, AI enables targeted training programs that can rapidly upskill individuals in response to industry demands. For example, AI-based simulations and virtual training environments are already being used to train healthcare, manufacturing, and IT workers. These technologies offer immersive, direct learning experiences that would be difficult or costly to replicate in traditional classroom settings (Bates, 2015). As AI continues to evolve, it will become an indispensable tool for equipping workers with the skills necessary to thrive in an increasingly digital economy.

19.1.4. Ethical Considerations and the Challenges of AI Implementation

Despite AI's many benefits, its integration into education presents significant ethical and practical challenges. One of the foremost concerns is the potential for bias in AI algorithms, which could perpetuate existing educational inequalities. AI systems are only as good as the data they are trained on. If these datasets reflect historical biases or structural inequalities, the AI may replicate and amplify these biases in decision-making processes (Binns, 2018). For example, AI used in admissions or grading systems could unintentionally favor certain demographic groups over others, exacerbating disparities in educational outcomes.

Data privacy and security also remain critical concerns. AI systems rely heavily on collecting and analyzing vast amounts of personal data, which raises issues of how this data is stored, shared, and protected. Educators and students need assurance that their data will not be misused or exploited and that AI systems comply with rigorous data privacy standards (Dastin, 2018). Moreover, as AI technologies become more integrated into the classroom, educators, policymakers, and tech developers must work together to establish clear guidelines and regulations that ensure AI is used ethically and responsibly in educational settings.

19.1.5. A Collaborative, Global Future

In the long term, AI's role in education could help create a more collaborative global learning ecosystem. By facilitating cross-border collaborations, AI can enable students and educators to engage in global classrooms where ideas, resources, and knowledge are shared seamlessly. AI technologies can help overcome language barriers, enable real-time communication, and foster collaborative projects that involve students from different cultural and geographic contexts (Anderson & Rainie, 2017). This collaborative learning environment will enrich the educational experience, offering students a broader perspective on global issues and helping them develop the critical thinking and intercultural skills necessary for success in a globalized world.

Reflecting on AI's role in shaping the future of education underscores its vast potential to transform the educational landscape. From personalizing learning to making education more accessible and inclusive, AI promises an education system that is more equitable, responsive, and adaptive to the needs of learners worldwide. However, the integration of AI into education must be done thoughtfully, ensuring that ethical considerations such as bias, privacy, and fairness are prioritized. The future of education will be marked by collaboration, innovation, and a commitment to ensuring that the benefits of AI are shared equitably across all learners.

19.1.6. Key Takeaways for Policymakers, Educators, and Technologists

As AI continues to shape the future of education, policymakers, educators, and technologists must collaborate to ensure that AI is deployed responsibly and effectively to benefit all learners. The following key takeaways outline the critical actions and considerations for these stakeholders in harnessing AI's potential in education.

19.1.6.1. Policymakers: Establishing Regulatory and Ethical Guidelines

Policymakers play a crucial role in shaping the landscape for AI in education. To ensure AI technologies are used responsibly, they must establish comprehensive regulatory frameworks that address data privacy, security, and bias issues. Policies should focus on protecting students' data while ensuring that AI systems comply with international data protection standards. Furthermore, policymakers should create inclusive policies that promote equitable access to AI-powered educational tools, especially for underserved and marginalized communities.

In addition to data protection and privacy, governments should incentivize the development of ethical AI tools that minimize biases. This includes setting up AI algorithms' transparency, accountability, and fairness standards. Policymakers must also ensure that AI solutions do not exacerbate existing educational inequalities but rather help bridge the digital divide by supporting schools with limited resources and access to technology (Williamson & Piattoeva, 2020).

19.1.6.1.1. Key Actions for Policymakers in AI and Education

19.1.6.1.1.1. Creating Clear Regulatory Frameworks for AI in Education

Policymakers are critical in establishing clear and comprehensive regulatory frameworks for using AI in education. These frameworks should prioritize ethics, privacy, and security to ensure that AI is used responsibly and equitably. Ethical considerations include preventing biases in AI algorithms that could reinforce existing inequalities and ensuring that AI tools respect the autonomy and dignity of learners. Privacy is paramount, especially when dealing with sensitive student data; robust data protection laws and guidelines should be enforced to safeguard against misuse. Security measures are equally crucial to protect educational institutions from cyber threats that could compromise AI-driven systems. By providing a solid regulatory foundation, policymakers can build trust among stakeholders and ensure that AI technologies are deployed to enhance, rather than hinder, the educational experience.

19.1.6.1.1.2. Promoting Equity and Inclusivity in AI Adoption

To harness the transformative potential of AI in education, policymakers must actively support initiatives that promote equity and inclusivity across all educational sectors. This entails addressing barriers that disadvantaged groups—such as low-income students, rural communities, and individuals with disabilities—face in accessing AI-driven tools. Policies should encourage the development of AI solutions tailored to diverse learning needs, ensuring that these tools are accessible and culturally relevant. Funding programs that subsidize AI tools for schools in underserved areas and creating partnerships with organizations working on inclusive AI innovations can help bridge the digital divide. By championing equity-focused policies, governments can empower all learners to benefit from AI, fostering a more inclusive and equitable educational system.

19.1.6.1.1.3. Investing in Infrastructure and Capacity-Building for Underserved Communities

One of the primary obstacles to leveraging AI in education is the lack of infrastructure and capacity in underserved communities. Policymakers should prioritize investments in digital infrastructure, such as reliable internet access and modern educational technologies, to enable these communities to benefit from AI-driven educational tools. Additionally, capacity-building initiatives, such as teacher training programs and workshops for school administrators, are essential to equip educators with the skills needed to integrate AI effectively into their teaching practices. Public-private partnerships can also be vital in mobilizing resources and expertise for these initiatives. By focusing on infrastructure and capacity-building, policymakers can create an environment where AI technologies enhance learning outcomes for all, regardless of socioeconomic or geographic disparities.

Integrating AI into education requires a multifaceted approach driven by clear policies, equity-oriented initiatives, and targeted investments in infrastructure and capacity. Policymakers have a unique opportunity to shape the future of education by ensuring that AI is used as a tool for empowerment and inclusion, contributing to a more equitable and innovative educational landscape.

19.1.6.2. Educators: Leveraging AI to Enhance Teaching and Learning

Educators are at the forefront of implementing AI in the classroom and must adapt their pedagogical practices to incorporate AI technologies effectively. AI can support personalized learning, provide real-time feedback, and help identify students at risk of falling behind. However, it is crucial for educators to receive appropriate training to use AI tools to complement, not replace, their expertise. AI should enhance the educational experience, providing teachers with data-driven insights into student performance that can inform instructional decisions (Brynjolfsson & McAfee, 2014).

Educators must also embrace the importance of teaching digital literacy, ensuring that students can navigate AI-powered environments and critically assess AI-generated content. This includes fostering critical thinking and ethical reasoning skills so students can understand the implications of AI in society.

19.1.6.2.1. Key Actions for Educators in AI and Education

19.1.6.2.1.1. Professional Development in AI Tools and Educational Applications

To effectively utilize AI in education, educators need ongoing professional development that focuses on both the technical and pedagogical aspects of AI tools. This training should equip teachers with the knowledge and skills to understand how AI operates, how to integrate it into their lesson plans, and how to evaluate its effectiveness. Professional development programs should include direct workshops, certifications, and collaborative learning opportunities encouraging educators to experiment with AI technologies and share best practices. Educators can confidently adopt AI tools to enhance teaching and learning outcomes by staying informed about the latest advancements and ethical considerations.

19.1.6.2.1.2. Integrating AI into Personalized Learning Strategies

AI has the potential to transform education by enabling personalized learning experiences that cater to diverse student needs. Educators can use AI-driven tools to identify learning gaps, track student progress, and tailor instructional approaches to individual preferences and abilities. For example, adaptive learning platforms can provide customized content and feedback, helping students learn independently. Teachers can also leverage AI to address the needs of students with disabilities by offering assistive technologies that make learning more accessible. By integrating AI into their teaching strategies, educators can create a more inclusive and supportive learning environment that empowers every student to succeed.

19.1.6.2.1.3. Teaching Digital Literacy and Responsible AI Use

Teaching students digital literacy is essential in a world increasingly shaped by AI. Educators are critical in helping students understand how AI tools work, their limitations, and their potential societal impacts. This includes fostering critical thinking skills so that students can evaluate the accuracy and bias of AI-generated information. Lessons on data privacy, ethical considerations, and the responsible use of technology should be integral to the curriculum. By equipping students with these skills, educators prepare them to use AI tools effectively and encourage them to become informed, ethical, and critical participants in an AI-driven world.

Educators are at the forefront of integrating AI into the classroom and preparing students for a future shaped by technological innovation. Through professional development, personalized learning strategies, and digital literacy education, they can harness the power of AI to enhance learning outcomes while fostering a culture of responsible and ethical technology use.

19.1.6.3. Technologists: Designing Ethical and Inclusive AI Solutions

Technologists and AI developers are responsible for designing effective and ethical AI tools. This includes creating transparent, interpretable algorithms free from biases that could perpetuate inequality. Technologists must also ensure that AI systems are adaptable to diverse learning contexts, including those that cater to different languages, cultural backgrounds, and special educational needs.

Collaboration with educators and policymakers is key for technologists to understand the practical needs of classrooms and the ethical concerns surrounding AI adoption. Developers should prioritize user-centered design and create easy-to-navigate AI systems for teachers and students. Furthermore, they should work to ensure that AI solutions remain accessible, scalable, and affordable, particularly in regions with limited resources.

19.1.6.3.1. Key Actions for Technologists: Prioritize Fairness and Inclusivity in AI Design to Avoid Algorithmic Biases

Technologists have a pivotal role in shaping the future of AI, particularly in education. To ensure that AI technologies contribute positively to diverse educational contexts, technologists must prioritize fairness and inclusivity in designing and deploying AI systems. A key aspect of this responsibility involves addressing algorithmic bias—where AI systems unintentionally favor certain groups over others based on factors such as race, gender, socio-economic status, or geographic location. Algorithmic bias can undermine the effectiveness and equity of AI-powered educational tools, potentially perpetuating existing inequalities in access to resources and opportunities (O'Neil, 2016).

To mitigate algorithmic bias, technologists must begin by implementing strategies during the development stage that promote fairness. This includes ensuring that the data used to train AI systems represents the diverse groups the system will serve. For example, training data must account for various cultural, linguistic, and socio-economic backgrounds to avoid systems that disadvantage underrepresented groups. Technologists should also critically assess the data used for AI training to identify and correct any imbalances or inherent biases in the data set. This process often involves performing bias audits, where datasets and models are assessed for fairness across multiple demographic factors (Barocas et al., 2019).

Moreover, technologists should develop and employ tools to explain AI decision-making processes, enhancing transparency and accountability. AI systems that are not interpretable can create a "black box" effect, where the decisions made by the algorithm are difficult for users to understand or challenge. By building explainable AI (XAI), technologists can help educators, students, and other stakeholders comprehend the logic behind AI recommendations or assessments. This transparency can contribute to trust in AI technologies and ensure that AI systems operate fairly, as stakeholders are more likely to accept decisions they understand and perceive as just (Ribeiro et al., 2016).

In addition to technical measures, technologists must engage with diverse stakeholders during the AI development process to ensure inclusivity. Collaboration with educators, students, and policymakers is crucial in identifying different groups' specific needs and challenges. For instance, understanding how AI-powered tools may affect students from various cultural backgrounds with different learning needs can help developers create more inclusive and effective systems. AI should be designed to accommodate students with disabilities, ensuring that accessibility features are integrated into the technology from the outset. This process may involve working with accessibility experts and disability advocacy groups to ensure that AI tools are usable by individuals with physical, sensory, or cognitive impairments (Binns, 2020).

Furthermore, technologists should be mindful of the ethical implications of AI systems in education. This includes ensuring that AI applications do not reinforce harmful stereotypes or discriminatory practices. For instance, facial recognition software used in classrooms may inadvertently reinforce racial or gender biases if it is trained on non-diverse datasets (Buolamwini & Gebru, 2018). Therefore, it is essential for developers to proactively avoid creating AI tools that could disproportionately impact marginalized or vulnerable groups. An essential aspect of this process is continuous evaluation, where AI systems are monitored and adjusted post-deployment to ensure that they remain fair, equitable, and aligned with ethical standards.

Finally, the education sector requires that technologists build inclusive AI systems and cultivate an environment of continuous improvement and adaptation. AI systems should be designed to evolve based on user feedback and real-world data, allowing for the identification and correction of biases that may arise after deployment. For example, AI tools that are used in diverse educational contexts should be regularly assessed to ensure that they continue to meet the needs of all learners, and modifications should be made based on this feedback. Engaging with communities of educators, learners, and other stakeholders to gather feedback and make improvements is essential to ensuring that AI remains a tool for equity and inclusivity (Crawford, 2021).

Prioritizing fairness and inclusivity in AI design is a fundamental responsibility for technologists when creating AI education tools. Technologists can minimize algorithmic biases and create more equitable and effective AI applications by ensuring diverse and representative datasets, developing explainable AI systems, collaborating with stakeholders, and addressing ethical considerations. These actions contribute to the broader goal of using AI to enhance learning experiences, empower students, and reduce educational inequalities. As AI continues to influence educational landscapes, technologists must remain committed to designing systems that serve the needs of all learners, fostering fairness, accessibility, and inclusivity in the process.

19.1.6.3.2. Collaborate with Educators to Understand the Classroom Needs and Challenges

Collaborating with educators to understand classroom needs and challenges is crucial for successfully developing and deploying AI technologies in education. Educators have firsthand experience with the complexities of student learning, classroom dynamics, and the varied challenges diverse student populations face. By collaborating closely with educators, technologists can ensure that AI tools are effective and aligned with the real-world needs of teachers and students. This collaborative approach can significantly enhance the design, implementation, and adoption of AI systems in educational settings.

19.1.6.3.2.1. Understanding Classroom Needs and Challenges

Educators possess deep insights into the specific challenges they encounter, such as managing diverse learning needs, maintaining engagement, addressing varying levels of academic achievement, and dealing with classroom behavior. Many AI applications can benefit from these insights, particularly in personalized learning. For instance, AI can track students' learning progress, provide real-time feedback, and recommend personalized learning pathways. However, such tools are only effective when they address fundamental issues in the classroom, such as the difficulty of tracking each student's progress in large, diverse classes. Through collaboration, educators can help identify the most critical aspects of classroom management that AI can support, ensuring that technology does not replace teachers but augments their capabilities.

A key aspect of this collaboration is recognizing students' varying needs regarding learning styles, disabilities, and language barriers. By engaging with educators, technologists can better understand how AI can help bridge these gaps. For example, AI-powered educational tools can assist students with disabilities by providing assistive technologies like speech-to-text, audio learning, and individualized learning plans. Understanding the specific needs of these students from an educator's perspective is vital for developing inclusive AI applications.

19.1.6.3.2.2. Co-Designing AI Tools with Educators

Collaborative efforts between educators and technologists can involve co-designing AI tools, where teachers actively shape the technology's features and functionalities. This collaboration can help ensure that AI systems align with pedagogical goals and fit into existing classroom workflows. Teachers can provide feedback on the usability of AI tools, suggest improvements, and help refine the technology to support the learning environment better. For example, a teacher might provide insights into how AI can best be used for formative assessments, where real-time data can inform teaching strategies, or how adaptive learning systems can be optimized to cater to individual learning speeds and styles.

By involving educators early in the design process, technologists can ensure that AI tools are practical, easy to use, and beneficial for enhancing teaching and learning. In contrast, if AI systems are developed in isolation without input from educators, there is a risk that the resulting tools will be disconnected from the classroom realities, potentially leading to poor adoption or underutilization. Co-designing these systems with educators can also help identify potential ethical concerns, such as the fairness of AI-driven assessments, privacy issues, and the protection of student data.

19.1.6.3.2.3. Continuous Feedback Loops for Improvement

Collaboration should not end with the design and deployment of AI tools. Establishing continuous feedback loops between educators and technologists is critical for the ongoing refinement and improvement of AI systems. Educators' feedback can reveal whether AI tools are meeting their expectations, helping to address classroom challenges, and supporting student outcomes. This feedback can be used to make iterative improvements to AI systems, ensuring they evolve in response to real-world classroom dynamics.

For instance, after an AI-powered system is deployed in a classroom, educators may notice specific patterns for which the AI fails to account, such as how students with specific learning challenges interact with the system or how the AI could be adjusted to accommodate cultural differences. By maintaining an ongoing dialogue, technologists can make necessary updates and adjustments, creating more adaptable AI tools that are responsive to changing classroom environments and educational needs.

19.1.6.3.2.4. Professional Development for Educators

In addition to collaborating on AI tool development, it is essential to support educators with professional development opportunities related to AI and its integration into the classroom. Technologists can work with educational institutions to create training programs that help teachers understand how to use AI tools effectively, interpret AI-generated data, and incorporate these technologies into their pedagogical practices. Educators need to feel confident in their ability to use AI systems and trust that the technology enhances rather than replaces their role in the classroom.

Such professional development initiatives should also build educators' capacity to critically evaluate AI tools for ethical concerns, biases, and equity issues. For example, educators need to be trained to recognize potential biases in AI-driven assessments or personalized learning systems and to act if these biases impact students' learning experiences. Technologists and educators can collaborate to ensure that teachers are equipped with the knowledge and skills to navigate the ethical complexities of AI in education.

Collaborating with educators is essential for the effective development, deployment, and use of AI in education. Educators' insights into classroom needs, their involvement in the co-design process, continuous feedback loops, and professional development opportunities are key to ensuring that AI technologies support learning in meaningful and equitable ways. By working together, technologists and educators can create AI systems that enhance educational outcomes and address teachers' real challenges in fostering inclusive and supportive learning environments.

19.1.6.3.2.5. Design scalable AI Solutions That Are Affordable and Accessible to Diverse Educational Contexts

Designing scalable AI solutions that are affordable and accessible to diverse educational contexts is critical for ensuring that AI-driven educational tools and systems can have a broad, inclusive impact. As the use of AI in education expands, these technologies must be developed with cost-effective strategies and equitable access in mind. AI has the potential to enhance educational outcomes by providing personalized learning experiences, improving accessibility, and optimizing teaching and administrative tasks. However, if AI solutions are prohibitively expensive or difficult to integrate into different educational settings, they may fail to reach underserved communities and lower-income schools, exacerbating existing inequalities.

19.1.6.3.2.6. Affordability in AI Design

Affordability is one of the primary barriers to widespread AI adoption in education, especially in underfunded schools or regions with limited technological infrastructure. To make AI solutions affordable, developers must design cost-efficient systems for development and implementation. One approach to achieving affordability is by adopting open-source AI frameworks, which reduce development costs and allow educators and institutions to modify the technology to fit their specific needs. Open-source platforms like TensorFlow and PyTorch, as well as educational tools built on top of these frameworks, can make AI more accessible by lowering the barrier to entry for schools and educational organizations that may lack the budget for proprietary software.

In addition to using open-source solutions, developers can design AI tools with cloud computing infrastructure in mind. By leveraging cloud-based AI solutions, educational institutions can avoid the need for expensive hardware and infrastructure investments. Cloud platforms allow users to access AI systems and tools remotely, offering flexibility and scalability. Schools and universities in developed and developing countries can use this technology without significant capital expenditure on IT infrastructure. AI-based platforms that can be accessed on low-cost devices like smartphones or low-end computers further enhance the affordability and accessibility of AI for education, especially in low-resource settings.

19.1.6.3.2.7. Scalability Across Diverse Educational Contexts

Scalability is another critical consideration when designing AI solutions for education. A solution that works well in one educational context, such as a highly resourced private school in an urban area, may not necessarily be applicable or effective in a rural public school with limited resources. Therefore, AI systems must be designed to be flexible and adaptable to different contexts, ensuring that they can be deployed effectively in diverse settings, including those with fewer resources. One way to achieve scalability is through modular AI systems, where different features or functionalities can be added or removed based on the educational institution's needs. For example, an AI-driven learning management system (LMS) could offer basic features like content delivery and assessment for schools with fewer resources.

In contrast, more advanced features such as adaptive learning and personalized feedback can be added for schools with greater technological capacity.

Furthermore, AI systems should be designed to support a range of pedagogical approaches, from traditional teacher-led instruction to more student-centered, collaborative learning environments. This flexibility ensures that AI tools can be integrated into various educational contexts, whether in classrooms, remote learning environments, or informal education settings. AI-driven educational platforms can also be designed to support multilingual capabilities, enabling them to be used in diverse cultural contexts. In regions where English is not the primary language, AI systems can offer content in local languages and adapt to specific cultural and educational practices, making the technology more relevant and accessible to a global audience.

19.1.6.3.2.8. Overcoming Technological and Digital Divides

To ensure that AI solutions are accessible, developers must also address the digital divide—the gap between those with access to modern technology and those without access. Access to high-speed internet, modern computers, and even basic digital literacy skills remain significant challenges in many parts of the world. To overcome these barriers, AI developers must design systems that can function in low-bandwidth environments and on less powerful devices. For instance, AI solutions could be optimized for mobile phones, which are more widely accessible in many low-income regions than desktop computers. These mobile-optimized systems can provide learning resources, tutoring, and assessment features without requiring high-end devices or fast internet connections.

Moreover, developers can collaborate with governments, non-governmental organizations (NGOs), and international organizations to facilitate the distribution of the necessary infrastructure for AI adoption in underserved regions. Public-private partnerships could be instrumental in providing schools with the resources they need to implement AI solutions, such as affordable devices and internet connectivity. International organizations like UNESCO and the World Bank have already recognized the importance of digital equity in education, and their initiatives can support the broader goal of making AI-driven learning tools universally accessible.

19.1.6.3.2.9. Ensuring Equity in AI Education Solutions

Beyond affordability and scalability, equity is a central consideration when designing AI solutions for education. AI tools must not exacerbate existing inequalities in the education system, whether based on socioeconomic status, geography, gender, or disability. AI solutions must be designed to be inclusive, providing equal opportunities for all students, including those from marginalized groups. For example, AI-driven platforms should be capable of adapting to different learning styles and providing personalized support for students with disabilities, such as those with visual or auditory impairments, learning disabilities, or autism. Educators and technologists can mitigate the risk of creating digital inequalities that further marginalize vulnerable populations by ensuring that AI tools are designed with inclusivity in mind.

Furthermore, AI solutions should promote diversity and cultural representation by incorporating content that reflects diverse student populations' backgrounds, identities, and experiences. AI systems should be designed to avoid reinforcing stereotypes or biases in their learning materials and assessments. By embedding ethical design practices, developers can create AI systems that are not only scalable and affordable but also promote fairness and inclusion, ensuring that all students can benefit from AI-enhanced education.

Designing scalable, affordable, and accessible AI solutions for education requires a multifaceted approach considering the diverse needs of educational contexts worldwide. By leveraging open-source frameworks, cloud-based solutions, and modular designs, AI tools can be made affordable and adaptable to different resource levels. Addressing the digital divide and ensuring that AI systems are designed for equity and inclusivity are also critical components of this process. As AI continues to transform education, developers must collaborate closely with educators, policymakers, and communities to ensure that these technologies are accessible, effective, and beneficial for all students, regardless of their background or location.

19.1.6.4. Collaboration Among Stakeholders

AI in education cannot thrive in isolation; it requires a multi-stakeholder approach. Policymakers, educators, and technologists must work together to ensure that AI adoption is aligned with educational goals and societal values. Policymakers should incentivize partnerships between tech companies and educational institutions, ensuring that AI tools are developed with the input of those who will use them most. Educators must share their classroom insights with developers to improve the usability and effectiveness of AI technologies. Technologists can provide valuable expertise on AI's potential and limitations, helping educators understand how best to integrate these tools into their teaching practices.

Collaboration should also extend internationally to bridge the digital divide between developed and developing regions. Global partnerships can ensure that AI technologies are accessible, culturally sensitive, and adaptable to a wide range of educational systems and languages.

19.1.6.4.1. Key Actions for Stakeholder

19.1.6.4.1.1. Foster Cross-Sector Collaboration to Design, Implement, and Monitor AI Systems in Education

Fostering cross-sector collaboration to design, implement, and monitor AI systems in education is crucial for successfully integrating artificial intelligence (AI) into educational frameworks. When effectively deployed, AI technologies can revolutionize the education sector by improving personalized learning, optimizing educational resources, and addressing systemic inequities. However, the complex nature of AI and its potential to impact various aspects of education—ranging from curriculum design to student outcomes—necessitates a collaborative approach. Collaboration across sectors such as technology, education, government, and civil society can help ensure that AI systems are ethically designed, contextually relevant, and aligned with educational goals. This multi-stakeholder collaboration is also essential for overcoming barriers related to accessibility, equity, and digital divides and monitoring AI systems' effectiveness in real-world educational environments.

19.1.6.4.1.2. The Role of Cross-Sector Collaboration

The first step in fostering effective collaboration is recognizing that AI in education is not just a technical issue but one that requires input from various sectors to address the complex social, cultural, and educational dynamics at play. Stakeholders in the educational sector—including policymakers, educators, school administrators, and researchers—bring critical insights into the pedagogical needs and challenges students and teachers face. However, they may lack the technical expertise required to design or implement AI systems effectively. Conversely, AI technologists with the technical knowledge to build and deploy AI systems may not fully understand educational contexts' specific needs and nuances. By fostering partnerships between these two groups, education systems can ensure that AI technologies are developed with an understanding of the educational system's technological potential and practical constraints.

Moreover, governmental bodies play a key role in shaping the policies that govern the use of AI in education. These policymakers are responsible for creating regulatory frameworks ensuring AI systems are deployed safely, equitably, and with proper data privacy and security safeguards. By collaborating with educators and technologists, governments can better align policies with the needs of the education system, ensuring that regulations do not stifle innovation but encourage responsible AI development. Non-governmental organizations (NGOs) and civil society groups also contribute to this dialogue by representing the interests of marginalized or underserved communities, ensuring that AI solutions are inclusive and equitable. Cross-sector collaboration, therefore, helps create a balanced approach where different perspectives and expertise come together to create AI solutions that are technically sound, pedagogically relevant, and socially responsible.

19.1.6.4.1.3. Benefits of Cross-Sector Collaboration

One of the primary benefits of cross-sector collaboration is the pooling of resources and expertise to develop AI systems that are both innovative and grounded in real-world educational practices. Collaboration between universities, tech companies, and educational institutions can lead to developing AI-driven learning tools that are more effective and tailored to diverse learner needs. For example, companies specializing in AI can partner with educational institutions to co-develop platforms that address specific learning challenges, such as providing support for students with disabilities, those with learning differences, or those in underfunded schools. These partnerships can ensure that AI systems are designed to be adaptable to various educational contexts, from urban schools with high-tech resources to rural or remote areas with limited access to technology.

Additionally, cross-sector collaboration can help bridge the gap between cutting-edge AI technologies and the day-to-day needs of classrooms. Teachers, who are the primary users of AI-powered educational tools, offer valuable feedback about the usability, effectiveness, and relevance of AI systems in actual learning environments. By involving educators in the design and testing phases, AI developers can ensure that the systems are user-friendly and aligned with educational goals, such as fostering critical thinking, creativity, and problem-solving skills. Furthermore, teachers' insights into student learning patterns can help refine AI systems to respond more to individual student needs, supporting differentiated learning approaches.

19.1.6.4.1.4. Monitoring and Evaluating AI Impact

The design and implementation of AI systems in education should not be seen as a one-off process but rather as an ongoing cycle of development, monitoring, and evaluation. AI systems in education need to be continuously assessed to ensure that they meet educational objectives and deliver measurable outcomes. Cross-sector collaboration plays a vital role in establishing frameworks for monitoring the effectiveness and impact of AI systems over time. This process involves evaluating how well AI tools support students' learning progress, identifying areas for improvement, and addressing unintended consequences such as algorithmic bias or a narrowing of learning experiences.

Collaboration between educational institutions, technologists, and policymakers is crucial to monitor AI systems effectively. Educational institutions can provide data on student outcomes, helping identify which AI systems deliver positive results and which may need to be refined. Technologists can analyze how well AI systems are functioning, detecting potential issues related to system performance, such as slow processing speeds or compatibility issues with other digital tools. Policymakers are responsible for ensuring that evaluation processes adhere to ethical standards, protecting student privacy, and ensuring data security. Involving all relevant stakeholders in these evaluation processes helps create a comprehensive feedback loop that leads to the continuous improvement of AI systems in education.

19.1.6.5. Overcoming Challenges Through Collaboration

Despite the promise of AI in education, its adoption faces several challenges, including concerns over data privacy, algorithmic bias, and the digital divide. Cross-sector collaboration can play a key role in addressing these challenges. By working together, stakeholders can create ethical guidelines and regulations that ensure AI systems are developed and deployed responsibly. For instance, technologists and policymakers can collaborate on data protection laws that govern how student data is collected, stored, and used. Furthermore, educators and NGOs can advocate for AI solutions that prioritize inclusivity, ensuring that the tools are accessible to all students, regardless of socioeconomic background, disability, or geographic location.

Cross-sector collaboration also provides an opportunity to address the digital divide, a persistent challenge in many parts of the world. In regions with limited internet access, cross-sector partnerships can help develop low-cost, offline AI solutions that provide educational resources to underserved communities. Governments, NGOs, and tech companies can work together to deploy AI-driven educational platforms that function in low-bandwidth environments and can be accessed through affordable mobile devices. Such collaborations can help bridge the gap in educational opportunities, providing quality learning resources to students in remote areas who otherwise would not have access to the benefits of AI-powered education.

Fostering cross-sector collaboration is essential for designing, implementing, and monitoring AI systems in education. By bringing together educators, technologists, policymakers, and civil society groups, stakeholders can develop AI solutions that are technically sound, pedagogically relevant, and ethically responsible. Collaboration ensures that AI systems are designed to meet the diverse needs of students, address challenges such as the digital divide, and promote equity and inclusivity. It also supports the ongoing evaluation of AI systems, ensuring that they continue to enhance educational outcomes and align with the evolving needs of the education sector. Moving forward, a concerted effort by all stakeholders is required to ensure that AI in education fulfills its potential to transform learning experiences and empower learners worldwide.

19.1.6.5.1. Engage in International Dialogues to Promote Global Equity in AI-Powered Educational Tools

Engaging in international dialogues to promote global equity in AI-powered educational tools is crucial to ensuring that the benefits of AI in education are distributed relatively and reach underserved populations worldwide. AI's transformative potential in education— from personalized learning experiences to enhanced accessibility for students with disabilities—offers unprecedented opportunities. However, these innovations risk exacerbating existing educational inequalities without global collaboration and dialogue. Many countries, particularly in the Global South, face significant challenges in accessing and adopting AI technologies due to limited infrastructure, digital literacy, and economic resources. International dialogues can help bridge these gaps by fostering collaboration among governments, educational institutions, technology companies, and civil society organizations to develop and deploy AI tools that are accessible, affordable, and effective for all students, regardless of their geographic location, economic status, or cultural context.

19.1.6.5.2. The Importance of International Dialogues

International dialogues provide a platform for stakeholders from diverse countries and regions to share experiences, challenges, and best practices regarding implementing AI in education. These dialogues promote a deeper understanding of different countries' unique needs and contexts, enabling the development of AI-powered educational tools that are both technologically advanced, culturally sensitive, and locally relevant. For example, while some countries may face challenges related to limited digital infrastructure, others may have concerns about data privacy or the risk of reinforcing biases in AI algorithms. Through international collaboration, stakeholders can work together to address these issues, ensuring that AI tools are designed to promote equity, inclusivity, and cultural sensitivity.

Moreover, such dialogues can help establish common standards and frameworks for AI in education, ensuring that the development and deployment of AI tools adhere to ethical principles and human rights. Establishing global norms and guidelines can help prevent the use of AI in ways that deepen societal inequalities or disproportionately benefit already advantaged populations. For instance, UNESCO's 2021 policy guidelines on AI in education emphasize the importance of ensuring that AI systems are developed in ways that align with the values of fairness, equity, and non-discrimination (UNESCO, 2021). International dialogue plays a critical role in advancing these goals, facilitating discussions on how to build AI tools that are universally beneficial, regardless of socioeconomic status or location.

19.1.6.5.2.1. Promoting Inclusivity and Access

One of the primary goals of international dialogues on AI in education is to promote inclusivity and ensure that AI-powered educational tools are accessible to all students, particularly those in underserved communities. In many parts of the world, access to technology is limited, and students in rural or low-income areas often lack the infrastructure to benefit from AI advancements in education. By engaging in international dialogues, stakeholders can work together to develop affordable and scalable solutions that address these disparities. For example, partnerships between international organizations, governments, and tech companies can create low-cost AI-powered learning platforms that function in offline environments or are compatible with basic mobile devices.

Furthermore, these dialogues can help identify the specific needs of marginalized groups, such as students with disabilities, minority ethnic groups, or girls in regions with low female education participation. By fostering global partnerships and collaborations, the international community can ensure that AI tools are designed to include these groups, offering them tailored learning experiences that address their specific educational needs. AI-driven solutions, such as speech recognition software for students with visual impairments or adaptive learning platforms for students with learning disabilities, are examples of how AI can be leveraged to support marginalized students. However, such tools must be accessible to all students, regardless of their geographic location or socio-economic background, and international dialogues are vital to creating solutions that meet these needs.

19.1.6.5.2.2. Addressing Digital Divides and Infrastructure Gaps

While AI holds great promise for transforming education, its impact is only as effective as the infrastructure that supports it. Many countries, particularly in the Global South, face significant barriers to accessing the internet, electricity, and the necessary digital tools to use AI technologies in the classroom. International dialogues can help address these infrastructure challenges by fostering partnerships between governments, tech companies, and international organizations to develop solutions that are suitable for regions with limited resources. For example, low-cost AI-powered educational platforms that do not require continuous internet access can help overcome connectivity issues in rural areas.

In addition, international collaborations can promote investment in the digital infrastructure needed to support AI in education, such as expanding broadband internet access and providing affordable devices for students. International development organizations, such as the World Bank and UNESCO, play a vital role in advocating for and funding such infrastructure projects. Engaging in dialogues with these organizations can help ensure that efforts to deploy AI in education are aligned with broader development goals and that investments in digital infrastructure prioritize equity and inclusion.

19.1.6.5.2.3. Establishing Global Standards and Ethical Frameworks

Establishing standards that ensure AI-powered educational tools are ethical, transparent, and aligned with global principles of human rights and fairness is essential for deploying them globally. International dialogues can facilitate the creation of these standards by bringing together stakeholders from diverse sectors, including academia, the tech industry, and civil society. By collaborating on global ethical frameworks, these dialogues can ensure that AI tools do not exacerbate biases or inequalities but instead promote fairness and justice in education.

Ethical considerations are particularly important in AI because, if not carefully designed; AI systems can perpetuate or exacerbate existing social inequalities. For instance, algorithms used in educational tools may unintentionally favor students from certain backgrounds or regions based on the data used to train them. Through international dialogues, stakeholders can work together to identify ways to mitigate these biases and ensure that AI systems are designed to promote inclusivity. Furthermore, these dialogues can help establish clear guidelines for using student data, ensuring privacy and security are prioritized in AI applications.

Engaging in international dialogues to promote global equity in AI-powered educational tools is essential for ensuring that the transformative potential of AI in education is realized in a fair and inclusive manner. By fostering collaboration among governments, educational institutions, technology companies, and civil society organizations, these dialogues can help address the challenges faced by underserved populations and bridge the digital divide. Additionally, international collaboration can lead to developing ethical guidelines and global standards that ensure AI tools are used responsibly and equitably. By prioritizing equity in the design, implementation, and monitoring of AI-powered educational tools, the international community can ensure that AI contributes to the realization of universal access to quality education, promoting social justice and empowering students worldwide.

19.1.6.5.3. Encourage Knowledge-Sharing and Capacity-Building Across Regions to Support the Ethical Development of AI In Education.

Encouraging knowledge-sharing and capacity-building across regions is essential for fostering the ethical development of AI in education. As AI technologies continue to reshape the educational landscape, it is crucial that all regions, particularly those in the Global South and underserved communities, could contribute to and benefit from these advancements. Knowledge-sharing and capacity-building efforts can help bridge the digital divide, promote equitable access to AI technologies, and ensure that AI applications in education are developed in ways that align with ethical principles, human rights, and global standards. By fostering cross-regional collaboration, stakeholders can learn from each other's experiences, share best practices, and collectively address the challenges and opportunities associated with AI in education.

19.1.6.5.4. The Importance of Knowledge-Sharing

Knowledge-sharing across regions is vital for ensuring that AI technologies are deployed in an inclusive and contextually relevant manner. Different regions have varying educational needs, challenges, and technological capabilities, and these differences must be considered when developing AI-powered educational tools. For instance, regions with limited infrastructure may need solutions that are low-cost, accessible offline, or can be accessed through mobile phones rather than expensive computers. Knowledge-sharing initiatives, such as regional forums, conferences, and partnerships between educational institutions, governments, and technology companies, provide a platform for stakeholders from diverse regions to exchange insights and collaborate on developing AI tools that meet local needs. This sharing of expertise ensures that AI tools are adaptable and culturally sensitive, reflecting the unique educational contexts in which they will be used.

Moreover, knowledge-sharing can also help identify and address common ethical concerns that arise in the deployment of AI in education. Ethical challenges such as algorithmic bias, data privacy, and equity in access to AI-powered tools are not confined to any one region but are global issues. By engaging in cross-regional dialogue, stakeholders can collaborate on developing solutions that address these concerns. For example, countries with advanced AI research capacities can share their experiences with developing ethical AI frameworks. In contrast, countries with emerging AI ecosystems can benefit from these insights to design AI tools that align with global ethical standards. In this way, knowledge-sharing helps promote AI's responsible and transparent development in education globally.

19.1.6.5.5. Building Capacity for AI in Education

Building capacity across regions is essential for ensuring that AI technologies are developed and implemented ethically and sustainably. Capacity-building efforts can help regions develop the technical, organizational, and policy frameworks necessary to integrate AI into their education systems. These efforts can range from providing training programs for educators and policymakers to developing local AI expertise in educational technology.

One effective way to build capacity is through collaborative training programs and workshops that bring together educators, researchers, and technology experts from different regions. These programs can focus on various topics, including AI literacy for educators, the ethical implications of AI in education, and the technical skills required to design and implement AI-powered educational tools. By building local expertise in these areas, capacity-building initiatives help ensure that AI technologies are developed and used in ways that are relevant to the local context and that they meet the needs of all students, including marginalized groups.

Furthermore, international partnerships can play a crucial role in supporting capacity-building. For example, collaborations between universities, research institutions, and international organizations can help provide technical expertise and financial support for developing AI tools tailored to specific educational contexts. These partnerships can also facilitate the development of regional AI hubs or centers of excellence, where researchers and educators can collaborate on AI research and development. By pooling resources and knowledge, such partnerships can accelerate the development of AI-powered educational tools that are both innovative and ethical.

19.1.6.5.6. Promoting Ethical Standards and Global Governance

As AI technologies become more widespread in education, ethical standards, and governance frameworks must be developed at national and international levels. Knowledge-sharing and capacity-building initiatives can be key in creating and implementing these frameworks. International organizations, such as UNESCO and the OECD, can lead efforts to develop global guidelines for the ethical use of AI in education, ensuring that AI systems are developed in ways that promote equity, transparency, and fairness.

By fostering collaboration across regions, stakeholders can work together to establish common ethical principles that govern the use of AI in education. These principles can address issues such as algorithmic bias, data privacy, and accountability in AI decision-making. Additionally, capacity-building initiatives can support the development of regulatory frameworks that ensure AI technologies are used responsibly in educational contexts. For example, by working together, governments and international organizations can create policies that require AI developers to adhere to ethical standards and provide transparency in how AI systems are trained, assessed, and deployed in educational settings.

Furthermore, international collaboration can help ensure that AI tools are developed in ways that respect the rights of students and teachers. Global partnerships can advocate for policies that protect the privacy and security of educational data and ensure that AI applications do not discriminate against vulnerable populations. By building capacity for ethical AI development across regions, stakeholders can help create a global ecosystem supporting responsible and equitable use of AI in education.

Knowledge-sharing and capacity-building are essential components of promoting the ethical development of AI in education. By fostering cross-regional collaboration, stakeholders can work together to develop AI-powered educational tools that are inclusive, culturally sensitive, and aligned with global ethical standards. These efforts help bridge the digital divide, promote equitable access to AI technologies, and ensure that AI applications in education are designed and deployed to benefit all students, regardless of their geographic location or socioeconomic status. Through international dialogue and cooperation, stakeholders can share best practices, address common challenges, and develop innovative solutions that ensure AI's responsible and ethical use in education. These efforts will contribute to creating a global education ecosystem that leverages the transformative potential of AI while promoting fairness, transparency, and social justice.

AI has the potential to reshape education by making learning more personalized, accessible, and inclusive. Policymakers, educators, and technologists must work together to ensure that AI enhances the educational experience while addressing ethical, equity, and access challenges. By establishing clear guidelines, fostering collaboration, and prioritizing the needs of diverse learners, AI can contribute to creating an education system that is more equitable, efficient, and adaptive to future demands.

References

Anderson, C. A., & Rainie, L. (2017). *The Future of Learning and Education: How Technology Shapes the Global Classroom*. Pew Research Center.

Barocas, S., Hardt, M., & Narayanan, A. (2019). Fairness and machine learning: Limitations and challenges. In *Fairness and Machine Learning: Limitations and Challenges* (pp. 3–27). ACM Press. https://doi.org/10.1145/3287560.3287598.

Bates, T. (2015). *Teaching in a Digital Age: Guidelines for Designing Teaching and Learning for a Digital Age*. Tony Bates Associates Ltd.

Binns, R. (2018). *On the Meaning of Privacy in the Age of Artificial Intelligence: A Framework for Ethical Design and Use*. ACM Digital Library.

Binns, R. (2020). The importance of accessibility in AI systems. *Journal of Technology and Disability*, 32(1), 19-35. https://doi.org/10.3233/TAD-200240.

Brynjolfsson, E., & McAfee, A. (2014). *The Second Machine Age: Work, Progress, and Prosperity in a Time of Brilliant Technologies*. W. W. Norton & Company.

Buolamwini, J., & Gebru, T. (2018). Gender shades: Intersectional accuracy disparities in commercial gender classification. In *Proceedings of the 1st Conference on Fairness, Accountability and Transparency* (pp. 77–91). ACM. https://doi.org/10.1145/3287560.3287593.

Cai, J., & Yang, J. (2021). Cross-sector collaboration for AI in education: Opportunities and challenges. *International Journal of Educational Technology in Higher Education*, 18(1), 22. https://doi.org/10.1186/s41239-021-00269-w.

Crawford, K. (2021). *Atlas of AI: Power, politics, and the planetary costs of artificial intelligence*. Yale University Press.

Dastin, J. (2018). *Amazon Scraps AI Recruiting Tool That Showed Bias Against Women.* Reuters.

Felder, R. M., & Silverman, L. K. (1988). Learning and teaching styles in engineering education. *Engineering Education*, 78(7), 674-681.

Hernandez, A., & Tan, L. (2022). Building inclusive AI systems in education: A framework for collaboration. *Journal of Artificial Intelligence in Education*, 32(3), 57-79. https://doi.org/10.1007/s40593-021-00267-4.

Hwang, G. J., & Chen, P. S. (2017). *The Convergence of AI and Education: A Review of Applications and Future Directions*. Springer.

Nussbaum, M. C. (2011). *Creating capabilities: The human development approach.* Harvard University Press.

O'Neil, C. (2016). *Weapons of math destruction: How big data increases inequality and threatens democracy*. Crown Publishing Group.

OECD. (2020). *Artificial Intelligence in Education: Challenges and Opportunities for Sustainable Development.* OECD Publishing. https://doi.org/10.1787/9789264489672-en.

O'Neil, C. (2016). *Weapons of math destruction: How big data increases inequality and threatens democracy.* Crown Publishing Group.

Popenici, S. A. D., & Kerr, S. (2017). Exploring the role of AI in education: A review of literature. *Educational Technology & Society*, 20(4), 35-45.

Punie, Y., & Cabrera, M. (2009). *The Future of Learning in the Knowledge Society. Institute for Prospective Technological Studies*.

Ribeiro, M. T., Singh, S., & Guestrin, C. (2016). Why should I trust you? Explaining the predictions of any classifier. In *Proceedings of the 22nd ACM SIGKDD International Conference on Knowledge Discovery and Data Mining* (pp. 1135–1144). ACM. https://doi.org/10.1145/2939672.2939778.

Schneider, E., & Shaffer, D. W. (2018). Lifelong Learning in the Digital Age: A Global Perspective. UNESCO.

Seldon, A., & Abid, I. (2019). Artificial intelligence in education: The future of learning and learning of the future. *Education Futures*.

Siemens, G. (2005). Connectivism: A Learning Theory for the Digital Age. *International Journal of Instructional Technology and Distance Learning*, 2(1), 3-10.

UNESCO. (2020). Global Education Monitoring Report 2020: Inclusion and Education: All Means All. UNESCO Publishing.

UNESCO. (2021). AI in Education: Policy Guidelines for Ethical and Inclusive Development. UNESCO. https://unesdoc.unesco.org/ark:/48223/pf0000377995

West, D. M. (2018). *The future of work: Robots, AI, and automation.* Brookings Institution Press.

Williamson, B., & Piattoeva, N. (2020). *The Global Education Race: Taking the Measure of PISA and International Testing*. Routledge.

Woolf, B. P. (2010). *Building Intelligent Interactive Tutors: Student-Centered Strategies for Revolutionizing E-Learning.* Morgan Kaufmann.

World Bank. (2018). World Development Report 2018: Learning to Realize Education's Promise. World Bank Group. https://doi.org/10.1596/978-1-4648-1161-4.

Zawacki-Richter, O., & Anderson, T. (2018). *Theoretical foundations of online learning: A research review. Springer*. https://doi.org/10.1007/978-3-319-51156-4.

Chapter 20

Case Studies of AI in Education Across Regions

20.1. Introduction

The integration of artificial intelligence (AI) into educational systems has the potential to transform education globally. The diverse approaches and outcomes across regions, depending on local needs, infrastructure, and educational contexts, illustrate this transformative potential. Case studies from different parts of the world show how AI can enhance education, address specific regional challenges, and promote equitable learning opportunities. These examples highlight how AI can revolutionize educational experiences by personalizing learning, improving access, and enhancing teacher support while also addressing barriers like geographical isolation, resource constraints, and socio-economic disparities.

20.1.1. Case Study 1: AI in Rural Areas of Sub-Saharan Africa

In Sub-Saharan Africa, limited resources, teacher shortages, and geographical barriers often hinder access to quality education. However, AI-powered tools are beginning to address some of these challenges. One notable example is the partnership between the African Development Bank (AfDB) and IBM to introduce AI-powered education systems in rural areas of countries like Kenya and Uganda. The initiative, known as the "AI for Education in Africa" project, uses AI-based platforms to support personalized learning and provide access to educational resources in remote areas.

AI-driven platforms, such as the IBM Watson-based "Teacher Advisor" system, offer personalized lesson plans, professional development resources, and feedback for teachers in under-resourced schools. By leveraging AI's ability to analyze data and recommend tailored instructional materials, the system enables teachers to improve their pedagogical skills and provide more targeted learning experiences for their students. This initiative addresses the scarcity of skilled teachers and creates a scalable solution for delivering high-quality education to regions with significant educational deficits (World Economic Forum, 2020).

This project is a testament to how AI can be a powerful tool in promoting educational equity. By overcoming barriers related to geographic isolation, resource scarcity, and professional development in developing regions, AI is playing a crucial role in making quality education more accessible. However, challenges remain, particularly regarding the affordability and sustainability of such technologies in areas with limited infrastructure.

20.1.2. Case Study 2: AI in China's "Smart" Education

China has made significant strides in integrating AI into its education system, particularly by implementing "smart classrooms" and AI-powered personalized learning platforms. One of the most notable examples is the use of AI by the education technology company Squirrel AI, which uses intelligent tutoring systems to offer personalized education to students. Squirrel AI's system analyzes students' learning behaviors and provides customized learning paths, adapting the difficulty of lessons based on real-time assessments of the student's progress. This adaptive learning technology is deployed in both primary and secondary schools, offering a personalized approach to education at a scale.

The widespread adoption of AI in China is part of a broader government initiative to integrate AI into education through initiatives like the "AI Education Action Plan" (2018). The government has also supported AI in education by funding research, providing data infrastructure, and encouraging private-sector participation. As a result, AI-driven education technologies are already becoming an integral part of the classroom experience, helping students learn at their own pace and enabling teachers to focus on providing targeted support to students who need it most (Xu et al., 2021).

While the implementation of AI in China's education system has shown positive results, particularly in terms of personalized learning, it has also raised important ethical considerations. Challenges around privacy, data security, and the ethical implications of AI in educational contexts are still emerging. The rapid adoption of AI in the country's education system underscores the need for careful regulation and responsible use of AI technologies to ensure that they are used ethically and inclusively.

20.1.3. Case Study 3: AI in Finland's Educational System

Finland has long been regarded as a global leader in education, with a strong emphasis on equity, teacher professionalism, and student-centered learning. The Finnish education system has embraced AI as a tool to enhance these values, focusing on augmenting, rather than replacing, teachers. A prime example is the AI-supported learning platform, "Kide Science," which was developed to teach young children complex scientific concepts through interactive storytelling and games. Kide Science uses AI to personalize content and adjust the difficulty level based on individual learners' progress, ensuring that every child receives the right level of challenge.

Another significant initiative is the use of AI in teacher professional development. Finland has invested in AI-driven tools to help teachers refine their skills by providing personalized feedback based on classroom interactions, student performance, and curriculum delivery. These tools are designed to support the development of reflective teaching practices and foster continuous improvement among educators. By focusing on both students and teachers, Finland's approach to AI in education aims to create a holistic learning ecosystem responsive to all stakeholders' needs (Heikkinen et al., 2020).

The Finnish approach contrasts with more centralized, top-down models of AI integration and emphasizes the importance of teacher autonomy, ethical decision-making, and student well-being. This balance between technological innovation and human-centered values serves as an important model for other countries looking to integrate AI in ways that align with social and educational goals.

20.1.4. Case Study 4: AI in Latin America

In Latin America, AI is being used to tackle some of the region's most persistent educational challenges, such as access to quality education, language barriers, and disparities between urban and rural areas. One of the leading examples is the "EdTech Colombia" initiative, which supports the development of AI-powered educational tools for public schools in Colombia. This initiative aims to provide underserved communities access to educational content and digital learning platforms that adapt to students' needs, allowing them to progress at their own pace. One such tool is the AI-based tutoring platform, "Aula Virtual," which provides personalized support for students in subjects like mathematics and language arts.

In Brazil, AI is also used to address language barriers and improve educational outcomes for marginalized populations. The AI-driven platform, "Cognitivo," is helping students learn Portuguese and other languages by using natural language processing (NLP) technologies to analyze spoken and written language. This technology is particularly important in a country with diverse linguistic groups and a large population of non-native Portuguese speakers. By offering real-time feedback and adapting learning materials to the linguistic abilities of each student, AI is helping to break down language barriers and promote inclusion in education (Faria et al., 2021).

The integration of AI in Latin America highlights its potential to address specific regional challenges, such as language diversity and educational inequality. However, challenges related to data privacy, digital literacy, and infrastructure must be addressed to ensure that AI-driven educational tools are implemented effectively and equitably across the region.

These case studies from Sub-Saharan Africa, China, Finland, and Latin America demonstrate the diverse ways in which AI is being integrated into educational systems worldwide. In each region, AI has the potential to address specific educational challenges, such as access to education, resource limitations, and language barriers. However, implementing AI in education has challenges related to infrastructure, ethical considerations, and ensuring equitable access. As AI technologies evolve, policymakers, educators, and technologists must collaborate across regions to share knowledge, address common challenges, and ensure that AI promotes inclusive, equitable, and high-quality education for all. Table 20.1. gives an overview of AI in education across different countries.

The table provides an overview of AI-driven educational initiatives across various countries, showcasing the diverse applications of AI to enhance personalized learning and improve educational outcomes.

- *United States: DreamBox Learning* leverages AI to provide adaptive math instruction for K-8 students. The platform adjusts the difficulty level based on real-time student performance, allowing for a personalized learning experience tailored to individual needs.
- *United Kingdom: Squirrel AI* delivers adaptive learning experiences across UK schools. The initiative focuses on personalized tutoring and assessments, adjusting content based on student performance to support optimal learning.

- *China: Squirrel AI* is similarly implemented in China's primary and secondary schools, offering personalized learning that adjusts to each student's individual pace. The goal is to bridge educational gaps by ensuring that each student receives instruction suited to their specific needs.
- *India: Byju's uses AI to create personalized learning paths for K-12* students and to assist with test preparation. Byju's platform emphasizes adaptive learning, where content and difficulty levels are adjusted based on student progress.
- *Finland: Kide Science* employs AI-powered personalized learning systems for young children. The focus is on early childhood education's interactive and play-based learning experiences, allowing for a creative, engaging, and adaptive learning environment.
- *South Korea: AI in Smart Education* integrates AI within South Korean classrooms to enhance personalized learning and provide teachers with real-time analytics. This initiative aims to optimize teaching effectiveness and student engagement.
- *Brazil: Cognitivo* focuses on AI for personalized language learning, especially Portuguese and other languages. The platform applies natural language processing (NLP) to adapt learning content to individual learners' proficiency levels.
- *Colombia: EdTech Colombia & Aula Virtual* utilize AI-based systems to support personalized learning, particularly targeting rural regions. These systems aim to improve the quality of education and increase student engagement through the use of adaptive technology.
- *Australia: AI-SEP (Smart Learning Environments)* applies AI to personalize learning paths in K-12 schools, providing data-driven insights for teachers. This initiative is designed to improve student engagement and learning outcomes and provide tailored learning experiences.
- *Kenya: AI for Education in Kenya* introduces AI-powered mobile learning platforms in rural and underserved areas. These platforms aim to provide students with accessible and personalized learning experiences, contributing to improving educational outcomes in regions with limited resources.

Each of these case studies represents how AI is being implemented across diverse educational systems globally, highlighting the potential of AI to foster personalized, efficient, and inclusive learning environments. These initiatives demonstrate the transformative potential of AI in enhancing education across different contexts, from K-12 schools to early childhood education, language learning, and rural areas.

Table 20.1. AI in education across different countries

Country	AI Initiative	Description
United States	DreamBox Learning	DreamBox uses AI to provide adaptive math instruction for K-8 students, adjusting difficulty levels based on student performance and providing a personalized learning experience.
United Kingdom	Squirrel AI	Squirrel AI uses AI to deliver adaptive learning experiences across UK schools, focusing on personalized tutoring and learning assessments.
China	Squirrel AI	Implemented across primary and secondary schools, Squirrel AI tailors lessons to individual students' learning paces, helping bridge educational gaps.
India	Byju's	Byju's platform leverages AI to deliver personalized learning paths for K-12 students and test preparation, emphasizing adaptive learning.
Finland	Kide Science	Kide Science uses AI-powered personalized learning for young children, focusing on interactive and play-based learning experiences in early childhood education.
South Korea	AI in Smart Education	South Korea's smart education initiative integrates AI into classrooms to enhance personalized learning and provide teachers with real-time analytics.
Brazil	Cognitivo	Cognitivo uses AI for personalized language learning, applying natural language processing to help students learn Portuguese and other languages.
Colombia	EdTech Colombia & Aula Virtual	EdTech initiatives in Colombia employ AI-based systems for personalized learning, particularly in rural regions, to improve educational quality and student engagement.
Australia	AI-SEP (Smart Learning Environments)	AI-SEP leverages AI to personalize learning paths and offer data-driven insights for K-12 schools in Australia, improving student engagement and learning outcomes.
Kenya	AI for Education in Kenya	In Kenya, AI-based mobile learning platforms are being implemented in rural and underserved regions to provide personalized learning experiences and improve educational outcomes.

Sources: Liu & Zhong, 2019; Xu et al., 2021; Gupta & Patel, 2020; Heikkinen et al., 2020; Lee & Kim, 2018; Faria et al., 2021; Chan & Kennedy, 2019; World Economic Forum, 2020, respectively.

References

Chan, W., & Kennedy, J. (2019). AI-driven personalized learning: The case of Smart Learning Environments in Australia. *Journal of Educational Research and Technology*, 23(2), 45-56.

Faria, D., Mota, J., & Barreto, M. (2021). Artificial intelligence for language learning: Challenges and opportunities in Latin America. *Journal of Educational Technology & Society*, 24(3), 10-21.

Gupta, S., & Patel, R. (2020). AI in education: Byju's and personalized learning in India. *International Journal of Educational Technology*, 17(2), 40-51.

Heikkinen, A., Niemi, H., & Rasku, M. (2020). AI in Finnish education: Supporting teachers and students. *International Journal of Educational Technology*, 19(4), 32-47.

Lee, H., & Kim, Y. (2018). AI-powered smart education in South Korea: Innovations and challenges. *Journal of Educational Innovation*, 25(1), 14-29.

Liu, S., & Zhong, Z. (2019). Adaptive learning systems powered by artificial intelligence: The case of DreamBox Learning. *Journal of Educational Technology & Society*, 22(3), 25-36.

World Economic Forum. (2020). *AI for Education in Africa: Leveraging technology to transform education in Sub-Saharan Africa*. https://www.weforum.org/agenda/2020/01/ai-africa-education-initiative/.

Xu, J., Wang, Y., & Zhang, L. (2021). *The future of AI in education in China: Opportunities and challenges*. *Journal of Artificial Intelligence in Education*, 31(1), 45-62.

Chapter 21

Conclusion: Reflections of AI Application in Education

The book AI Applications in Education and Empowerment is a comprehensive resource that examines the intersection of artificial intelligence (AI), education, and empowerment. It systematically explores AI's transformative potential, ethical considerations, and societal implications. By combining theoretical insights with practical applications and case studies, this book aims to inspire and motivate educators, policymakers, and technologists to harness AI responsibly and effectively, thereby empowering individuals and communities. This expanded elaboration builds on the existing chapters to underscore the book's depth and significance.

21.1. AI Applications in Education and Empowerment

The introductory chapter contextualizes AI's transformative role in reshaping education and empowerment. It highlights AI's capacity to personalize learning experiences, automate administrative tasks, and create equitable access to quality education. The chapter also introduces empowerment as a central theme, linking AI's potential to enhance individual agency and societal equity. Drawing on recent developments, it emphasizes that AI in education is not just a tool but a paradigm shift toward adaptive, inclusive, and future-ready learning systems.

21.2. The Age of Artificial Intelligence

This chapter offers a dual focus: the historical evolution of AI and its growing intersection with education. It chronicles AI's journey from conceptual theories in the 20th century to its practical applications today, such as adaptive learning platforms and intelligent tutoring systems. The chapter also explores how AI can empower marginalized communities, democratize access to education, and enable lifelong learning opportunities. The chapter weaving historical context with current trends sets the stage for understanding AI's role as a transformative force in education.

21.3. The Need for Transformation in Education and Empowerment

Acknowledging the systemic challenges in traditional education systems, this chapter builds a case for transformative approaches driven by AI. It identifies critical gaps, such as unequal access, outdated curricula, and a lack of personalization, and explores how AI can address these issues. The chapter argues that education is a cornerstone of empowerment, enabling individuals to break poverty, inequality, and exclusion cycles. AI's capacity to scale solutions and foster inclusion is framed as a critical component of global efforts toward achieving equitable and quality education.

21.4. Foundations of AI in Education

21.4.1. AI and Learning Paradigms

This chapter examines the theoretical foundations of AI in education, focusing on its ability to transform traditional learning paradigms. AI-driven tools like intelligent tutoring systems, virtual assistants, and gamified learning platforms are analyzed for their role in enhancing student.

21.4.2. AI in Curriculum Design and Development

Educators can create dynamic, adaptive, and inclusive learning materials by leveraging AI for curriculum design. This chapter explores how AI algorithms analyze learning data to design curricula that meet diverse student needs. The focus is AI's ability to align educational goals with real-world skills, fostering innovation in curriculum development.

21.4.3. Bridging Gaps with AI

The potential for AI to bridge educational gaps extends beyond addressing current disparities. Looking ahead, AI's integration with technologies like blockchain can ensure credentialing transparency and enable recognition of skills across borders. Collaborative global initiatives, such as open AI-powered education platforms, can further democratize access, empowering learners in even the most remote regions. Bridging gaps is not just about access; it's about creating equitable systems where diverse learners thrive. AI can redefine the educational landscape by amplifying voices, addressing systemic inequities, and fostering a global shared knowledge and innovation culture.

This book serves as a critical resource for bridging the knowledge gap and understanding the profound implications of artificial intelligence in the educational landscape. The book addresses existing theoretical and practical knowledge gaps by comprehensively exploring AI's potential, challenges, and practical applications. It synthesizes interdisciplinary insights from education, technology, ethics, and societal development, offering a holistic understanding of how AI can transform learning and empowerment systems.

Each chapter contributes to closing the knowledge gap by breaking down complex AI concepts into actionable insights tailored for educators, policymakers, researchers, and students. For instance:

- *Historical Context* (Chapter 2) equips readers with a nuanced understanding of AI's evolution and its intersection with education and empowerment.
- *Innovative Applications* (Part IV) showcases real-world examples of how AI-driven tools can revolutionize learning processes and expand opportunities, especially for underserved communities.
- *Ethical Considerations* (Chapter 10) ensures a critical evaluation of AI's implications, fostering an informed approach to its integration in education.

By blending academic rigor with practical case studies, the book creates a blueprint for knowledge-sharing that is inclusive, accessible, and forward-looking. It empowers readers to understand AI and leverage its transformative potential to address systemic inequities and unlock opportunities for all.

21.5. Empowerment Through AI-Driven Learning

21.5.1. Skills Development for the Future Workforce

AI equips learners with skills for a rapidly changing job market. This chapter discusses how AI-driven tools facilitate skill development in critical thinking, problem-solving, and digital literacy. It also explores AI's role in fostering creativity and innovation, preparing learners for Industry 4.0 and beyond.

21.5.2. AI and Lifelong Learning

Lifelong learning is critical in an era of rapid technological change. This chapter explores AI's role in enabling continuous learning by offering flexible, adaptive, and personalized learning opportunities. The chapter highlights innovations supporting learning across all life stages, from professional upskilling platforms to AI-powered mentorship systems.

21.5.3. Empowering Underserved Communities

Education is a powerful tool for empowerment, and AI can amplify its impact. This chapter examines case studies of AI-driven educational initiatives that have transformed underserved communities. Examples include mobile learning apps for remote areas, AI tutors for non-native speakers, and AI tools to support learners with disabilities.

21.6. Societal Impacts of AI in Education and Empowerment

21.6.1. Ethics and Equity in AI for Education

Ethics and equity are central to responsible AI deployment. This chapter discusses algorithmic bias, data privacy, and digital divides. It advocates for ethical AI design principles and governance frameworks to ensure that AI-driven education systems are fair, inclusive, and transparent.

21.6.2. Cultural Sensitivity and Representation in AI Systems

AI systems must reflect cultural diversity and sensitivity. This chapter explores how cultural biases in AI systems can undermine equity and empowerment. It calls for inclusive AI development processes prioritizing cultural representation, ensuring AI tools resonate with diverse populations.

21.6.3. Global Collaboration for AI in Education

Global challenges require collaborative solutions. This chapter highlights international efforts to leverage AI in education, such as partnerships between governments, NGOs, and private organizations. It explores how cross-border collaborations can address shared challenges, promote innovation, and build inclusive educational ecosystems.

21.7. Future Possibilities—The Next Generation of AI in Education

The future of AI in education is poised to be transformative. As generative AI becomes more sophisticated, it can create customized educational content, such as interactive simulations and virtual reality experiences, that adapt to individual learners' preferences and goals. Innovations in neurotechnology and AI can also explore how students learn, enabling the development of tools that align with brain-based learning principles. For instance, AI-powered real-time assessments could identify what a learner knows and how they think, offering deeper insights into cognitive processes.

Integrating AI with emerging fields like quantum computing and 5G connectivity promises global learning ecosystems where students can interact with peers and educators across the globe in immersive, real-time environments. These advancements also raise critical questions about governance, ethics, and the human-AI relationship, urging stakeholders to anticipate and address challenges proactively. The next generation of AI in education has the potential to go beyond solving existing problems—it could fundamentally reshape our understanding of learning itself.

21.8. Reflections on AI's Role in Shaping the Future of Education

Reflecting on AI's transformative impact, its role in shaping the future of education becomes clear: it is both a tool and a catalyst. As we advance, AI offers a means to personalize education, foster creativity, and develop global competencies, ensuring learners are informed and empowered. However, the reflection must also recognize the complexities AI introduces. Issues such as algorithmic bias, digital dependency, and the risk of dehumanizing education highlight the need for thoughtful integration.

This reflection also emphasizes the importance of collaborative governance and multi-stakeholder engagement. The future of AI in education must be co-created, drawing insights from educators, technologists, policymakers, students, and communities. Ethical considerations should guide every AI development and deployment stage to ensure education remains human-centered.

AI's role in education is not an endpoint but an ongoing journey. As we navigate this journey, we must remain committed to leveraging AI for equity, innovation, and empowerment. The future of education, shaped by AI, is an opportunity to redefine learning and reimagine a world where knowledge, opportunity, and empowerment are accessible to all.

This book goes beyond bridging knowledge gaps; it lays a solid foundation for the right pathways to address pressing global challenges. This book is a guiding framework for navigating complexities in a rapidly evolving world where AI shapes the future of work, learning, and societal interactions.

21.8.1. Equipping Stakeholders with Tools for Innovation

The book offers concrete strategies for educators to enhance personalized learning, policymakers to create equitable frameworks, and researchers to push the boundaries of innovation. This collective knowledge ensures that stakeholders are well-equipped to foster resilient, adaptable, and inclusive systems.

21.8.2. Empowering Underserved Communities

Through a dedicated focus on empowerment (Chapter 9), the book highlights pathways to integrate AI in underserved regions, ensuring equitable access to education and opportunities. It emphasizes the transformative power of AI to break cycles of poverty and exclusion by making high-quality education universally accessible.

21.8.3. Fostering Ethical and Inclusive Growth

Chapters on ethics, equity, and cultural sensitivity emphasize the importance of an inclusive and human-centered approach to AI adoption. This ensures that AI systems reflect diverse cultural contexts, uphold human dignity, and prevent the perpetuation of systemic biases.

21.8.4. Preparing for a Sustainable Future

The final chapters, which explore future possibilities and global collaboration, set a vision for sustainable, lifelong learning ecosystems. They emphasize the integration of AI with emerging technologies, fostering a world where education is continuous, collaborative, and capable of addressing the needs of an unpredictable future.

By offering a well-rounded exploration of AI's transformative role in education and empowerment, this book addresses the immediate needs of the contemporary world and anticipates future challenges and opportunities. It inspires readers to think critically and proactively leverage AI for equitable development and empowerment. The knowledge and pathways presented in this book provide the necessary foundation to create a world where learning is a catalyst for progress, empowerment, and

The book concludes with a call to action for stakeholders to collaborate in building ethical, inclusive, and innovative AI applications in education. By bridging knowledge gaps and providing actionable insights, this book aspires to serve as a foundational text for the emerging field of AI in education and empowerment.

Glossary of AI and EdTech Terminologies

Adaptive Learning Technology

Adaptive learning technology refers to software or platforms that dynamically adjust educational content and activities based on a learner's progress, performance, and individual needs. This type of technology uses algorithms to analyze data from students' interactions and tailor the learning experience to provide personalized support, such as altering the difficulty of questions, recommending supplementary resources, or presenting new topics based on mastery. Adaptive learning helps ensure that each student moves at their own pace and receives targeted instruction that addresses their specific learning gaps.

Adaptive Learning

Adaptive learning is an educational approach that uses AI to modify the difficulty and style of content based on a learner's progress, behavior, and needs. The system continuously assesses student performance and adjusts the curriculum, ensuring that learners receive materials that are appropriate for their current level of understanding. This personalized approach helps optimize learning efficiency, enhance engagement, and ensure that students are challenged without being overwhelmed.

Adaptive Learning

Adaptive learning refers to a technology-driven approach in education where the content, pace, and style of teaching are customized based on the individual needs of the learner. It leverages data about student performance, learning preferences, and progress to adjust instructional strategies in real-time. This ensures that each student receives a personalized learning experience that addresses their strengths, weaknesses, and preferred learning methods. For example, an adaptive learning system might provide additional practice for a student struggling with a particular concept while accelerating lessons for a student who has mastered the material. This approach is widely used in digital learning platforms, such as DreamBox Learning and Knewton, where algorithms continuously adapt the learning path for each student based on their interactions.

Adaptive Testing

Adaptive testing is a type of assessment where the difficulty of questions adjusts in real time based on the student's responses. The system analyzes the student's performance as they progress through the test and adapts the questions to reflect their knowledge and skill level. This ensures that each student is appropriately challenged, providing a more accurate measure of their abilities. Tools like the GRE and other standardized tests have incorporated adaptive testing technology to create a personalized assessment experience that better matches each student's proficiency.

AI Chatbot

An AI chatbot is a software tool powered by artificial intelligence that simulates human conversation through text or voice interactions. In educational settings, AI chatbots can assist learners by answering questions, providing study material, offering feedback, and even guiding them through lessons. These chatbots use natural language processing and machine learning algorithms to understand and respond to student inquiries, helping to create a personalized learning experience and support students 24/7.

AI in Learning Disabilities

AI tools are increasingly being used to support students with learning disabilities by providing personalized, adaptive content and interventions. These tools can analyze individual learning patterns, identify specific challenges, and offer targeted resources or modifications to help students succeed. Examples include text-to-speech applications, speech recognition, and AI-driven tutoring systems tailored to students' needs.

AI in STEM Education

AI in STEM education involves the application of artificial intelligence technologies to enhance the teaching and learning of Science, Technology, Engineering, and Mathematics (STEM) subjects. AI can be used to create personalized learning experiences, analyze student performance, provide instant feedback, and simulate complex scientific and engineering concepts. By integrating AI into STEM curricula, educators can better engage students, improve problem-solving skills, and foster deeper understanding in these critical fields.

AI Tutor

An AI tutor is a software application that leverages artificial intelligence to provide personalized tutoring to students. These AI-powered tutors are often used in subjects like mathematics, languages, and science, offering customized lessons, feedback, and problem-solving assistance. AI tutors can adapt to individual students' learning styles and needs, track their progress, and provide real-time support, helping to enhance learning outcomes and offering a supplementary tool to traditional teaching methods.

AI-Driven Content Creation

AI-driven content creation refers to the use of artificial intelligence to generate educational materials automatically, such as quizzes, videos, assignments, and lesson plans. AI can analyze curriculum requirements, student performance data, and learning objectives to produce personalized, adaptive content. This technology helps reduce the workload for educators and ensures that content is tailored to the needs of individual students, improving engagement and learning outcomes.

AI-Driven Personal Learning Assistant

An AI-driven personal learning assistant is a virtual assistant that helps guide students through their learning journey. These assistants provide personalized content recommendations, manage schedules, remind students of tasks, and answer questions. By adapting to each learner's needs, these assistants offer a more customized learning experience.

AI-Enhanced Collaboration Tools

AI-enhanced collaboration tools are designed to support teamwork and group learning by optimizing group dynamics and suggesting tasks, resources, or activities for teams. These tools use AI to assess individual and group performance, recommend collaborative tasks, and facilitate communication, ensuring that students are effectively working together toward common educational goals.

AI-Enhanced Content

AI-enhanced content refers to educational material that has been personalized, modified, or created using artificial intelligence (AI) algorithms. AI can be used to adjust the difficulty of tasks, recommend specific resources, or tailor the content to a learner's progress and preferences. For instance, AI can analyze a student's interactions with the material and suggest targeted exercises or explanations to address learning gaps. This personalization enhances the learning experience by making the content more relevant and engaging for each individual learner.

AI-Enhanced Teacher Support

AI-enhanced teacher support involves the use of artificial intelligence tools to assist educators with tasks like grading, lesson planning, student engagement, and data analysis. AI can automate administrative tasks, analyze student performance, and provide insights that help teachers tailor their instruction to meet individual needs. By leveraging AI, teachers can focus more on instructional quality and student interaction, improving overall teaching effectiveness and reducing burnout.

AI-Powered Assessments

AI-powered assessments are evaluations that use artificial intelligence to measure a student's performance and progress. These assessments can automatically grade assignments, analyze student responses, provide personalized feedback, and even predict future learning outcomes. AI can adapt the difficulty of questions in real time based on the learner's performance, creating a more accurate and personalized evaluation of student abilities and helping educators identify areas where students need further support.

AI-Powered Content Curation

AI-powered content curation involves the use of AI algorithms to select, organize, and recommend educational materials based on a learner's individual preferences, needs, and learning history. By analyzing data from students, AI systems can suggest personalized resources, such as articles, videos, exercises, and assessments, making it easier for students to access relevant materials and enhance their learning experience.

Algorithm

An algorithm is a precise, step-by-step procedure or set of rules that are followed to perform a task or solve a problem. Algorithms are at the heart of most computer programs, including AI systems, where they define how data is processed, analyzed, and used to generate outcomes. In the context of AI, algorithms enable machines to learn from data, make predictions, or solve specific problems. For instance, recommendation algorithms in e-commerce platforms suggest products based on customer behavior, while machine learning algorithms in education personalize learning experiences based on a student's progress.

Artificial Intelligence (AI)

Artificial Intelligence (AI) is a field within computer science that focuses on creating machines and systems capable of performing tasks that typically require human intelligence. These tasks include problem-solving, decision-making, language understanding, and perception. AI systems use algorithms to analyze data, learn from it, and make predictions or decisions. AI can be categorized into narrow AI, which is designed for specific tasks (such as facial recognition or language translation), and general AI, which would be capable of performing any intellectual task that a human can do. In education, AI is applied in various ways, including personalized learning platforms, automated grading systems, and intelligent tutoring systems.

Artificial Neural Network

An artificial neural network (ANN) is a computational model inspired by the structure and functioning of the human brain. It consists of layers of interconnected nodes (or "neurons") that process information by recognizing patterns and relationships within data. ANNs are widely used in AI applications such as image and speech recognition, natural language processing, and decision-making. They are a fundamental technology in machine learning, enabling systems to improve and "learn" from experience without being explicitly programmed.

Asynchronous Learning

Asynchronous learning is an educational approach where students engage with learning materials, such as videos, readings, or assignments, independently and on their own schedule. In this mode, students can access the content at any time, without the need for real-time interaction with the instructor or classmates. This flexibility allows learners to progress at their own pace, making it ideal for working professionals, adult learners, or students with varying time commitments. Asynchronous learning is commonly facilitated through platforms like MOOCs, pre-recorded lectures, and self-paced courses.

Augmented Reality (AR)

Augmented Reality (AR) is a technology that overlays digital content—such as images, videos, or 3D models—onto the physical world through the use of devices like smartphones, tablets, or AR glasses. Unlike VR, which creates a completely immersive environment, AR enhances the user's view of the real world by adding virtual elements. In education, AR can be used to make learning more interactive and engaging. For example, students studying anatomy could use an AR app to see 3D representations of organs overlaid on a physical textbook, or history students could explore historical landmarks by pointing their devices at images in their textbooks.

Automated Grading

Automated grading refers to the use of AI systems to grade assignments, quizzes, tests, and other assessments automatically. These systems evaluate students' work, provide timely feedback, and offer insights into their strengths and areas for improvement. Automated grading helps reduce educators' workloads and allows for more consistent and immediate assessment, particularly for large-scale testing environments.

Autonomous Learning

Autonomous learning refers to self-directed learning where students take responsibility for their own educational journey. This approach emphasizes independence, critical thinking, and the ability to set goals, select resources, and manage time. Technology tools, such as online courses, interactive platforms, and educational apps, often support autonomous learning by providing students with the flexibility to learn at their own pace and choose their learning paths. Autonomous learning is often seen in higher education and lifelong learning contexts, where students engage in self-guided study and use resources like MOOCs or learning management systems.

Big Data

Big data refers to extremely large datasets that are difficult to process using traditional data management tools due to their size, complexity, and speed. Big data is often characterized by the "three Vs": volume (large amounts of data), velocity (fast data generation), and variety (data from various sources). In education, big data can be leveraged to improve learning outcomes by analyzing data from various sources, such as online assessments, social media interactions, and learning management systems. For example, universities can use big data to analyze student engagement and predict which students are at risk of dropping out.

Blended Learning

Blended learning is an educational approach that combines traditional face-to-face teaching with online learning elements. This approach allows for flexibility in how content is delivered, enabling students to engage with lessons both in physical classrooms and through online platforms. Blended learning can take many forms, such as rotating through different learning modalities, integrating online lessons into a typical classroom setting, or offering self-paced online courses alongside scheduled face-to-face interactions. The goal of blended learning is to provide students with a more flexible and personalized learning experience. For example, a student might attend weekly in-person lectures and complete online modules for homework or self-paced learning.

Blockchain for Education

Blockchain technology in education is used to securely and transparently manage academic records, credentials, and certifications. By using blockchain, student data and achievements are stored in an immutable ledger, preventing tampering and enabling secure verification of educational qualifications. This technology also enables the creation of decentralized platforms for issuing and validating credentials, offering a solution to the challenge of diploma fraud and providing greater trust in the accuracy of academic records.

Blockchain in Education

Blockchain technology in education is used to securely store and manage educational records, such as student credentials, academic achievements, and course completions. It allows for transparent, tamper-proof records that can be easily verified and shared, enhancing trust and security in the management of academic data and reducing the risk of fraud.

Blockchain

Blockchain is a decentralized digital ledger technology that securely records transactions across multiple computers so that the records cannot be altered retroactively. In the context of education, blockchain can be used to verify and store credentials such as diplomas, certificates, and transcripts. This ensures the authenticity of academic qualifications and prevents fraud. For example, blockchain-based systems like the “Learning Machine” can enable universities to issue digital diplomas that can be easily verified by employers and other institutions.

Chatbot

A chatbot is an AI-powered tool designed to simulate conversation with users through text or voice. Chatbots are commonly used in customer service, but in education, they serve as virtual assistants that can provide students with answers to frequently asked questions, help with assignments, offer guidance on course materials, and provide personalized feedback. Educational chatbots can be available 24/7, ensuring that students have continuous access to support and resources. For example, a university might use a chatbot to answer questions about course registration or provide guidance on library resources.

Chatbots for Education

Chatbots in education are AI-powered conversational agents designed to engage with students via messaging platforms. These chatbots can answer questions, provide information on course materials, offer tutoring in certain subjects, and assist with administrative tasks. They provide immediate, round-the-clock support for students, enhancing their learning experience.

Cloud Computing

Cloud computing is the delivery of computing services—such as storage, processing power, and software—over the internet. Instead of using local servers or personal devices, users can access these services remotely via cloud platforms like Amazon Web Services (AWS), Google Cloud, and Microsoft Azure. In education, cloud computing allows for scalable and flexible access to resources like learning management systems (LMS), collaborative tools, and online courses. Cloud-based platforms also enable real-time data sharing and collaboration among students and educators, facilitating remote learning and the integration of AI-powered educational tools.

Cloud-Based Learning

Cloud-based learning refers to educational practices that are facilitated through cloud computing technologies, where content, resources, and tools are stored and accessed remotely over the internet. Students and educators can access learning materials, collaborate, and track progress through cloud-based platforms such as Google Classroom, Microsoft OneDrive, or learning management systems like Moodle. Cloud-based learning allows for flexibility, as students can access their lessons, assignments, and resources from any device with an internet connection, fostering collaboration and continuous learning.

Cognitive Computing

Cognitive computing refers to AI systems designed to simulate human thought processes in order to solve complex problems. Cognitive computing systems can analyze large amounts of unstructured data, such as text, speech, and images, and make decisions based on that analysis. These systems are often used to enhance human decision-making, support problem-solving in real-time, and create personalized user experiences. In education, cognitive computing can be applied to create adaptive learning systems that respond to students' needs and offer personalized learning paths. For example, IBM's Watson is a cognitive computing system that has been applied in healthcare and education to provide intelligent tutoring and data-driven insights for educators.

Cognitive Load

Cognitive load refers to the amount of mental effort required to process information during learning. It is based on the idea that the brain has a limited capacity for processing information at any given time. In educational settings, instructional strategies should aim to minimize extraneous cognitive load (unnecessary distractions) and optimize intrinsic cognitive load (the inherent complexity of the material). This can be done through techniques like chunking information, providing clear instructions, and using visuals to support understanding, which ultimately helps students retain and apply knowledge more effectively.

Cognitive Tutoring

Cognitive tutoring is an AI-driven approach to personalized learning that focuses on understanding a student's cognitive processes and providing targeted support. This type of tutoring system adapts in real-time, offering hints, explanations, and feedback to guide students through problem-solving, helping them build deeper understanding and critical thinking skills.

Collaborative Filtering

Collaborative filtering is an AI-based recommendation system that predicts a user's preferences based on the behaviors and preferences of other similar users. In education, this can be used to suggest learning materials, courses, or resources to students based on what peers with similar learning profiles have engaged with. Collaborative filtering enhances personalized learning by helping students discover relevant content that they might not have otherwise found on their own.

Collaborative Learning

Collaborative learning is an educational approach where students work together in groups to solve problems, complete tasks, and achieve learning goals. This method encourages active engagement, critical thinking, and the development of social skills as students share ideas, debate, and help each other understand new concepts. Collaborative learning can take various forms, including group projects, peer review, and discussion-based activities. Technology often enhances collaborative learning by enabling virtual teams to connect and collaborate through online platforms, video calls, and shared digital workspaces.

Competency-Based Education

Competency-based education (CBE) is an educational approach that focuses on students demonstrating mastery of specific skills or knowledge, rather than progressing through a set of courses based on seat time or credit hours. In CBE, students move forward only when they have demonstrated sufficient proficiency in a particular subject or skill, which allows for personalized pacing and a more flexible learning experience. This approach is gaining popularity in higher education and workforce training, where students can gain credit for mastering skills relevant to their careers or goals.

Competency-Based Learning

Competency-based learning is a personalized educational approach where students advance based on their mastery of specific skills or knowledge, rather than the time spent in a class. AI systems often support this model by continuously assessing students' performance, identifying areas for improvement, and ensuring that they only progress when they demonstrate proficiency.

Content Curation

Content curation in the context of education refers to the process of selecting, organizing, and presenting educational content to learners. This involves identifying high-quality, relevant, and up-to-date resources, such as articles, videos, research papers, and interactive tools, and then organizing them in a meaningful and accessible way. Educators use content curation to help learners engage with materials that are specifically tailored to their needs, enhancing the learning experience by providing structured and relevant content without overwhelming students with irrelevant or excessive information.

Curriculum Mapping

Curriculum mapping is a process that involves aligning the curriculum with learning objectives, standards, and assessments. It is a strategic approach to ensuring that what is taught in the classroom is directly linked to educational goals and outcomes. This process helps educators visualize how different units or lessons connect to broader learning objectives and ensure that all necessary content is covered throughout the course. Curriculum mapping can also help identify gaps or redundancies in instruction and guide improvements in teaching practices.

Curriculum Personalization

Curriculum personalization involves tailoring educational content and delivery methods to meet the specific needs, preferences, and learning styles of individual students. By using technologies such as adaptive learning software, data analytics, and student profiles, educators can create customized learning pathways that cater to each student's pace, interests, and strengths. This approach helps ensure that all students have an engaging and effective learning experience, addressing their unique challenges and allowing for greater ownership of their educational journey.

Data Mining

Data mining is the process of analyzing large datasets to discover patterns, correlations, and useful insights that were previously hidden. Using algorithms and statistical techniques, data mining helps to extract valuable information from raw data. In education, data mining can be used to understand student performance, predict future trends in learning outcomes, and optimize teaching methods. For instance, by analyzing patterns in student assessments, educators can identify at-risk students and intervene early to provide additional support.

Data Privacy

Data privacy refers to the protection of personal and sensitive information from unauthorized access, use, or disclosure. In educational contexts, data privacy involves safeguarding student data, such as academic records, personal identifiers, and learning behaviors, from breaches or misuse. Institutions and educators must comply with privacy regulations, such as FERPA (Family Educational Rights and Privacy Act) in the United States or GDPR (General Data Protection Regulation) in the European Union, to ensure that students' privacy rights are upheld and their data is securely managed.

Data-Driven Instruction

Data-driven instruction refers to the practice of using data collected from various sources, such as student assessments, behavior metrics, and engagement levels, to inform and guide teaching practices and decisions. This approach enables educators to identify students' strengths and weaknesses, track their progress over time, and adjust teaching strategies to improve learning outcomes. Tools like Google Classroom and various learning management systems (LMS) provide educators with access to real-time student performance data, allowing them to tailor instruction accordingly.

Data-Driven Instruction

Data-driven instruction refers to the practice of using data from student performance (such as test scores, assignments, and feedback) to inform teaching decisions. By analyzing data, educators can identify students' strengths and weaknesses, adjust the curriculum, and tailor teaching methods to meet individual needs, ultimately improving learning outcomes.

Deep Learning

Deep learning is a specialized subset of machine learning that involves neural networks with many layers (hence "deep"). These neural networks are designed to simulate the way the human brain processes information, allowing them to recognize complex patterns in large datasets. Deep learning has been particularly successful in areas such as image recognition, speech recognition, and natural language processing. For example, deep learning algorithms are used in self-driving cars to recognize pedestrians, traffic signs, and obstacles, and in voice assistants like Siri and Alexa to interpret spoken commands.

Deep Learning

Deep learning is a subset of machine learning that uses artificial neural networks with multiple layers to analyze and process complex data. It is particularly effective in handling tasks such as natural language processing, image recognition, and speech recognition. In education, deep learning models can be used to improve personalized learning, automate grading, and analyze large datasets to predict student performance.

Digital Assessment

Digital assessment refers to the use of technology to assess and evaluate students' learning through tools such as online quizzes, tests, assignments, and simulations. These assessments may include a variety of formats, such as multiple-choice, short-answer, essays, and performance-based tasks. Digital assessment tools allow for real-time feedback, efficient grading, and data collection, helping educators identify areas where students are excelling or struggling. Additionally, they offer opportunities for personalized assessments, which can adapt based on a learner's progress.

Digital Badge

A digital badge is a form of digital recognition awarded to individuals for achieving specific skills, competencies, or milestones in an educational program. These badges serve as verifiable credentials that can be shared, stored, and displayed on digital platforms, such as professional networks or learning management systems. Digital badges are often used in gamified learning environments to motivate students, recognize achievements, and provide evidence of accomplishment in areas like problem-solving, creativity, or technical skills.

Digital Content Creation

Digital content creation is the process of developing educational materials in digital formats, such as videos, podcasts, eBooks, blogs, or infographics. This content is used in a variety of learning environments, from classrooms to online courses and self-paced learning platforms. Digital content creation empowers educators to produce interactive, engaging, and multimedia-rich learning experiences that can cater to different learning styles and improve student engagement.

Digital Divide

The digital divide refers to the gap between individuals who have access to modern technology and the internet and those who do not. This divide can be influenced by factors such as socioeconomic status, geographic location, and educational background, often leading to disparities in access to information, learning opportunities, and technological resources. In the context of education, the digital divide means that some students may lack the necessary tools or infrastructure to participate in online learning or benefit from technology-enhanced education. Efforts to bridge the digital divide include providing affordable internet access and distributing devices to underserved communities.

Digital Literacy

Digital literacy refers to the ability to effectively and responsibly use technology to access, analyze, evaluate, and create information. It encompasses a broad range of skills, from understanding how to use basic digital tools such as word processors and spreadsheets to evaluating the credibility of online content and using digital platforms for communication. Digital literacy is an essential skill in the modern world, enabling individuals to participate fully in the digital economy, engage with online education, and navigate the complexities of the information age.

Digital Pedagogy

Digital pedagogy refers to the integration of digital tools, platforms, and technologies into teaching practices to enhance and transform the learning experience. This approach focuses on leveraging technology to improve how students learn, how educators teach, and how the educational content is delivered. Digital pedagogy includes using various technological tools like multimedia, interactive platforms, and online resources, all aimed at promoting student engagement, collaboration, and personalized learning. It encourages innovative instructional strategies and fosters greater accessibility, flexibility, and inclusivity in education.

Digital Portfolio

A digital portfolio is an electronic collection of a student's work, achievements, and assessments that showcases their learning progress and accomplishments over time. It typically includes various types of content, such as essays, projects, multimedia presentations, and assessments, organized to demonstrate the student's skills, strengths, and growth. Digital portfolios are increasingly used in educational settings to assess students' learning in a more holistic and comprehensive manner. They can also be shared with instructors, peers, or prospective employers as a representation of the student's capabilities.

Digital Twin

A digital twin in education refers to a virtual representation of a physical student, classroom, or educational environment. It is used to simulate, analyze, and optimize learning experiences. Through real-time data and AI, digital twins can track a student's progress, preferences, and interactions, providing personalized feedback and supporting adaptive learning strategies. In classrooms, digital twins can model classroom dynamics, helping educators improve the learning environment and address individual needs more effectively.

EdTech Ecosystem

The EdTech ecosystem refers to the interconnected network of educational technology tools, platforms, policies, and stakeholders that collaborate to enhance learning. This ecosystem includes technology providers, educators, students, policymakers, and other stakeholders who interact with educational technologies to improve teaching and learning. It involves a dynamic set of resources, including Learning Management Systems (LMS), digital content, analytics, and instructional tools, all designed to support diverse educational needs and settings.

EdTech Integration

EdTech integration is the process of incorporating educational technology tools and systems into existing teaching practices, curricula, and institutional frameworks. Successful integration involves aligning technology with pedagogical goals, ensuring accessibility, and providing professional development for educators. By effectively integrating EdTech, schools and universities can enhance student engagement, improve learning outcomes, and streamline administrative tasks, making education more efficient and personalized.

EdTech Platform

An EdTech platform is a software environment or application designed to facilitate various aspects of the educational process, such as content delivery, learning management, student tracking, and communication. These platforms often integrate tools for assessment, collaboration, and reporting, allowing educators to manage their classrooms and students to access learning resources and track their progress.

EdTech Policy

EdTech policy refers to the set of rules, regulations, and strategies that guide the use and integration of technology in educational settings. These policies are designed to ensure that educational technology is used effectively, equitably, and ethically to enhance learning outcomes. They cover aspects like data privacy, accessibility, digital literacy, teacher training, funding, and the selection of appropriate technology tools. EdTech policies play a key role in shaping how schools, universities, and other educational institutions incorporate technology into their curricula.

EdTech Startup

An EdTech startup is a new business focused on the development and implementation of technology-based tools, platforms, and services designed to improve education. These startups often focus on creating innovative solutions to address specific challenges in the education sector, such as personalized learning, access to educational resources, or teacher professional development. Examples of successful EdTech startups include Byju's, which offers personalized learning paths for students, and Duolingo, a language-learning platform that uses gamification to teach languages effectively. These startups contribute to the growing ecosystem of educational technology, shaping the future of learning.

EdTech

EdTech, short for Educational Technology, refers to the use of digital tools and technologies to enhance, support, or facilitate the learning process. These technologies range from software and applications that support classroom management, instructional design, and learning outcomes to more complex systems like virtual classrooms, digital textbooks, and learning analytics platforms. EdTech also includes hardware tools such as interactive whiteboards, tablets, and computers. The goal of EdTech is to improve educational practices, streamline teaching and learning processes, and enable more personalized and accessible education. For example, platforms like Moodle and Canvas are used by schools and universities to create and manage online courses, track student progress, and facilitate communication between teachers and students.

Edutainment Apps

Edutainment apps are mobile applications that combine educational content with entertainment to create engaging, interactive learning experiences. These apps often use game-like features, storytelling, and interactive activities to make learning more enjoyable and motivating. Edutainment apps are designed for learners of all ages and cover a wide range of subjects, from math and science to languages and history. By blending fun with education, these apps encourage learners to actively participate and engage with the material, making learning enjoyable while also achieving educational outcomes.

Edutainment

Edutainment is a combination of education and entertainment, designed to engage students while teaching important concepts or skills. The goal of edutainment is to make learning enjoyable and interactive, often by incorporating game mechanics, storytelling, and multimedia content. Examples of edutainment include educational video games, interactive apps, and television programs that teach subjects like math, history, or language. An example is the educational game "Osmo," which uses physical objects and digital interactions to teach children basic skills like math, spelling, and art.

E-learning

E-learning, or electronic learning, refers to the process of learning that is conducted through digital platforms, typically over the internet. E-learning can take many forms, including fully online courses, virtual classrooms, webinars, and self-paced modules. It enables students to access educational content at any time and from anywhere, making it flexible and accessible. E-learning has grown in popularity due to its ability to support a wide range of learners, including remote students, working professionals, and those with diverse learning needs.

Exponential Learning

Exponential learning refers to the rapid acquisition of knowledge and skills facilitated by technology-enhanced methods. With the help of AI, big data, and interactive tools, students can access and absorb vast amounts of information at a much faster pace than traditional learning methods allow. Exponential learning emphasizes continuous learning cycles, where the learner can build upon previous knowledge and adapt quickly to new information, enhancing overall learning efficiency.

Flipped Classroom Model

The flipped classroom model is a teaching approach that reverses the traditional learning structure. In this model, students first engage with instructional content (such as videos, readings, or online lessons) outside the classroom, often at home or during independent study time. Then, during class time, they participate in interactive activities such as discussions, group projects, or problem-solving exercises. This model promotes active learning, student-centered engagement, and more efficient use of classroom time for hands-on learning and collaboration.

Flipped Classroom

The flipped classroom is an instructional model in which traditional learning structures are inverted. In this model, students are assigned to study content independently outside of class—typically through videos, readings, or interactive modules—before attending class. During class time, instead of delivering lectures, teachers facilitate collaborative activities, discussions, problem-solving exercises, and projects. This shift allows for deeper engagement and more active learning during class sessions. For example, in a flipped classroom for a science course, students may watch a video about chemical reactions at home, and then in class, they engage in hands-on experiments to explore the concepts in more depth.

Flipped Learning

Flipped learning is a pedagogical model that inverts traditional teaching methods. In this model, students engage with instructional content (e.g., video lectures, readings) at home or independently, while class time is used for interactive, hands-on activities such as discussions, group projects, or problem-solving exercises. This approach encourages active learning and allows for more personalized, collaborative, and deeper learning experiences in the classroom, while also promoting student autonomy.

Gamification

Gamification refers to the application of game design principles and mechanics—such as points, rewards, levels, challenges, and leaderboards—to non-game contexts, including education. In the context of education, gamification aims to increase student engagement, motivation, and participation by making learning more interactive and fun. For instance, educators might use point systems to reward students for completing assignments or create competitive challenges that encourage students to solve problems or answer questions. Popular platforms that incorporate gamification include Kahoot! and Duolingo, where students earn points or progress through levels based on their learning achievements.

Gamified Assessment

Gamified assessment involves incorporating game design elements, such as points, badges, levels, and leaderboards, into educational assessments to increase engagement, motivation, and participation. The use of gamification in assessments turns traditional testing into a more interactive and enjoyable experience, encouraging students to perform better and stay engaged. For example, platforms like Kahoot! and Quizizz use game mechanics to make quizzes more exciting and competitive, motivating students to participate actively and learn in a fun, dynamic environment.

Gamified Learning

Gamified learning incorporates game elements, such as points, levels, badges, and rewards, into educational activities to increase engagement, motivation, and participation. By adding elements of competition and achievement, gamified learning transforms the educational experience into a more interactive and enjoyable process, encouraging students to stay focused and strive for mastery.

Haptic Feedback

Haptic feedback is a technology that provides tactile sensations to users, simulating touch or offering feedback in virtual environments. This can be used in educational settings to enhance learning experiences, particularly in virtual or augmented reality environments. For example, students may feel vibrations or pressure in response to actions they take in a virtual lab or interactive simulation, making the experience more immersive. Haptic feedback helps bridge the gap between the digital and physical worlds, adding an additional layer of sensory engagement to the learning process.

Instructional Design

Instructional design is the process of creating educational content, experiences, and assessments that foster effective learning. It involves analyzing learning needs, defining learning objectives, designing materials, and evaluating the effectiveness of the instructional approach. Instructional designers use theories of learning, pedagogy, and technology to develop courses and training programs that are engaging, efficient, and accessible. For example, designing an online course involves structuring lessons, selecting multimedia tools, and creating assessments to ensure that learners achieve the desired learning outcomes.

Instructional Software

Instructional software consists of digital programs designed to support the teaching and learning process by delivering content, assessing students, and aiding in instructional activities. These programs can range from simple educational games to complex learning management systems (LMS) and adaptive learning platforms. Instructional software helps streamline classroom management, provides interactive and engaging ways to learn, and often includes built-in analytics to help instructors monitor and adjust the learning process to better suit the needs of students.

Instructional Video

Instructional videos are educational videos designed to teach or explain specific concepts or skills to students. These videos may include demonstrations, lectures, animations, and visual explanations to facilitate understanding. Instructional videos are used to supplement classroom teaching, provide asynchronous learning opportunities, and offer visual learning aids for complex topics. They can be accessed at the student's convenience, allowing for flexibility and personalized learning. Instructional videos are commonly used in online courses, flipped classrooms, and blended learning models.

Intelligent Learning Systems

Intelligent learning systems use AI to personalize and optimize learning experiences in real-time. These systems analyze student data, including performance, preferences, and behavior, to adjust the content, pace, and teaching methods. By continuously learning from student interactions, intelligent learning systems aim to create dynamic and individualized educational pathways, enhancing student engagement and performance.

Intelligent Tutoring System (ITS)

An Intelligent Tutoring System (ITS) is a computer-based learning system designed to provide personalized tutoring to students by adapting to their individual learning needs. ITS systems use artificial intelligence to simulate one-on-one instruction, providing real-time feedback, hints, and explanations. These systems assess students' responses and modify instructional content based on their level of understanding, ensuring a tailored learning experience. For example, programs like Carnegie Learning use ITS to teach mathematics by adjusting problem difficulty according to a student's performance, helping them progress at their own pace.

Interactive Learning

Interactive learning is an educational approach that emphasizes active participation by students, encouraging them to engage with content, instructors, and peers through various activities. These activities can include discussions, group projects, simulations, hands-on experiments, and problem-solving tasks. Interactive learning fosters deeper understanding and critical thinking by involving students in the learning process rather than passive consumption of information. It often incorporates technology tools like interactive whiteboards, collaborative platforms, and gamified elements to enhance engagement.

Interactive Whiteboard

An interactive whiteboard (IWB) is a large digital display used in classrooms to present lessons, conduct activities, and engage students. The board can be connected to a computer and uses touch-sensitive technology that allows users to interact directly with the screen, making it more dynamic than traditional whiteboards. Teachers can use IWBs to display multimedia content, annotate lessons, and facilitate interactive activities, such as quizzes and problem-solving exercises, making lessons more engaging and interactive for students

Interactivity

Interactivity refers to the level of engagement and active participation that students can have with learning materials, instructors, and peers. In an interactive learning environment, students are not passive recipients of information but instead engage in tasks, discussions, simulations, and collaborative activities that require active input and feedback. The degree of interactivity can vary, but higher levels typically lead to deeper engagement, increased motivation, and improved learning outcomes. Interactivity is often supported by technology, such as interactive quizzes, discussion forums, live polls, and collaborative platforms.

Knowledge Graphs

Knowledge graphs are a way to represent knowledge in a visual format that links different data points, concepts, and relationships. They are typically organized as a network of nodes (representing concepts or entities) and edges (representing relationships between them). Knowledge graphs are used in education to structure and visualize complex information, making it easier for students to understand connections between ideas and concepts. They can be integrated into educational tools to help learners navigate large bodies of knowledge and enhance learning through more intuitive and interactive exploration.

Learning Analytics

Learning analytics involves the collection, measurement, and analysis of data related to learners and their learning environments. It aims to provide insights into learning behaviors, identify trends, and support data-driven decision-making to improve educational practices and outcomes. By analyzing student data, educators can personalize learning experiences, intervene when necessary, and continuously enhance teaching strategies.

Learning Analytics

Learning analytics refers to the measurement, collection, analysis, and reporting of data related to learners and their learning environments. By examining data such as student performance, engagement, and behavior patterns, educators can gain insights into how students learn, identify at-risk students, and improve teaching strategies. Learning analytics tools are often used to track progress over time, personalize learning, and ensure that educational interventions are effective. Examples include platforms like Blackboard Analytics and Tableau for Education, which allow educators to analyze student data to improve educational outcomes.

Learning Ecosystem

A learning ecosystem is a dynamic system comprising various interconnected learning resources, tools, platforms, and environments that support the educational experience. It includes formal (classrooms, courses, instructors) and informal (social media, online communities, self-study tools) elements, all working together to provide a rich and diverse learning experience. A well-designed learning ecosystem promotes flexibility, collaboration, and continuous learning by integrating technology, content, people, and processes in a seamless way that adapts to the needs of learners.

Learning Experience Platform (LXP)

A Learning Experience Platform (LXP) is a software platform designed to deliver personalized learning experiences by curating content, tracking learners' progress, and offering interactive learning paths. LXPs use artificial intelligence and data analytics to provide tailored learning recommendations, supporting learners' needs, interests, and goals. Unlike traditional Learning Management Systems (LMS), which focus on course delivery, LXPs emphasize a more learner-centered experience by integrating diverse learning resources, such as videos, articles, podcasts, and social collaboration tools.

Learning Management System (LMS)

A Learning Management System (LMS) is a software application or platform designed to manage, deliver, and track educational courses and training programs. An LMS typically allows educators to create and manage content, monitor student progress, and assess learning outcomes. It also provides tools for collaboration, communication, and feedback, enhancing the overall learning experience. Examples of LMS platforms include Blackboard, Moodle, and Canvas. These systems are often used in both K-12 schools and higher education institutions to deliver content in a digital format, track student engagement, and integrate with other learning tools such as multimedia resources and quizzes.

Learning Pathway

A learning pathway is a personalized trajectory or roadmap that outlines a sequence of lessons, activities, and assessments tailored to an individual learner's needs, progress, and interests. Learning pathways are designed to guide students through their educational journey, providing a clear structure while allowing for flexibility in how they move through content. These pathways can be adjusted based on student performance and learning preferences.

Learning Pathways

Learning pathways are personalized routes that guide students through an educational program or curriculum, based on their preferences, progress, and goals. These pathways are dynamic and can be adapted to each learner's pace, skills, and interests. Learning pathways often leverage data analytics to provide customized recommendations, helping students navigate through a course or degree program by selecting the most relevant courses, resources, and assignments that align with their learning objectives.

Machine Learning (ML)

Machine learning is a subset of AI that focuses on developing algorithms that allow computers to learn from data and improve their performance over time without explicit programming. In education, ML can be used to predict student performance, personalize learning experiences, and automate tasks such as grading and content recommendation. Machine learning models continually improve as they process more data, helping to refine educational practices and outcomes.

Machine Learning

Machine learning (ML) is a subset of AI that allows systems to automatically learn and improve from experience without being explicitly programmed. ML algorithms use statistical methods to analyze data, recognize patterns, and make decisions. Over time, as the system is exposed to more data, it becomes more accurate in its predictions or decisions. For example, an ML system used in adaptive learning platforms might improve its ability to assess a student's understanding of a topic after analyzing their past responses. Key types of machine learning include supervised learning (where the model is trained on labeled data), unsupervised learning (where the model finds patterns in unlabeled data), and reinforcement learning (where the model learns through trial and error).

Micro-Credentials

Micro-credentials are digital certifications or badges that are awarded for the completion of small, focused learning modules or the demonstration of specific competencies. These credentials allow learners to gain recognition for mastering particular skills or knowledge areas and can be shared digitally on platforms such as LinkedIn or personal portfolios. Micro-credentials provide an alternative to traditional degrees, offering flexible and targeted learning opportunities that cater to the needs of both students and employers.

Microlearning

Microlearning is a learning strategy that delivers content in small, focused segments, usually lasting a few minutes. This approach is designed to provide bite-sized lessons that target specific skills or knowledge areas, enhancing learner engagement and retention. Microlearning is often used in mobile learning apps, online tutorials, and just-in-time training modules. Its concise nature makes it ideal for learners who need quick, focused information on a particular topic, making it especially effective in fast-paced environments and for learners with short attention spans.

Mobile Learning

Mobile learning, or m-learning, refers to the use of mobile devices like smartphones and tablets to access educational content and participate in learning activities. It is often used in informal contexts, such as on-the-go learning or when students are away from traditional classrooms. Mobile learning supports flexibility, allowing learners to access resources, videos, quizzes, and other educational tools anytime and anywhere. This approach is particularly effective for lifelong learning, microlearning, and the delivery of bite-sized educational content.

MOOC (Massive Open Online Course)

A Massive Open Online Course (MOOC) is an online educational course that is designed to accommodate a large number of participants, often with no formal entry requirements. MOOCs are typically offered by universities or online platforms such as Coursera, edX, and Udacity. They provide flexible learning opportunities, often for free or at a low cost, and cover a wide range of subjects. For example, courses like "Introduction to Computer Science" on edX or "Machine Learning" on Coursera are MOOCs that allow students from all over the world to access world-class education.

MOOC Platforms

MOOC platforms are websites or online services that host and deliver massive open online courses (MOOCs). These platforms allow learners from around the world to access courses on a wide range of subjects, typically for free or at a low cost. MOOCs are designed to be scalable, often allowing thousands of participants to take the same course simultaneously. Popular MOOC platforms include Coursera, edX, and Udacity, which collaborate with universities, institutions, and experts to provide high-quality educational content in formats such as video lectures, quizzes, assignments, and discussion forums.

Natural Language Processing (NLP)

Natural Language Processing (NLP) is a branch of AI that focuses on enabling machines to understand, interpret, and generate human language. It encompasses tasks such as speech recognition, language translation, sentiment analysis, and text summarization. In education, NLP is used in tools like chatbots that assist students by answering their questions, providing feedback on assignments, or translating educational content into different languages. NLP also powers virtual assistants like Google Assistant and Siri, which can understand and respond to natural language queries.

Natural Language Processing (NLP)

Natural Language Processing (NLP) is a field of AI focused on enabling machines to understand, interpret, and generate human language. In education, NLP can be used to analyze written or spoken content, provide feedback on student writing, support language learning, and enable voice-powered assistants. It plays a crucial role in applications such as automated essay grading, language translation, and conversational agents for learning.

Neural Networks

Neural networks are computational models inspired by the structure of the human brain, consisting of layers of interconnected nodes (or neurons). These networks process data by passing it through multiple layers of nodes, where each node performs a mathematical operation. Neural networks are particularly effective at identifying patterns in data, making them essential for deep learning applications. In education, neural networks can be used to analyze student performance, predict outcomes, and personalize learning experiences based on patterns in student behavior and progress.

Open Educational Resources (OER)

Open Educational Resources are freely accessible and openly licensed materials used for teaching, learning, and research. OERs include textbooks, videos, quizzes, lesson plans, and other educational resources that can be used, shared, and modified by educators and learners without significant costs. They promote equitable access to quality education by eliminating financial barriers and encouraging collaborative learning. Platforms like OER Commons or Creative Commons host a variety of OER materials.

Peer Assessment

Peer assessment is a process in which students evaluate the work or performance of their peers to provide constructive feedback and encourage learning. This process helps students develop critical thinking, self-reflection, and communication skills while also gaining different perspectives on their own work. Peer assessment can be facilitated by both in-person interactions and digital platforms, where students assess each other's assignments, projects, or presentations. It fosters collaboration and a deeper understanding of the subject matter, as students often learn from the strengths and weaknesses of their peers' work.

Personalized Assessment

Personalized assessment refers to an assessment approach that adapts to each student's learning progress, ability level, and preferences. By using AI and data analytics, personalized assessments can adjust the difficulty of questions, provide targeted feedback, and identify areas of improvement. This approach ensures that assessments are more accurate and reflective of a student's capabilities, enhancing the learning experience and supporting personalized learning pathways.

Personalized Learning

Personalized learning is an educational approach that tailors learning experiences to the individual needs, interests, and abilities of students. This method allows learners to progress at their own pace, with content and resources adjusted to meet their specific strengths and weaknesses. Personalized learning can be facilitated through technology, such as adaptive learning systems and data analytics tools, which help customize lessons. For instance, platforms like Khan Academy and Duolingo allow students to learn at their own pace by offering personalized practice exercises based on their progress.

Real-Time Analytics

Real-time analytics refers to the immediate processing and analysis of data as it is generated, allowing for rapid insights and timely interventions. In educational settings, real-time analytics can track student engagement, performance, and behavior during lessons or online activities. This data helps educators make informed decisions, adapt teaching strategies on the fly, and provide immediate feedback to students, enhancing learning outcomes and improving instructional practices.

Self-Directed Learning

Self-directed learning refers to a learning process in which students take the initiative in diagnosing their own learning needs, setting goals, finding resources, and evaluating their progress. In self-directed learning, students are responsible for their own educational journey, which promotes autonomy, critical thinking, and a sense of ownership over their learning. Technology plays a significant role in facilitating self-directed learning by providing access to resources like online courses, tutorials, forums, and educational apps that empower learners to explore topics of interest at their own pace.

Sentiment Analysis

Sentiment analysis in education involves the use of AI techniques to assess and interpret students' emotions, opinions, or attitudes toward learning content, activities, or teaching methods. By analyzing text, speech, or social media interactions, sentiment analysis can gauge student engagement, satisfaction, and emotional response. This data helps educators adjust their teaching methods, identify students in need of support, and enhance the overall learning experience.

Smart Classroom

A smart classroom is a technology-enhanced learning environment equipped with digital tools such as interactive whiteboards, projectors, tablets, and computers that support teaching and learning. These tools facilitate interactive lessons, real-time feedback, and collaborative learning experiences. Smart classrooms are designed to integrate various forms of technology to enhance engagement, improve information delivery, and support personalized learning. The use of tools like digital quizzes, online resources, and collaborative platforms allows for a more dynamic and interactive learning experience.

Social Emotional Learning (SEL)

Social Emotional Learning (SEL) refers to educational practices aimed at developing students' emotional intelligence, self-awareness, empathy, and interpersonal skills. SEL helps students manage emotions, set positive goals, show empathy for others, and build strong relationships. AI-powered tools can support SEL by analyzing students' emotional states and providing tailored activities or interventions to foster emotional growth and resilience, contributing to overall academic and personal development.

Social Learning

Social learning is a process by which learning occurs through interaction with others, typically within a social context such as online communities, peer groups, or collaborative platforms. It involves sharing knowledge, collaborating on tasks, and learning from the experiences and feedback of others. Social learning can be facilitated by digital tools such as discussion forums, social media platforms, wikis, and group projects, which help students engage with each other and learn from their peers. It emphasizes the importance of communication, collaboration, and the sharing of diverse perspectives in the learning process.

Speech Recognition

Speech recognition is an AI technology that converts spoken language into written text. This technology enables voice-driven learning applications, such as virtual assistants, voice-controlled search, and transcription services. In educational contexts, speech recognition can help students with disabilities, support language learners, and provide a more accessible learning experience. It is also used in assessments, enabling voice-based interactions and real-time feedback.

Student Data Analytics

Student data analytics refers to the use of data collection, analysis, and interpretation to understand student behavior, performance, and learning trends. By analyzing data such as test scores, attendance records, engagement metrics, and learning preferences, educators can gain insights into individual and group learning patterns. This information helps identify at-risk students, personalize learning pathways, and improve overall teaching strategies. For example, a school might use student data analytics to identify which students need additional support in math or reading and then provide targeted interventions. Additionally, these analytics can be used to predict outcomes like graduation rates or identify factors that contribute to student success.

Student-Centered Learning

Student-centered learning is an educational approach that focuses on the individual needs, interests, and abilities of the student, rather than the traditional teacher-centered model. In this approach, students take a more active role in their learning, with the teacher acting as a facilitator or guide. This model promotes personalized learning, collaboration, critical thinking, and self-directed learning. The use of technology, such as adaptive learning platforms, collaborative tools, and interactive content, can enhance student-centered learning by offering more tailored learning experiences that align with students' preferences and learning styles.

Synchronous Learning

Synchronous learning refers to educational activities that occur in real-time, where students and instructors interact simultaneously. Examples of synchronous learning include live video lectures, webinars, online discussions, or virtual classrooms where students engage with instructors and fellow learners in a real-time, interactive setting. This format allows for immediate feedback, questions, and discussions, and it replicates the traditional classroom environment. Synchronous learning often requires participants to be present at a specific time, which can be both an advantage for structured learning and a limitation for students with scheduling conflicts.

Video-Based Learning

Video-based learning is an educational approach where content is delivered through videos. This format allows students to learn through both visual and auditory means, enhancing comprehension and retention. Video-based learning can include recorded lectures, animated tutorials, interactive videos, or screencasts. It is widely used in both formal and informal learning environments and is often paired with other interactive elements like quizzes or discussions to reinforce learning.

Virtual Classroom

A virtual classroom is an online environment where students and instructors can interact in real-time, simulating a traditional classroom experience. Virtual classrooms often include features such as video conferencing, live chats, virtual whiteboards, screen sharing, and collaborative tools. They allow students to engage with instructors and peers, ask questions, participate in discussions, and receive real-time feedback, all while learning remotely. Virtual classrooms are commonly used in online courses, corporate training programs, and blended learning environments, offering a flexible way for educators and learners to connect across geographical boundaries.

Virtual Classrooms

Virtual classrooms are online environments where students and instructors interact, either in real-time or asynchronously, to conduct lessons. These classrooms are supported by technologies such as video conferencing, AI-powered tools, and digital whiteboards. They provide a flexible, accessible way for students to learn remotely while maintaining interaction with their peers and instructors.

Virtual Lab

A virtual lab is a digital simulation of a laboratory environment that allows students to conduct scientific experiments or engage in hands-on learning experiences in a virtual setting. Virtual labs enable students to explore complex concepts and carry out experiments that may be too costly, dangerous, or time-consuming to perform in a traditional physical lab. These tools provide a safe and accessible space for learners to practice skills, manipulate variables, and observe outcomes without the constraints of a physical classroom or lab environment.

Virtual Reality (VR)

Virtual Reality (VR) is a technology that creates a fully immersive, simulated environment that users can interact with using specialized hardware, such as headsets, controllers, and motion sensors. In education, VR is used to create engaging, interactive learning experiences that would be difficult or impossible in the real world. For example, VR can be used to take students on virtual field trips to historical sites, simulate scientific experiments, or allow them to explore the human body in 3D. VR helps promote experiential learning, providing a more interactive and engaging alternative to traditional classroom instruction.

Virtual Reality Learning

Virtual reality (VR) learning immerses students in simulated environments where they can explore complex concepts, conduct experiments, or practice skills in a safe, controlled space. VR technology creates highly engaging, interactive experiences that can simulate real-world scenarios or abstract concepts, such as historical events, scientific phenomena, or architectural design. This approach enhances learning by providing hands-on experiences and fostering deeper understanding, especially in subjects like science, medicine, engineering, and art.

Voice Assistants

Voice assistants are AI-powered tools that use speech recognition and natural language processing to interact with users. In education, these tools assist students by answering questions, providing explanations, setting reminders, and helping with assignments. Voice assistants can support personalized learning, especially for students with disabilities, and provide an interactive, hands-free approach to accessing information and learning resources.

Wearable Technology

Wearable technology refers to devices that are worn on the body and designed to collect and analyze data to enhance learning experiences. Examples of wearable tech in education include smartwatches, fitness trackers, and augmented reality glasses. These devices can monitor students' physical activity, health metrics, or provide interactive learning experiences in real time. For instance, smartwatches can be used to track student activity during physical education lessons, while AR glasses can provide immersive learning experiences in science or history by overlaying information on the physical world.

About the Author

Professor Medani P. Bhandari, PhD
Akamai University, USA, Sumy State University, Ukraine,
Kathmandu Forestry College and Gandaki University, Nepal

Short Biography

Dr. Medani P. Bhandari is a widely recognized humanitarian, professor, author, and editor who has significantly contributed to social and environmental sciences. With expertise in social equity, inequality, inclusion, innovation, feminism, sustainability, climate change, and social and environmental policies and management, Dr. Bhandari has dedicated his career to these important areas. In addition to his extensive scholarly work, Dr. Bhandari is a poet, essayist, and advocate for the environment and social causes. His expertise expands to global and international environmental politics and justice, climate change, sustainable development, public/social policy, the non-profit sector, renewable energy, nature, culture, and power. He has gained field experience across diverse regions, including Asia, Africa, North America, Western Europe, Australia, Japan, and the Middle East. Dr. Bhandari has authored and co-edited several books, including Green Web-II: Standards and Perspectives from the IUCN, 2nd Edition, Getting the Climate Science Facts Right: The Role of the IPCC, Reducing Inequalities Towards Sustainable Development Goals: Multilevel Approach, Educational Transformation, Economic Inequality – Trends, Traps, and Trade-offs, Social Inequality as a Global Challenge, The Unbeatable Challenges of Inequality, Perspectives on Sociological Theories, Methodological Debates, and Organizational Sociology, The Past, Present, and Future Directions of Migration/Immigration, Theories, and Practices of Global Journeys, Transforming Futures – Navigating Society, Environment, and Governance, Live and Let Others Live – In Reference to Sustainability and Environment Conservation, Navigating Sustainability: A Comparative Analysis of Micro vs. Macro Strategies in the least Developed Countries, The Nexus of Climate Change and Land-use – Global Scenario with Reference to Nepal, Women and Society etc.. Social Inequality- Past, Present, and Future (in which 15 African Countries' case studies are included), etc. Furthermore, Dr. Bhandari\'s creative writing encompasses a vast collection of poems and essays. He has published three volumes of poetry in collaboration with Prajita Bhandari. Dr. Bhandari\'s multifaceted contributions to academia, humanitarianism, and creative writing have solidified his reputation as an esteemed figure in social and environmental sciences, profoundly impacting social equity, sustainability, climate change, and beyond. Professor Bhandari holds five master's degrees in social and environmental sciences and a PhD in sociology. For 45 years, he has been actively involved in environmental conservation and humanitarian efforts through nonprofit and academic platforms. Guided by the philosophy that all living and non-living beings are interconnected ("Vasudhaiva Kutumbakam") and the principle of "Live and Let Others Live," his work reflects a deep commitment to the well-being of our planet and its inhabitants.

He serves as an International Program Director at the New York-based NGO Atlantic State Legal Foundation in Syracuse, NY; a professor at Akamai University, USA, and Sumy State University, Ukraine; and Kathmandu Forestry College, and advisor to Gandaki University, Nepal. He is also the UNEP Civil Society Regional Facilitator for North America and the Corresponding Lead Author of UNEP GEO 7, as well as the Lead Author of Integrated Biodiversity-Inclusive Spatial Planning and Ecological Connectivity (Spatial Planning and Connectivity Assessment) of the UN Intergovernmental Science-Policy Platform on Biodiversity and Ecosystem Services (IPBES). He is also the editor-in-chief of Strategic Planning for Energy and the Environment, the books series editor at the River Publisher, and the books series editor at Nova Publishers.

https://www.amazon.com/Books-Medani-P-Bhandari/s?rh=n%3A283155%2Cp_27%3AMedani+P.+Bhandari

https://novapublishers.com/?s=medani+bhandari&post_type=product (books link)

https://english.dcnepal.com/category/opinion/ (opinions)

https://www.linkedin.com/in/medani-bhandari-ph-d-8611a018/

Index

I

K

L

M

N